CHAMPIONS OF FLIGHT

Skyways

NOVEMBER, 1942
twenty-five cents

HESLIP

CHAMPIONS OF FLIGHT

Clayton Knight and William Heaslip

Artists Who Chronicled Aviation
from the Great War to Victory in WWII

Sheryl Fiegel and Theodore Hamady

With an introduction by Dominic A. Pisano, PhD
Curator of Popular Culture, Emeritus, Aeronautics Department, Smithsonian Institution,
National Air and Space Museum, Washington, DC

CASEMATE

Philadelphia & Oxford

Published in the United States of America and Great Britain in 2019 by
CASEMATE PUBLISHERS
1950 Lawrence Road, Havertown, PA 19083, USA
and
The Old Music Hall, 106–108 Cowley Road, Oxford OX4 1JE, UK

Hardcover Edition: ISBN 978-1-61200-779-3

A CIP record for this book is available from the British Library

Typeset in the UK by Frabjous Books
Printed and bound in India by Replika Press

For a complete list of Casemate titles, please contact:

CASEMATE PUBLISHERS (US)
Telephone (610) 853-9131
Fax (610) 853-9146
Email: casemate@casematepublishers.com
www.casematepublishers.com

CASEMATE PUBLISHERS (UK)
Telephone (01865) 241249
Email: casemate-uk@casematepublishers.co.uk
www.casematepublishers.co.uk

Frontispiece: *Skyways* magazine cover, illustrated by William Heaslip.

Contents

This book is dedicated to the memory of the preeminent aviation artists Clayton Knight and William Heaslip, who captured the transformative years of aviation history from World War I through World War II; and also to their sons, Hilary Knight and Allan M. Heaslip, who preserved their fathers' work and graciously shared it with us.

Clayton "Joey" Knight Jr. and Hilary Knight

Allan M. Heaslip

Vought-Sikorsky YR4 Helicopter.

Acknowledgments

We are grateful to many new and old friends who assisted our research over a decade of work. Librarians, curators, and archivists were especially helpful and always saw their work as something more than just a job. Terri J. Goldich (curator, University Libraries, University of Connecticut), Becky Simmons (archivist, Wallace Memorial Library, Rochester Institute of Technology), Ann Y. Evans (Springs Close Family Archives), Tom Belton (archivist, Western University, London, Ontario), Jeff Causier (London Room, London Public Library), Leah Smith (librarian, National Air and Space Museum) and John V. Alviti (senior curator, the Franklin Institute) were always there and available to assist.

Those who knew the artists were generous with their recollections and we are grateful for their contributions. Of particular note is World War I historian and author Peter Kilduff, whose knowledge of Clayton Knight was invaluable. The Reverend Clarence Sickles filled in with personal stories about William Heaslip's later life in Hackettstown, New Jersey. We would also like to acknowledge Owen Billman, who never got to write that article about William Heaslip. His research, which was passed on to us, gave us access to information unavailable any other way.

We benefited from sage advice offered by aviation artists, historians and eminent collectors, including award-winning military and aviation artist James Dietz; Dom Pisano, PhD, curator emeritus of the National Air and Space Museum; Michael O'Neal, past president of the American Society of Aviation Artists and current president of the League of World War I Aviation Historians; Charles Walthall, PhD; and Tom Heitzman.

Those who shared their collections and special knowledge with us include Willis M. Allen Jr., of Allen Airways Flying Museum, on early Clayton Knight illustrations; and Allen McHenry and Mark Finn, concerning Heinz aviation trading cards. A special thank you goes out to Michael G. Conley, former colleague of Sheryl's at the U.S. Air Force; and to Holly Brady, our gracious, patient, and immensely helpful review editor. Holly guided us through the process of melding aviation and aviation art history into a scholarly and readable book.

Michael Hamady, our gifted graphic artist, demonstrated his consummate skill in the restoration of the photographs and illustrations throughout our book. Also, Andrea Fiegel was always there with professional design advice, Leland Fiegel with technical expertise, and John Fiegel with a valuable final review.

We are especially indebted to the artists' families. Clayton Christopher Knight has been most generous with his kind assistance on all aspects of retrieving information about his grandfather. We also thank members of the Heaslip family: Chris and Meghan (Heaslip) Blake and Heatheré M. Heaslip. Allan's wife, Eileen Heaslip, was unfailingly considerate and helpful to us over many years.

And finally, a small army of friends freely gave of their time to undertake researches into nooks and crannies holding important bits of information. They include Jeff Mandel, Ray and Ellen Voss, Barry Martin, and members of the Coca-Cola Collector's Club.

We humbly apologize to those helpers whom we have failed to recognize.

—Sheryl Fiegel and Theodore Hamady

Introduction

Though it may seem improbable to the jaded and now uneasy air traveler of today, the airplane remained during its first four decades of existence, a magical contrivance that had little to do with most people's everyday lives. To the extent that the general public had contact with flight ... largely through the form of spectacle. Hence, they experienced flight vicariously through the public celebration of the exploits of aviation heroes and images diffused by various forms of mass culture. ... Aviators, like sports figures and actors, became celebrities, and subsequently the early history of aviation has to be understood within the framework of the rise of a certain type of mass culture. ... World War II (1939–1945) immediately followed the Golden Age during which time aviation achieved global significance.[1]

—Robert Wohl, *The Spectacle of Flight: Aviation and the Western Imagination 1920–1950*

The aviation illustrations of William Heaslip and Clayton Knight, two of aviation's greatest and most prolific commercial artists, can only be understood if one places them in the context of the period described above. Both were Great War airmen and formally trained artists, and both were creative during a uniquely exciting, formative period of aviation history—rich with significance technologically, politically, and culturally.

An impressive amount of aviation-related popular culture was created during the quarter-century between 1919 and 1945. Pulp fiction, advertising, popular film, the comics, industrial and automotive design, vernacular architecture and the commercial illustration movement—the latter led by Heaslip and Knight—were just a few of the areas that celebrated aviation between the end of World War I and the end of World War II.

To provide further context for their work, one must examine the history of commercial art and illustration in the United States during the 1920s and 1930s, because aviation illustration falls squarely within that context. From the turn of the century, journalism had developed a strong pictorial emphasis—via photographs, cartoons and comic strips, graphic illustration, and Sunday supplements. This journalistic revolution was aided by the development of technologies such as the Linotype machine, and later, the Teletypesetter.

Advertising, another enterprise that Heaslip and Knight benefited from, had begun to gain prominence during the period, aided by the development of the multicolor rotary press at the turn of the century. By 1948, almost 50 percent of the advertising pages in prominent American magazines were printed in two or more colors.[2]

In the final analysis, historians might argue that the period in question was characterized by two equally significant developments: political and legislative influences that enabled

Opposite: Charles A. Lindbergh with the *Spirit of St. Louis* shortly before departure from Long Island, NY on solo flight to Paris May 20, 1927. (Theodore Hamady)

aviation technology to grow into a commercial and military enterprise; and deep public interest in both civil and military flight. Without both, aviation might never have developed in the way that it did.

1919–1926: The Period of Incorporation

During World War I, aviation became a useful tool for the military, and it was employed by all the major combatants—in observation, pursuit, bombardment, and ground attack roles. This war also brought about interest in a new aviation celebrity-hero.

The ace—a fighter pilot who gained prominence by the number of victories (aircraft shot down) scored against the enemy—was celebrated as a heroic knight of the air. Businessmen like André Michelin, the French tire mogul, established a million-franc fund for aviators who had distinguished themselves in battle. By 1916, governments had begun to celebrate aviators and exploit their celebrity for nationalistic and propagandistic value. German ace Manfred von Richthofen—with 80 victories—was the most prominent member of this new fraternity of heroes, with France celebrating René Fonck (75 victories); Britain, E. C. "Mick" Mannock (73 victories); and the United States, Edward V. "Eddie" Rickenbacker (26 victories).[3]

Immediately after the war, aces were largely forgotten. The market for aircraft—at least in the United States—declined, and the aircraft industry struggled to the keep itself alive militarily and commercially. Nevertheless, a number of significant flights managed to keep aviation in the public eye: in 1919, the transatlantic voyage of the U.S. Navy's Curtiss NC-4 Flying Boat, and in 1925 the round-the-world flight of the U.S. Air Service's Douglas World Cruisers both held the public's interest.

The period between 1919 and 1926 was even more important because it was marked by aviation's struggle to become a business. During that time, four significant developments took place.

First, a 1909 patent dispute between the Wright brothers and Glenn Curtiss (and subsequently others) was settled, and a cross-licensing agreement with the Manufacturers Aircraft Association was created, allowing the industry—with the assistance of the newly formed National Advisory Committee for Aeronautics—to begin paving the way toward legitimizing aviation as a business.

Second, during World War I, Howard Coffin of the Hudson Motor Car Company and other executives in the automotive industry promoted an alliance between automobile manufacturers and the fledgling aviation industry.

The idolization of ace Baron von Richthofen, the Red Knight of Germany, was greatly enhanced by the publication of Floyd Gibbons's book in 1927. (Doubleday, Page & Company, an imprint of Penguin Random House)

PATHE NEWS
1910—FIFTEENTH ANNIVERSARY—1925

1924
Four American fliers circumnavigate the globe for the first time in the history of aviation. Eager crowds inspect the craft of Lieut. Smith.

Left: The U.S. Air Service contracted with the Douglas Aircraft Company in 1923 to build four Douglas World Cruisers (more simply, DWCs) whose mission was to circumnavigate the earth. The aircraft were named *Boston*, *Chicago*, *New Orleans*, and *Seattle*. All four DWC aircraft departed from Seattle on April 6, 1924, and flew a carefully prescribed and well-provisioned 23,942-mile route, with three surviving aircraft returning to Seattle on September 28, 1924. (The *Boston* crashed en route.) The success of this flight proved a boon to the U.S. Air Service, to the young Douglas Aircraft Company, and to aviation generally.[4]

Below: Lindbergh's Paris flight caused many investors to seek stakes in the exciting aviation industry. Massive capital investment infused the industry, and smaller companies merged to produce larger ones. Among the merged companies were aerial pioneers Wright Aeronautical and the Curtiss Airplane and Motor Company.[5] (Theodore Hamady)

Third, Clement M. Keys, head of the Curtiss Aeroplane and Motor Company, drew on his knowledge of management and finance to lay the groundwork for the merger of Curtiss and Wright Aeronautical corporations, and to forge alliances with other aviation corporations and with Wall Street.

And finally, through the pioneering efforts of the Guggenheim Fund for the Promotion of Aeronautics, the corps of aeronautical engineers became professionalized, developing a systematized technological base of knowledge and institutionalizing professional education. These new professionals contributed greatly to the public's acceptance of aviation by building aircraft that flew higher, faster, longer, and safer.

Equally important was the growth of air mail. Initially accomplished by the military and the federal government, the Air Mail Act of 1925 authorized private operators—such as Ford, Colonial Air Transport, Robertson, and Western Air Express—to fly the mail along eight key routes.

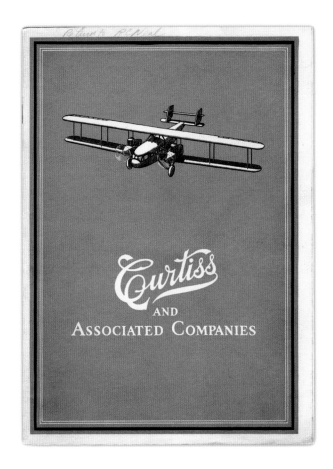

Curtiss AND ASSOCIATED COMPANIES

Parcels being loaded aboard a TWA Ford Trimotor. The passage of the Air Mail Act in 1925 authorized the postmaster general to contract with private aviation companies, which could deliver mail across country in three days, as opposed to being shipped by train. When night flying became an important contributor to speeding the mail, navigational aids became a necessity. The U.S. government's growing involvement in aviation resulted in the passage of the first aviation regulations.[6]

1913–1939: Air Racing Draws the Crowds

After a series of legislative firsts paved the way for larger aircraft, with space replacing weight as a way of computing subsidies, passenger flight began to take center stage. While this was going on, aviation manufacturing companies, such as the Curtiss Aeroplane and Motor Company, struggled to stay alive, mostly with contracts from the military for fighter and racing aircraft, which competed in air races—including the Pulitzer and Schneider Trophy races.

The Pulitzer and Schneider aircraft races were responsible for keeping aviation in the public eye and for providing a platform for the development of military aircraft. The Pulitzer Trophy race was originated in 1920 by American newspaperman Ralph Pulitzer and his two brothers, Joseph Jr. and Herbert, owners of the *New York World* and the *St. Louis Post Dispatch*. Ralph Pulitzer envisioned the race as a long-distance transcontinental event designed "to induce the equipment of military and civilian aviators for national defense; to demonstrate the practical uses of aero planes for the transportation of passengers and mail; and to open the first transcontinental aerial highway."[7] However, at the urging of the Aero Club of America, the purpose of the contest quickly changed into an all-out speed race that seemed more suited to the times and that could generate headline stories.

The Schneider Cup race, an over-water aviation event begun in 1913 by Frenchman Jacques Schneider, was intended to spur international competition. Schneider envisioned

a world connected by transoceanic seaplanes, an idea that achieved some currency in the subsequent development of the long-range flying boat. The Schneider races, however, quickly evolved into a hotly contested and prestigious nationalistic competition among the world's greatest air powers: France, Great Britain, the United States, and Italy. Thus, neither the Pulitzer Trophy race nor the Schneider Cup race fulfilled its originator's utilitarian conception, and the races evolved into speed contests that were undertaken largely by the military. Despite this unintended evolution, the races did have a peripheral impact on the technological development of military aircraft in the 1920s. While the Pulitzer-Schneider racing regimen was limited to high-speed flying at low altitudes,

racing provided an environment where engines and airframes could be tested and proven under strenuous competitive circumstances, and where relationships between the military and the industry could be developed.[8]

Competition between the army and navy for racing prizes was fierce, and it was often necessary for the military to camouflage racing activity as research and development to obtain necessary funds from congressional watchdogs.

Perhaps the most important event during this era was the enactment of the Air Commerce Act in 1926. This significant piece of legislation, which had been debated fiercely since the end of World War I, ushered in an era of government regulation supervised by the Aeronautics branch of the U.S. Department of Commerce. The branch was authorized to certify aircraft to insure their safety, to issue licenses to pilots, and to investigate aircraft accidents. Former Federal Aviation Administration historian Nick Komons has called the Air Commerce Act "a cornerstone on which to erect a commercial air transport system" and "perhaps the only genuine legislative achievement of the [Calvin] Coolidge presidency."[10]

The U.S. Army and Navy recognized the growing importance of aviation by creating the positions of Assistant Secretary of War for Air and Assistant Secretary of the Navy for Air. The former position was filled by F. Trubee Davison (left), a founder of the First Yale Naval Aviation Unit before the Great War, and the latter by David Ingalls, the U.S. Marine Corps' only ace during the war. Both men served under President Herbert Hoover while assisting the war and navy secretaries with the promotion of military and naval air issues.[9]

1927–1930: The Era of Spectacle and Speculation

While aviation struggled to become a business and the government attempted to enforce the mandates of the Air Commerce Act, spectacular aviation events began to focus the public's eye. One such event, in 1919, was the frenzy to be the first person to pilot an aircraft across the Atlantic, thus winning the $25,000 Orteig Prize offered by wealthy hotelier Raymond Orteig. This competition drew the attention of such famous aviators as René Fonck, Richard E. Byrd, Clarence Chamberlin, Charles Nungesser, François Coli, and, of course, Charles A. Lindbergh. In May 1927, Lindbergh flew the Ryan NY-P *Spirit of St. Louis* from New York to Paris, capturing the prize amid huge public acclaim and adulation.[11]

The Atlantic Ocean had been crossed by air several times before 1927. But the fact that a young, unheralded Midwesterner—a former barnstormer and airmail pilot—did it solo and nonstop, thereby capturing a large monetary prize, dazzled the American public and ushered in the Lindbergh era of aviation.

In 1927, Lindbergh and the *Spirit of St. Louis* journeyed throughout the United States in a 23,350-mile cross-country tour sponsored by the Guggenheim Fund for the Promotion of Aeronautics. Americans had seen movie serials and heard Lindbergh's voice

BREAKFAST IN HONOUR OF
CAPTAIN CHARLES A. LINDBERGH
on the presentation of the
RAYMOND ORTEIG 25,000 DOLLAR PRIZE
New York to Paris non-stop flight
FRIDAY, JUNE 17, 1927
HOTEL BREVOORT
NEW YORK

VALOUR

MALCOLM & HAYES, NY

Left: The $25,000 Orteig Prize was awarded to Charles Lindbergh at the Hotel Brevoort in New York City by hotelier Raymond Orteig. (Theodore Hamady)

over the radio, but over 30 million of them in 82 cities across the country were to see him flying overhead or speaking to promote aviation.[12]

Among the many Americans who remembered Lindbergh's overflight of their family's home, was a five-year-old boy named Bob Cavanagh, who lived near Kalamazoo, Michigan. Many years later, Cavanagh related the personal impact that Lindbergh's flight had on him to author Ted Hamady. Like several generations of boys and girls, Cavanagh became an avid model airplane builder and continued to closely monitor aviation developments, which led to a passion for aviation history and a lifetime career in the aviation industry.[13]

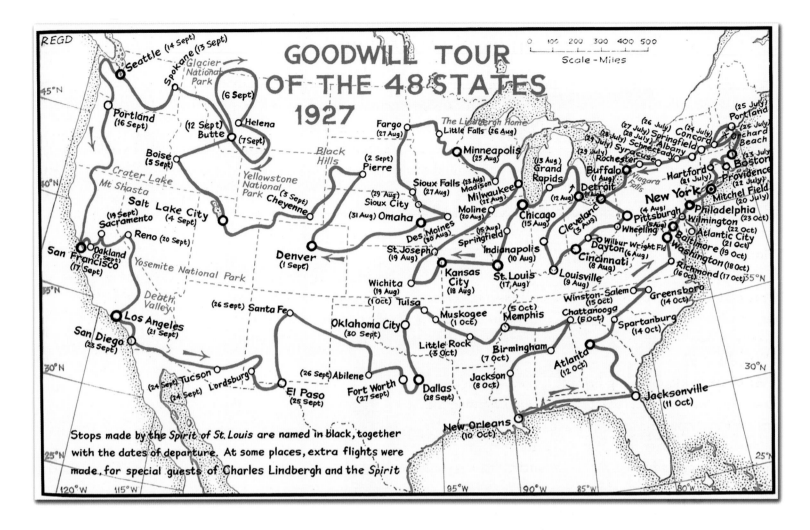

GOODWILL TOUR OF THE 48 STATES 1927

Stops made by the *Spirit of St. Louis* are named in black, together with the dates of departure. At some places, extra flights were made, for special guests of Charles Lindbergh and the *Spirit*

Goodwill Tour Map. (National Air and Space Museum)

In late 1927 and 1928, Pan American began exploring routes to Latin America, which influenced American aviation in the Southern Hemisphere and helped usher in an era of transoceanic commercial aviation. In 1931 and 1933, Lindbergh and his wife, Anne Morrow Lindbergh, made important flights, which provided valuable route information for commercial aviation. As Lindbergh biographer Kenneth S. Davis points out, "Future historians might have difficulty determining how much of the great aviation boom was due to Lindbergh and how much to other factors … but none could doubt that he was a major cause of it."[14]

During this time, the "Lindbergh Boom" also began to affect aviation finance, although historians have argued that Lindbergh was not the only factor for the increased interest in aviation stocks. In 1929, aircraft production increased almost four-fold over the previous year. Nevertheless, aviation felt the effects of the Great Depression and a number of companies confronted with overexpansion were forced to close their doors.

At the same time, aviation companies began a period of consolidation and merger. Four large holding companies were formed, the first and largest of which—United Aircraft and Transport—was created by William Boeing and Frederick Rentschler, the chief executive of engine manufacturer Pratt & Whitney. Other consolidations quickly followed: North American Aviation and the Curtiss-Wright Corporation were put together by investor Clement Keys; and the Aviation Corporation was put together by aerial photographer Sherman Fairchild, together with Averill Harriman and Robert Lehman.

1931–1939: The Era of Commercial and Military Aviation

The years from 1931 to 1939 saw the development of the aviation industry, the birth of air travel in the United States, and the growth of army and navy aviation doctrine. The so-called "Spoils Conference" of 1930, presided over by Postmaster General Walter Folger Brown of Herbert Hoover's administration, began the process of rationalizing the route structure of the major airlines in the United States. The introduction of the Boeing 247 and Douglas DC-series aircraft in the early to mid-1930s paved the way for the modern airline era, although air travel was still only available to those who were rather well off. And the romantic aura that surrounded air travel, largely as a result of colorful and attractive advertising posters, flourished.

Inspired by Lindbergh's flight, Walt Disney introduced Mickey Mouse in a six-minute silent cartoon (later converted to sound) entitled *Plane Crazy*. Comic strip pilot hero Tailspin Tommy was introduced in 1928, and by the early 1930s this feature appeared in over 450 newspapers. A 12-chapter movie serial, produced by Universal Studios, followed in 1934.

Airplane model building became a craze among young boys (and some girls) when *American Boy* magazine created the Airplane Model League of America in 1927. Membership benefits included opportunities for young modelers to get advice from aeronautical experts and participate in national model competitions.

The area on which the Lindbergh era had the greatest influence was Hollywood. Shortly after Lindbergh's transatlantic flight in 1927, the first true aviation genre film, *Wings,* appeared. The film was so popular that it won the first Academy Award ever given in the category Outstanding Picture for 1927–28. Reviewers marveled at the realism of the scenes: "Nothing in the line of war pictures ever has packed a greater proportion of real thrills into an equal footage. As a spectacle, *Wings* is a technical triumph. It piles punch upon punch until the spectator is almost nervously exhausted."[16]

At about the same time that *Wings* appeared, Howard Hughes, a man who was destined to become a pilot celebrity-hero himself, began working on *Hell's Angels,* the first version of which—a silent film—Hughes scrapped because talking pictures had begun to dominate the Hollywood scene. Hughes was considered a neophyte filmmaker, but when *Hell's Angels* finally appeared on June 30, 1930, it was a box-office success. As one critic later wrote, the film is "dramatically commonplace, clumsily strung together and without clear authorship, but the aerial photography is superb."[17]

William Boeing established an airline in 1927, merging it with Pratt & Whitney to establish the United Aircraft and Transport Company (UATC) in 1929. United Airlines was formed in 1931 as a holding company for UATC's airline subsidiaries when the U.S. government decreed that airplane manufacturing interests could no longer control airlines.[15] The aircraft pictured in the United Air Lines brochure include a Boeing-built single engine transport and two variants of the Boeing Model 80 trimotor. (Theodore Hamady)

Right: Juan Trippe, founder of Pan American Airlines, quietly and astutely worked with the U.S. government to further Pan Am's interests in establishing international routes. Charles Lindbergh, as company technical representative, helped lay out and fly the routes. Pan American used the Sikorsky S-42 flying boat on the Flying Cruises to Rio. (Theodore Hamady)

Below: The Trimotor provided reliable, cross-country transportation but still had to rely on rail connections. Once airliners flew higher, safer, and farther—comfortably and reliably—they became the preferred mode of long-distance travel.[18] (Theodore Hamady)

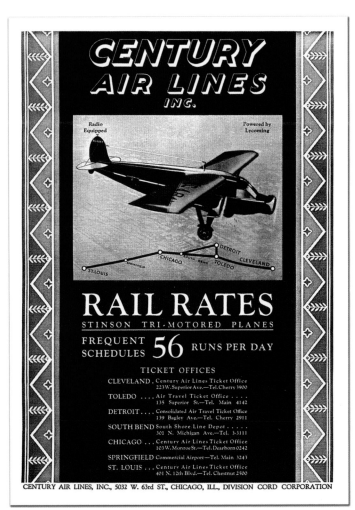

What characterized these films and made them like no others were their aerial sequences. It was as though Hollywood directors were painting aviation on the largest canvas yet available.

Although there may not be an apparent connection between the earliest aviation films and aviation art and illustration, the cinematographic quality of the work is apparent in both formats. Heaslip produced a 1930 newspaper advertisement for *Hell's Angels*, and Knight created the cover design of the film's opening night program—and both used their cinematographic flair to tell exciting stories with dynamic images. Although their canvases were restricted in comparison to film, they managed to compress into small frames the cinematographic aspects of film, and, more to the point, the cinematographic qualities of the aviation genre—lighting and contrast, foregrounding and backgrounding, motion, verticality and horizontality.

Another significant development was the rise of an aviation celebrity culture. Pilots like Lindbergh, Amelia Earhart, Jimmy Doolittle, Jacqueline Cochrane, Wiley Post, Roscoe Turner, and Howard Hughes performed feats of courage that inspired a generation of Americans and made aviation a revolutionary and exciting technology capable of erasing the barriers of time and space. In his book *Celebrity*, Chris Rojek explains:

This comic strip was inscribed to Allan Heaslip, son of the artist William Heaslip. *Tailspin Tommy*, created by Hal Forrest, first appeared in newspapers in 1928 not long after Lindbergh's epochal flight. Within three years, 250 newspapers, movie serials, and Big Little Books were featuring Tailspin Tommy and his aerial adventures.[19] (Allan M. Heaslip)

Left: William Heaslip created this newspaper ad for Howard Hughes's 1930 aviation film *Hell's Angels*. (Allan M. Heaslip)

Right: The 1938 pre–World War II National Air Races was among the most exciting of all: Roscoe Turner won his third Thompson Race and retired the Trophy, and Jacqueline Cochrane won the Bendix Trophy. Within a year, several of the international performers would be at war. (Theodore Hamady)

To the anthropologist Mircea Eliade, nearly all religions posit the existence of sky gods or celestial beings. Human experience is typically divided into three realms: sky, earth and underworld. Men and women are of the earth, but their lives are invested with heightened meaning by the journeys—offered through religious rites and ceremonies—to the sky or the underworld. Most religions can be structurally reduced to a combination of rites and ceremonies of ascent and descent. Journeys above and below are associated with ecstatic experience.[20]

Pilots' passages into the air and back to earth in an attempt to conquer time and space reflect the arduousness of human existence; simultaneously, their journeys give them a heroic and even godlike aspect. Given this archetypal significance, it is not surprising that government, industry, and the media, using the techniques of mass communication,

The cover of this issue of *Literary Digest* features some of the aviation celebrities of the day: Amelia Earhart, Charles A. Lindbergh, Rear Admiral Richard E. Byrd (a renowned naval pilot and polar explorer from the air); and Major General Benjamin Foulois, chief of the U.S. Army Air Corps.

fashioned heroic-celebrity personas for pilots, attributing glamorous status to them and making them into public figures, often for nationalistic and propagandistic purposes.

It was in the 1920s, however, when all of the conditions for modern-day celebrity—radio, newspaper journalism, newsreels, motion pictures, magazines—became commonplace, and that a veritable sea change in the way celebrities were perceived by the public took place. During that time, columnists like Walter Winchell created an obsession with celebrity, and the public hungered for information about famous people as never before. The communications technology that enabled what we now call the media to transmit information to masses of people paved the way for Lindbergh, arguably the most renowned aviation celebrity of the 20th century, and other pilot figures of the era.[21]

Equally important during the 1930s was the beginning of what might be called the "democratization" of aviation. Although flying was predominantly the domain of white men, inroads were being made by famous women pilots, including Amelia Earhart, Louise Thaden, and Jacqueline Cochran. Many African-Americans—also fascinated by the thrill of aviation—attempted to join this white-male-dominated activity and for a short time, both women and African-Americans were welcomed into the Civilian Pilot Training Program (CPTP). But the program eventually closed its doors to both groups as the nation prepared for war. Nonetheless, the CPTP greatly enhanced the popularity of flying in the immediate pre-WWII period—by the end of 1941, 100,000 licensed pilots were on their rolls.[22]

Left: U.S. Army recruiting poster, 1941

Right: U.S. Navy recruiting poster, 1941

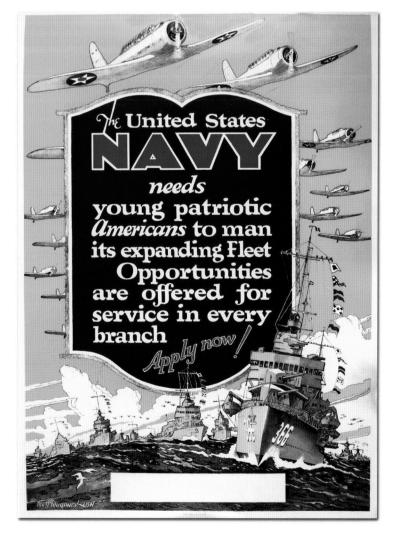

This period also saw the development of an army and navy aviation doctrine that had its origins in the intense rivalry between the two military services for supremacy in the air. The U.S. Navy air effort, let by Admiral William Moffett, focused on integrating naval aviation into fleet operations. Milestone naval aviation events were the construction of the first aircraft carrier, the USS *Langley*, and the development of dive-bombing, which would become a staple of World War II naval air operations.

The Army Air Corps (formerly the U.S. Air Service), created in 1926 by the Air Corps Act legislation, took its cue from General William "Billy" Mitchell, a fierce advocate of air power and of air service independence from the U.S. Army. The path to independence was the development of a discrete strategic bombardment mission and long-range bombardment aircraft. The army and navy carried on a long and bitter struggle over mission, which resulted in the MacArthur-Pratt Agreement in 1931, signed by General Douglas MacArthur, Army Chief of Staff; and Admiral William Veazie Pratt, Chief of Naval Operations. The agreement specified that the army would have aerial jurisdiction over the land and the navy would have aerial jurisdiction over the seas. Nevertheless, the Army Air Corps interpreted the pact loosely enough to assert its privilege in defending the coasts of the United States against invasion. This interpretation gave the Air Corps broad leeway to develop long-range bombardment aircraft and to train bomber crews to go beyond coastal defense and seek out potential enemy invaders before they could reach American shores.

1940–1945: Air Power and Total War

While U.S. military and naval aviation had found a purpose in World War I, it had certainly grown in importance during the inter-war years, becoming significantly refined during the 1920s and 1930s. This was particularly true with the Air Corps' new doctrine of strategic daylight, high-altitude bombing, and the Navy's development of independent carrier offensive operations. The Air Corps' doctrine, intended to eliminate the stalemated warfare so prevalent in World War I, would provide quick-strike capabilities; and the Navy's doctrine would take the air war to the enemy across vast stretches of ocean.

By the attack on Pearl Harbor on December 7, 1941, the U.S. military and naval air services had begun to field a far more sophisticated and potent weapon of war. And when coupled with industry's prodigious wartime production effort, America's air forces became a full partner in achieving victory in World War II.

It is my sincere hope that this book will revive interest in the work of Clayton Knight and William Heaslip, which was so intimately bound up with the world of aviation in the 1920s, 1930s, and the war years of the 1940s, and reintroduce the public to a significant aspect of aviation's social and cultural history.

—Dominic A. Pisano, PhD
Curator of Popular Culture, Emeritus, Aeronautics Department,
Smithsonian Institution, National Air and Space Museum, Washington, DC

Our country's growing strength fulfilled President Roosevelt's prophecy that the United States would become the "arsenal of democracy." This "Defense in the Air Begins on the Ground" poster was designed by Ralph Iligan. (National Air and Space Museum)

U.S. Air Service

September, 1920 Price 25c

Volume 4 Number 2 $3.00 a Year

COLONEL GORRELL ON RULES OF THE AIR

In this Issue **LT.-COMDR. LEIGHTON—RALPH H. UPSON—"DIARY OF A FLYING CADET"**

Published monthly by the Air Service Publishing Co., Inc., 130 West 42nd Street, New York, N. Y. Application pending for entry as second class matter at the Postoffice, New York, N. Y.

CHAPTER ONE

Clayton Knight: The Formative Years

The only newspaper in Rochester, New York, to headline the Wright brothers' first flight was the evening *Union & Advertiser* on December 18, 1903:

> SUCCESSFUL TEST OF A FLYING MACHINE
> Traveled Three Miles in the Face of a Wind—
> Navigated with the Aid of an Engine

Years later, accomplished artist and author Clayton Knight (1891–1969) would refer back to that event with some reverence as he promoted aviation to a generation of future fliers. For him, the story of aviation was not just the story of flying machines, but the story of courageous individuals whose love of flight would change the world. His talent and ambition would later distinguish him first in Chicago as a student at the School of the Art Institute and then as a successful illustrator in New York City, 300 miles from his hometown in western New York.

Above: A studio portrait of Clayton Knight in his finest Knickerbocker suit, *c.* 1900. (Clayton Christopher Knight)

Becoming an Artist/Illustrator

In 1903, however, Knight was just another impressionable 12-year-old boy with high aspirations. His creative side was probably derived from his father, Frederick (Fred) Clayton Knight, a bright man of varied interests whose business ventures were in many ways directed by the booming economy in Rochester on the banks of the Erie Canal. In 1910, the city boasted a population of 218,149 and was home to Bausch & Lomb Optical Company, Eastman Kodak, Western Union Telegraph, and R.T. French & Company. City directories indicate Fred was proprietor of a "fancy goods" store until 1909. There is no mention of him during the years 1909–10, but in 1911–12, he is listed as secretary and treasurer at Harry Versprella Glazier; and in 1913–14, at Easterly & Rothaug Glaziers.[1] Later in life, family members would fondly remember him as a gifted carpenter whose craft revealed great skill and attention to detail.

Opposite: The most inspiring of his three covers for *U.S. Air Service* magazine, this image from September 1920 portrays a lieutenant sporting a ribbon bar and three chevrons denoting 18 months of overseas service. The fighter planes in the background have insignia—a U.S. star in a blue field—that was reinstated on U.S. military aircraft after World War I. The illustration, based on a stand-alone painting, is unrelated to any internal content.

Bisecting downtown Rochester, the 363-mile Erie Canal created a navigable water route from New York City to the Great Lakes.

At the turn of the century, Rochester was a thriving city, ranked 24th in the nation based on population.

Clayton's mother, Elizabeth (Brooks), was by all accounts a kind woman who provided stability for young Clayton and his sister, Lou, in a working-class home on Parsells Avenue.[2] If Clayton's artistic instincts were inherited from his father, his mother certainly nurtured and encouraged them. An entry in Clayton's journal dated May 5, 1903, reveals that he met his mother and aunt in uptown Rochester to purchase paintbrushes—an activity that seems to portend the future.

Young Clayton was gifted with both innate talent and the good fortune to be in the right place at the right time. Sometime in late 1909 or early 1910, he enrolled at the Mechanics Institute, founded in 1885 by a group of enterprising Rochester businessmen to establish "free evening schools in the city for instruction in drawing and such other branches of studies as are most important for industrial pursuits of great advantage to our people." Its first president was Henry Lomb, one of the founders of Bausch & Lomb.[3]

The Mechanics Institute's Department of Applied & Fine Arts provided Knight with an introduction to the study of life drawing and illustration,[4] and, ultimately, a purpose and direction as a commercial artist. As described in the school bulletin, these studies offered "particular advantages to those wishing to enter the field of newspaper or magazine illustration, or those desirous of obtaining practical training in drawing for advertisements or lithography and other work of a similar nature."[5] Primary instruction was provided by Frank Von Der Lancken, whom Knight later acknowledged in biographies as an influential teacher. Clayton's work during that period reveals a competent draftsman with a highly developed aesthetic.[6] And the practical skills he learned in class were put to the test when he apprenticed as a lithographic designer for the Stecher Lithograph Company, one of the many companies producing advertising for local businesses in the Rochester area.

Rochester had become a center for lithography years before, due to the efforts of an influx of skilled emigrants who left Germany in response to social unrest there and resettled in upstate New York. This fact, plus the abundance of horticultural publishing which serviced the large number of major nurseries in the area, provided a steady supply of business

Prior to 1911, all art classes at the Mechanics Institute were held either in the Eastman Building or the Eastman Annex (pictured). The Eastman Annex, which opened December 9, 1894, was the first building erected by the Institute. (RIT Archive Collections, Rochester Institute of Technology)

opportunities for lithograph companies of national scope. Technical aspects of the commercial lithographic process were jealously guarded by the craft-union printers, who resisted the presence of outsiders, including artists, in the pressrooms.[7] Knight's early training and familiarity with this process would serve him well later on, when artist and future teacher George Bellows would become a leader in emancipating lithography from mere commercial endeavors and establishing it as a legitimate medium for fine art printmakers.

During this period, current events—especially technological advances in aviation—provided an enticing distraction for young Clayton. In 1910, Glenn Curtiss of Hammondsport, New York, 90 miles from Rochester, won the *Scientific American* Trophy and a $10,000 prize offered by the *New York World* newspaper for flying down the Hudson River from Albany to New York City.[8] And in July 1911, John J. Frisbie, a well-known local balloonist, flew his Curtiss biplane, powered by an engine made by the local Elbridge Engine Company, from an airfield located between Rochester's Highland and Elmwood Avenues to the New York Central Railroad Depot and back. Days after Frisbie's flight, the Moisant International Aviators, flying Bleriot monoplanes, demonstrated how the airplane could be used in wartime by dropping paper bags filled with flour on a company of National Guard troops. Knight must have been acutely aware of these events as they were unfolding.

Seated in the back with a fellow student looking over his shoulder, Clayton Knight studies illustration techniques, probably in the Eastman Annex Building, c. 1910. (Clayton Christopher Knight)

In the fall of 1911, Knight moved to Chicago to start his studies at the School of the Art Institute, one of the premier art schools in the country. He followed a standard illustration curriculum with courses in lettering, anatomy, perspective, and block drawing. Favored teachers included John W. Norton (drawing, life, and illustration), Allen E. Philbrick (junior composition, still life, and figure), and Fred De Forrest Schook (illustration).[9] Records indicate that Knight shifted to afternoon and evening classes during his second year (1912–13) and was retained by the school as a Saturday teacher.[10] In a 1942 interview, he revealed that he worked his way through school doing five jobs at once: he was a part-time commercial artist, an art teacher, a lunchroom waiter, a theater ticket taker, and a night watchman for an undertaker.[11]

Outside of his academic pursuits, Knight experienced two significant events while studying in Chicago—one personal and the other professional. On a personal level, he met and began a lifelong friendship with the illustrator Lucille Patterson (Marsh), who introduced him to Katharine Sturges, the woman he would eventually marry. Sturges's success as an illustrator would parallel his own, and he would often collaborate with her.[12] Of professional significance was the appearance at the Art Institute of the "International Exposition of Modern Art"—the famous "Armory Show." The exhibit came straight from

John J. Frisbie making a demonstration flight over Genesee Valley Park in a Curtiss biplane. After this success, Frisbie moved to the Midwest where he became the first aviator to fly over Detroit. He fell to his death during an air exhibition in Norton, Kansas, on September 2, 1911, after being taunted by a jeering crowd to fly a plane he knew was impaired. (Albert R. Stone Negative Collection, Rochester Museum & Science Center, Rochester, NY)

Right: The Art Institute of Chicago was originally planned as both a museum and a school. Located in Grant Park on the east side of Michigan Avenue, the building was funded through a collaboration of the museum and the 1893 World's Columbian Exposition. When the World Congress Auxiliary of the World's Columbian Exposition vacated the building, the Art Institute took over.

Below: Studio portrait of Clayton Knight, signed by "Pearson" (possibly Mrs. Emma J. Pearson, 64 Spring, Rochester, NY). By pose, clothing style and estimated age, Knight probably had this taken while home on break from his studies in Chicago. (Clayton Christopher Knight)

its sensational month-long venue in New York—in abbreviated form, but with the same radical modern art that had sent shock waves throughout the New York art world.

It is unlikely that the Armory Show did much to alter Knight's artistic bent, but it did signify revolutionary change in the art world. Now there was an alternative to the traditional classical imagery promoted by the academies, imagery that sought to disguise reality through idealization. This dramatic change in approach had been launched a few years earlier by a group of newspaper illustrators—among them George Luks, William Glackens, John Sloan, Everett Shinn, and teacher/artist Robert Henri—dedicating their work to bringing a new social realism into public view.

In 1908, this group, whose work was derisively known as the "Ash Can School," joined leading artists Arthur B. Davies, Ernest Lawson, and Maurice Prendergast to show their work at the Macbeth Gallery in New York City. The seminal exhibition, titled "The Eight," introduced the American public to a new aesthetic. The group soon formed the Association of American Painters and Sculptors (AAPS), which quickly expanded to 25 artists,[13] including some of the more open-minded members of the National Academy of Design, and began to hold "exhibitions of the best contemporary work that can be secured, representative of American and foreign art."[14]

The group's first exhibit, held at the 69th Infantry Regimental Armory on Lexington Avenue at 25th Street, came to be known as the Armory Show. The exhibit displayed over 1,300 works of art representing avant-garde painting, sculpture, and prints, a third of which were produced by foreign-born artists.[15] Cubism, including work by Marcel Duchamp and Pablo Picasso, was one of the movements on display—and Cubists' multiple perspectives of a single subject seem to have garnered the most criticism.[16] When the exhibit moved to Chicago, Arthur B. Davies, the organization's leader and one of the most knowledgeable advocates of European modernism, exerted his influence over the exhibit so that the American component was almost entirely eliminated in favor of the controversial foreign core.

From March 24 through April 16, 1913, a total of 634 works were exhibited at the Art Institute—including 312 oil paintings, 57 watercolors, 120 prints, 115 drawings, and 30 sculptures. According to the catalogue, there were on display 4 sculptures by Constantin Brancusi (1876–1957); 15 oils and prints by Paul Cezanne (1839–1906); 4 oils by Marcel Duchamp (1887–1968), including *Nude Figure Descending a Staircase*; 14 oils, watercolors, prints, and sculptures by Paul Gauguin (1848–1903); 18 oils by Vincent Van Gogh (1853–1890); 16 oils, drawings, and sculpture by Henri Matisse (1869–1954); 7 oils by Pablo Picasso (1881–1973); and 70 oils, pastels, and prints by Odilon Redon (1840–1916).

Even though editorials and articles in Chicago publications urged fair play in the consideration of the "greatest exhibition of insurgent art ever held," the faculty and students at the School of the Art Institute were incensed by the exhibit. They made plans to hang in effigy Matisse, Brancusi, and American expatriate artist Walter Pach (who had assisted the organizers in Paris) at the end of the exhibit, but their efforts were blocked by the school's administrators. Instead, the students (as individuals, not as members of the Chicago Art Students League) staged a mock trial of "Henri Hairmattress" and

Clayton Knight produced this work in a life drawing class while studying at the School of the Art Institute of Chicago, *c.* 1913. (Clayton Christopher Knight)

The Armory Show in Chicago was housed in seven galleries of the Art Institute. Gallery 53 displayed many Cubist artists, including Pablo Picasso, Alexandre Archipenko, Francis Picabia, and Marcel Duchamp. (The Art Institute of Chicago/Art Resource, NY)

burned replicas of Matisse's works, all of which they followed with dancing and song. The exhibit then traveled to a disappointing stay in Boston, after which accounts were closed and art was returned.

Although the success of the Armory Show destroyed the power of the academies, some founding members of AAPS came to believe that the social realism of the "Ash Can School" had been marginalized. As a result, 8 of the 24 members at what was to become the last official meeting of the Association resigned with apparent displeasure over the heavy-handed administration of Arthur B. Davies. Among them were Robert Henri, George Luks, John Sloan, and George Bellows.[17] This philosophical schism divided the most progressive of American artists into two opposing groups.

The impact of the Armory Show on Knight was certainly not stylistic, as his artistic expression was firmly planted in the realist camp. However, the unbridled energy of some of the Cubists' works—notably those of Marcel Duchamp, who effectively captured movement in painting—may have been stored away in Knight's subconscious to be retrieved years later in his aviation art. Cubism also found its way into Knight's later design work in the decorative arts. The show's focus on European art might also have pointed Knight's attention to the unfolding Great War, which was to engulf the world in one of the bloodiest conflicts in history and would be the defining event of his life.

By the time Knight moved to New York City in 1914, great illustrators such as Howard Chandler Christy (1873–1952), James Montgomery Flagg (1877–1960), and Joseph Christian Leyendecker (1874–1951) were well established; and the Big Four magazines—*Century*, *Harper's*, *McClure's*, and *Scribner's*—as well as smaller magazines provided much opportunity.[18] He found a position as assistant art director at a company that turned out drawings for various advertising agencies.[19] In a 1938 publication he described this early period of his life as "tranquilly making a living in New York, painting what was known as still life." He made light of his endeavors, claiming he could "turn out as fine a plate of beans or dish of wrinkled prunes or tube of toothpaste with toothbrush and bowl of flowers as was being done in those days, and the checks that paid for them were often and satisfying."[20]

Never complacent and always looking for new challenges, Knight soon signed up for art courses from none other than the two icons of American realism Robert Henri and George Bellows. There is no known reference as to where or when these courses were offered, but based on chronology, Knight probably joined others flocking to classes at the Modern School, 63 E. 107th Street, also known as the Ferrer Center.[21] Both Henri and Bellows admired the founder of the school, self-proclaimed anarchist Emma Goldman, who was a strong supporter of artistic freedom.[22] And while the school moved to Stelton, New Jersey, in 1914, the Ferrer Center lasted in New York until 1918, and Henri taught there from 1911–18.[23]

Becoming an Aviator

Beginning in 1916, photographs of the Escadrille Americaine, later known as the Lafayette Escadrille, found their way into American newspapers. Piloting machines made of wood and canvas in aerial combat over France without the benefit of parachute, volunteer American aviators were pictured displaying great courage in the face of overwhelming odds. Not surprisingly, their adventurous exploits captured the imagination of the American public, including Clayton Knight and his studio mate, Norman Borchardt, both of whom tried to join the military—but both lacked the required two years of

Members of the Lafayette Escadrille flew combat missions for France before the United States entered World War I. Pilots here include James Rogers McConnell (1887–1917) standing with Captain Georges Thenault (1887–1948).

Left: Gervais Raoul Lufbery (1885–1918), credited with 17 victories, was the most successful member of the Lafayette Escadrille. French-American by birth, he transferred to the U.S. Air Service in 1918 where he imparted his knowledge and wisdom about aerial combat to apt pupils of the 94th Pursuit Squadron, including Eddie Rickenbacker, who later became the U.S. Ace of Aces. Major Lufbery was killed in action on May 19, 1918.

Right: Menu from the SS *Havana*, with a notation by Clayton Knight next to Cuban Coffee: "Black stuff, believe me." The SS *Havana*, part of the New York and Cuba Mail Steamship Company (commonly called the Ward Line), was requisitioned for use by the Army and Navy during WWI. (Clayton Christopher Knight)

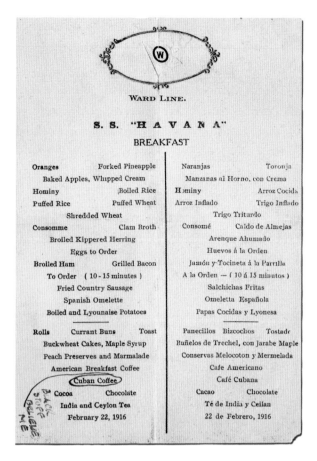

Clayton Knight arrives in Austin, Texas, with fellow recruits. The University of Texas was one of eight Schools of Military Aeronautics (private and state-run universities) offering preflight (ground) training for aviators in World War I. (Clayton Christopher Knight)

Clayton Knight with illustrator Lucille Patterson on the beach in Havana. Lucille was primarily known for her depictions of children on the covers of national magazines and in ads. Not long after their return from this trip, Knight made the *New York Times* (March 13, 1917) for chasing away an intruder from the Patterson home.
(Clayton Christopher Knight)

Since recruits were expected to be athletic, physical fitness was part of their training. They were also taught the basics of flight, airplane operation and maintenance, meteorology, astronomy, military science, and officer behavior. Knight would later recount that he found training to be quite difficult: he had been out of school for some time, whereas others were fresh out of college.
(Clayton Christopher Knight)

college. Discouraged, and probably drawn to a warmer climate during the winter of 2016, Knight instead joined fellow artists on a cruise to Havana, Cuba, returning through New Orleans and Charleston.

Once America declared war on Germany in April 1917, Knight was able to enlist. He joined a class of approximately 30 recruits at ground school in Austin, Texas. There, he proved his mettle against recent college graduates and finished among the top 10 in his class, qualifying him for duty in France.

It was only upon gathering with others in Mineola, New York, that he learned that Italy was their destination. Sailing on the RMS *Carmania* to Liverpool, he learned some Italian from Fiorello LaGuardia, a captain in his outfit, and met a roster of memorable individuals, among them Elliot White Springs, who would later figure prominently in the legendary lore of World War I.[24]

After disembarking in Liverpool, Knight was reassigned with others in his group to Oxford and Grantham for additional ground training, some with Lewis and Vickers machine guns. Although these men still wore American uniforms, they came under British orders. On May 18, 1918, Knight and most others in his group were commissioned as first lieutenants; Elliott White Springs, George Vaughn and Field Kindley were captains. After 60 hours of solo training, Knight received orders to proceed directly to France where he was assigned to No. 206 Squadron of the Royal Air Force.

No. 206 was an Intelligence Squadron of the British Second Army, a group made up of three

The identity card of Lieutenant Clayton Knight, American Expeditionary Forces, Pilot, American Air Service.
(Clayton Christopher Knight)

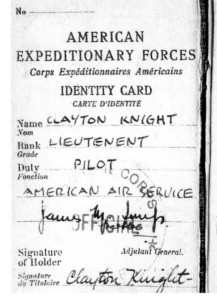

Left: British and American cadets at Christ Church College, Oxford University, October 1917. (Springs Close Family Archives)

Right: Clayton Knight in Grantham, England, late in 1917. After his training at Oxford, Knight was unable to secure a seat in flying school. Instead, he enrolled in a course on ground training of Lewis and Vickers machine guns in Grantham. (Peter Kilduff)

flights of six planes each, tasked with reconnaissance over enemy lines without fighter coverage.

After several close calls, Knight and his observer, Second-Lieutenant J. H. Perring, found themselves on the morning of October 5, 1918, in an unfamiliar plane over German territory. There he encountered Oberleutnant Harald Auffarth, who was about to earn his 23rd of 29 aerial victories.[25]

According to firsthand accounts of the battle, Knight and Perring, who had been flying lower than the others in formation because of engine problems, were the first to see the oncoming Fokker D. VIIs. Their attempts to signal the others of the approaching enemy

Clayton Knight was assigned to No. 206 Squadron, which was made up of British, Canadians, South Africans, Australians, and six Americans. Knight is seated in the front row, third from left, over the initials "C. K." Photo taken in France, 1918. (Peter Kilduff)

Above left: Designed by Geoffrey de Havilland in 1917, the Airco D.H.9 was a biplane daytime bomber crewed by pilot with observer seated directly behind. The aircraft was armed with a flexible Lewis gun for the observer's use and a fixed Vickers machine gun for use by the pilot. The aircraft was maneuverable and easy to land.

Above right: Oberleutnant Harald Auffarth next to his Fokker D. VII in late 1918.

Left: Oil painting labeled by its artist Clayton Knight: "Oberleutnant Harald Auffarth, C. O. of Jastr 29, leads flight of Fokker D. VII fighters down on a flight of D.H.9 Bombers ... October 4, 1918." The yellow comet insignia on Auffarth's fuselage is clearly in view. This painting is currently displayed on the Clayton Knight wall at the Wings Club, New York, NY. (Clayton Christopher Knight)

Clayton Knight in uniform in Rochester, New York, after his return from World War I. (Clayton Christopher Knight)

went unnoticed, and they were attacked. Shots fired into the floorboards of Knight's plane ignited and spattered grease and oil. By the time Knight stamped out the fire, the plane was spinning out of control. It dove to 1,500 feet, followed by two or three Fokker D. VIIs, which peppered the disabled plane with a stream of bullets. Perring fired back until his guns gave out, at which time Knight took over the front gun, providing the aircraft's only protection. Thinking the end was near, Knight set his sights on the Fokker D. VII flown by Oberleutnant Auffarth. In a last-ditch effort, he flew his plane over his opponent's aircraft, a maneuver that resulted in a wound to his leg. The engine finally quit, and the pair crash-landed in a field of newly planted wheat.

Unfortunately, the site of the crash was behind a small German headquarters building.[26] Knight was transported with other wounded prisoners to Courtrai, Deynze, Ghent, and finally to a hospital in Antwerp. There the prisoners worried constantly that one of their fellow pilots would bomb the installation. But they soon received news that the war was over. The Belgian Red Cross took over from the Germans and moved the patients to a clinic staffed by French nuns. A few weeks later, they were transported to Brussels and then to Wimereux, on the coast of France, where Lady Hadfield had established a British hospital. Their status as former prisoners of war gave cause for a grand celebration replete with the requisite champagne.[27]

Knight's convalescence continued in England, where crutches afforded him greater mobility and where he ran into old friend Elliot White Springs at the Savoy Bar. Springs, the son of a wealthy South Carolina textile mill owner, had survived the war as flight commander of the 148th Squadron based at Dunkirk. His squadron finished the war with a record number of enemy kills for an American unit, second only to that of Captain Eddie Rickenbacker, which had been in action three months longer.[28]

Both Springs and Knight returned to the United States in February 1919. That summer in New York, as Knight was returning to his previous life as an illustrator and Springs was escaping from the demands of an autocratic father, they would run into each other again.[29] And a few years later, when their paths crossed for a fourth time, the meeting would be life-altering for both.

Becoming an Aviation Artist & Illustrator

Soon after his return to the States, Knight began producing covers for publications such as *La France* and *House & Garden* magazines. These early works—colorful, decorative, and conventional—demonstrate the influence on Knight of the Brandywine School, which dominated the New York commercial art scene at the time. The Brandywine School was a style of illustration developed by Howard Pyle (1853–1911) and passed on to his many influential students, including N. C. Wyeth (1882–1945) and Harvey Dunn (1884–1952). It was natural for Knight to adopt this style before developing his own distinctive look.

But coming back to a career illustrating "jelly jars and canned soup"[30] must have been dull fare for a man who had survived numerous adventures as a World War I aviator. Early in 1920, Knight produced some covers for the *U.S. Air Service* magazine (February, June, and September). In two of these illustrations, an airplane appears as a supporting prop (see page 16); and in the third, the plane looks as if it is floating, rather than moving through the sky.

From these early assignments, Knight must have anticipated the potential for aviation art. In June 1920, he traveled to Antwerp to see the Aero Show, which displayed military planes used during World War I, as well as commercial and experimental planes developed in the years after the war. He also attended an aeronautical meet held in conjunction with

One of two cover illustrations produced by Clayton Knight for *House & Garden*, a popular interior design, entertaining, and gardening magazine published by Condé Nast, July 1922.

Clayton Knight took this sketchbook on his summer 1920 trip to the Aero Show at Olympia in London and the Aeronautical Meet in Antwerp, Belgium. The inspiration for the cover image is unknown, but it is based on the Bronze Horseman, an equestrian statue of Peter the Great in St. Petersburg, commissioned by Catherine the Great and created by the French sculptor Étienne Maurice Falconet. (Clayton Christopher Knight)

Left: In describing the hangars at the airdrome in Antwerp, Clayton Knight observed there were "a half-dozen canvas ones, and two huge wooden sheds that were up before the war and which the Germans used for Zeppelins." July 25, 1920. (Clayton Christopher Knight)

Right: These sketches were made from a sequence of 781 photographs that form Eadweard Muybridge's series "Animal Locomotion," published by the University of Pennsylvania in 1887. The South Kensington Museum (later the Victoria & Albert Museum) subscribed to "Animal Locomotion" when it was produced. (Clayton Christopher Knight)

the Olympics. During this two-month trip, he observed an international collection of aircraft competing with one another, and he updated his knowledge of the state of aviation in Europe. He also made many connections and answered many questions about flying in America. A detailed letter to *U.S. Air Service* magazine (September 1920) describes the airplanes he saw and the people he met.[31] His sketchbook reveals a drawing of the Antwerp airdrome, dated July 25.

On the way back to New York, Knight spent time in London where he focused on the pioneering studies of animal locomotion by English photographer Eadweard Muybridge. Knight seemed keenly interested in the stages of a bird in flight. One can easily speculate that he was analyzing the nature of movement for later application in making an airplane appear to fly. Then, sailing from Southampton, he returned to New York on August 21.

It is at this point that Knight's old friend Lucille Patterson (Marsh) from the School of the Art Institute introduced him to Katharine Sturges, who had attended the Chicago Academy of Fine Arts and subsequently studied in Japan before moving to New York. While in Chicago, she had found some success as an illustrator for Volland Publishers, founded by German-born Frederick Volland to publish greeting cards. The company soon became known for publishing high-quality, mass-produced children's books written by notable authors and illustrated by equally accomplished artists. After her studies in Japan, she continued her work with Volland in New York, where Japanese influences, notably the flat areas of color characteristic of woodblock prints, found their way into her stylistic renderings. The relationship between Knight and Sturges quickly evolved into a serious one. They married in July 1922 and soon thereafter started a family.

This drawing of Katharine Sturges was done by family friend and illustrator Maud Tousey Fangel, who was known primarily for her appealing drawings of babies, most always done from life. In addition to her illustrations, she also produced portraits. (Clayton Christopher Knight)

WOMEN'S LIFE CLASS, SEPTEMBER, 1907.
CHICAGO ACADEMY OF FINE ARTS.
6 MADISON STREET, CHICAGO.

Postcard of a Women's Life Class at the Chicago Academy of Fine Arts (6 Madison Street), a school with a commercial focus. Katharine Sturges identifies herself in a penciled note. September 1907. (Clayton Christopher Knight)

The cover of Sturges's children's book *Mimi, Momo and Miss Tabby Tibbs* reveals the stylistic influences of her studies in Japan. The whimsical story is based on the adventures of a little girl and a group of toys brought to life in the attic of an abandoned house. The book includes 6 full-page illustrations and a group of smaller, colored drawings. (Clayton Christopher Knight)

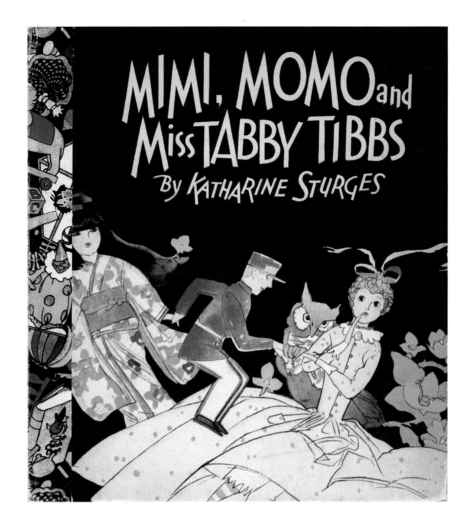

The dedication page for *Mimi, Momo and Miss Tabby Tibbs* features the Japanese doll Momo with the author's two children, Joey (Clayton Jr.) and Hilary. (Clayton Christopher Knight)

Knight and Sturges continued to work individually, but they also found ways to collaborate professionally, integrating their respective travels and experiences into their work. In 1925, *Little Pictures of Japan* (edited by Olive Beaupre Miller as part of the "My Travelship" series) was published by Book House for Children, with over 190 pages of poetry and folk tales, half of which were lavishly illustrated by Sturges. A couple of years later, she wrote and illustrated her own book about three dolls, one of them Japanese: *Mimi, Momo and Miss Tabby Tibbs* was published by Gordon Volland and the Buzza Company, with a charming dedication to "two little Knights, Joey and Hilary, by an extravagantly devoted parent."

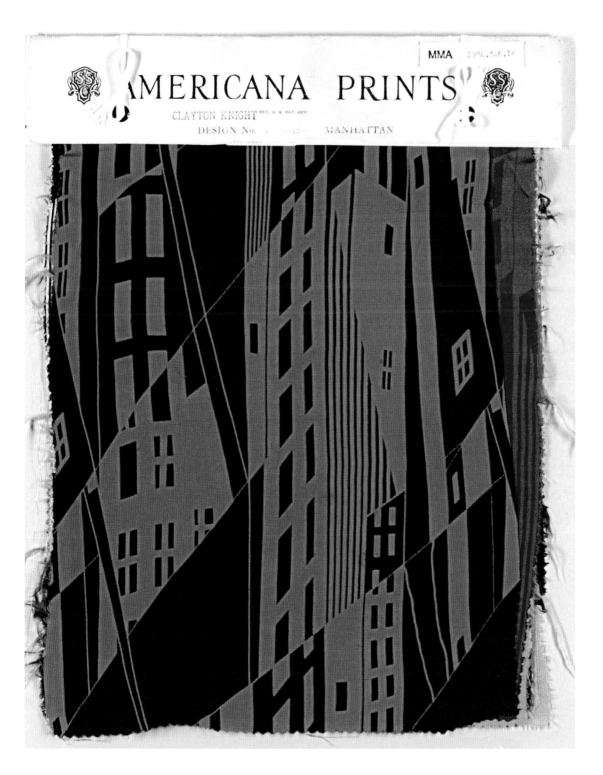

Kneeland (Ruzzie) Green, art director for Stehli Silk Corporation, developed an Americana Print series to celebrate everyday life, while emphasizing important people and trends in American culture. He successfully merged art and industry, marketing the new series as fine art. (The Metropolitan Museum of Art)

AMERICANA PRINTS

Stehli Fabrics Corporation

DESIGN ·712 MID-OCEAN

ARTIST CLAYTON KNIGHT

A HUNDRED PER CENT. AMERICAN
DESIGN: "THE SKYSCRAPERS OF
NEW YORK,"
an Americana Print in Silk by Clayton Knight,
Made Into a Smart Palm Beach Model.
(Bonney, From Times Wide World Photos.)

April 17, 1926 THE Price 15 cents
NEW YORKER

Left: A *New York Times* article, which appeared soon after the debut of the Americana Print series, declared Clayton Knight's design "Manhattan" to be the most successful, noting that "it is so modern that it suggests a view of all our skyscrapers piled up together, seen from an elevated train rounding a sharp curve." November 1, 1925. (The Metropolitan Museum of Art)

Right: Clayton Knight's sophisticated portrayal of the newly independent and fashionable woman of the 1920s continues to be one of the most popular of *New Yorker* covers since the magazine launched as a weekly in 1925. Appropriately, an interior story profiled F. Scott Fitzgerald. April 17, 1926.

Left: This simple, two-color block-print proof—without the additional hand-coloring that would eventually be incorporated— became an illustration for *War Birds: Diary of an Unknown Aviator*. (Clayton Christopher Knight)

Opposite: This design, titled "Mid-Ocean," was one of two aviation-related designs by Clayton Knight for the Stehli Silk Company. The second, titled "War Birds," was introduced in series two. (The Metropolitan Museum of Art)

During this period, Sturges and Knight also created textile designs for the Stehli Silk Company, which sought the talents of well-known artists to design fabric for women's fashion.[32] Knight's close professional association with his wife was pulling him out of the bread-and-butter work of advertising and into more creative pursuits.

Knight's training at the School of the Art Institute of Chicago had included instruction in block printing and lettering in classes on book illustration. And Sturges developed a deep appreciation for this particular set of skills during her stay in Japan, where a long tradition of woodblock printing contributed greatly to the development of modern art in the late 19th century. The couple was also influenced by family friend and established illustrator C. B. Falls, best known for designing patriotic posters during the war, and for a popular 1923 alphabet book based on a series of original woodblock prints depicting letters with corresponding animals. Both Knight and Falls greatly admired modern German printmaker and poster designer Ludwig Hohlwein, whose flat, interlocking shapes of brilliant color were a frequent point of reference.[33]

It's not surprising, then, that Knight soon began

Bunk

Seventh Paper in the Series "Back in Seventeen"

ELLIOTT SPRINGS

Illustrations by Clayton Knight

Copyright, 1926, by Elliott Springs

AS THE United States Magazine tells us on every page every month, "If you work hard you will succeed, provided you have the right stuff in you and use good judgment." Yea, and if you've got four aces and everybody else drops you're going to win the pot. And if you own the right kind of African dominoes you can't roll a seven. Otherwise the story about this horny-fisted son of toil donning the royal purple and pushing the button for the board of directors to gather round him is just so much bunk. And the successful Ali Babas don't count the day well spent unless they can tell some unsuspecting stranger how they got where they are by the honest sweat of a brainy brow. They don't say whose brow but the intimation is clear. More bunk! When those birds clean out the boys at stud poker they want their pictures in the paper and claim they invented the game and made all the chips with their own hands. It hasn't ever occurred to them that some poor benighted fallen arch has GOT to win. The plain truth is that some bozos can't be kept out of a bank by anything but a scarlet fever sign and others trip all over their own dogs when they're walking up to get their cup. I remember a case to point. ·

You've heard all about how some sterling youths put on a uniform and before the fracas petered out they were weighted down with medals and waiting for a new rank to be created for them. Well,

"In an old Farman pusher"

don't think it was because they did all the dirty work and had an extra large cranial capacity. Not that they don't tell it to the reporters as such.

There was a young fellow in England who got mad when the Germans broke into Belgium and he signed on the dotted line the next day. He was sufficiently peeved to want to fight, so picked the flying corps as offering the best opportunity of coming to grips with Bismarck's other herrings. It wasn't long before he got his wish and was out at the front popping off a rifle in an old Farman

"Then they gave him Sop Camels"

pusher. When the Farman gave out he got an Avro and went skidding about the sky again with a shot gun. That was back in the days when you flew by ear and got your instructions out of prayer book. He spent a while in hospital and when he got put back together they made him a captain and sent him out again to fly those funny little D. H. Twos in which he sat out front and tried to work a Lewis gun in between shivers from his spine and splutters from his monosoupape motor. He was doing well with the Taubes, and was spending half his time in the sky and the other half under the table, when the Baron dropped on his tail with one of the new synchronized guns that fire through the propeller and made a casualty out of him.

HE DID another tour in Blighty and then they made him a major and gave him a squadron. He ran a fair outfit when his pilots were sober enough and led them all over the Somme valley in those little Bristol Scouts. They they gave him Sop Camels with two Vickers guns on them and he did so well that by 1918 he was a colonel. He didn't bother much about the war but fighting men were scarce and it looked as though he was going right on up the ladder by the well-known blistered route. All the birds with brains had got themselves soft jobs where there wasn't any exposure to

TO ELLIOTT SPRINGS   CLAYTON KNIGHT

Hand-colored woodcut from *War Birds* (1926), depicting a pilot sitting on his wrecked pursuit plane and carelessly smoking a cigarette. Inscribed to Elliot Springs and signed by Clayton Knight. *(Springs Close Family Archive)*

experimenting with woodblock prints depicting action scenes of World War I aviation. His early woodblock prints—colorful, succinct and energetic—may have been intended for a children's book, but a fortuitous meeting with Elliot White Springs at the Dutch Treat Club in 1926 provided a mutually beneficial alternative.[34] At that meeting, Springs told Knight of a story he had written for the U.S. Air Services about Allan F. Bonnalie, a war veteran who had been awarded the United States Army Distinguished Service Cross and decorated by the British with the Distinguished Service Order, and Knight showed Springs the colored woodcuts of war planes he had done for fun. "That made my eyes pop out and pulse speed up. I knew that was just what I needed to persuade the editors to publish my stories," Springs later said. They went to the offices of the periodical *Liberty Weekly,* and according to Springs, the magazine bought the story as an excuse to print one of Knight's drawings. Knight later remembered that this illustration, which appeared in June 1926, was "my first published airplane sketch."[35]

The Bonnalie story was soon followed by the serialization "War Birds: Diary of an Unknown Aviator" in *Liberty* magazine and a book by the same name published by the George H. Doran Company and heavily illustrated with both woodcuts and drawings.

The "unknown" aviator referred to in the book's title was John McGavock Grider, a pilot well known to both Knight and Springs as a fellow member of the training group at Oxford University and a squadron mate of Springs in No. 85 Squadron, RAF. Grider's diary, completed and embellished by Springs after Grider's death in combat on June 18, 1918, became the substance of *War Birds*.

War Birds spread the fame of Clayton Knight and Elliot White Springs beyond their small aviation audience at a time when Charles Lindbergh was about to electrify the world as the first man to fly nonstop across the Atlantic in 1927. The role of aviation in popular culture was about to take off, with Knight and Springs bringing authenticity to the genre. Those skeptical of whether Clayton Knight considered this to be a seminal moment for him professionally need only look at his log book,[36] which meticulously records all of his jobs with associated dates and payments over a 16-year period. It starts in 1927, as if nothing before was of any significance.

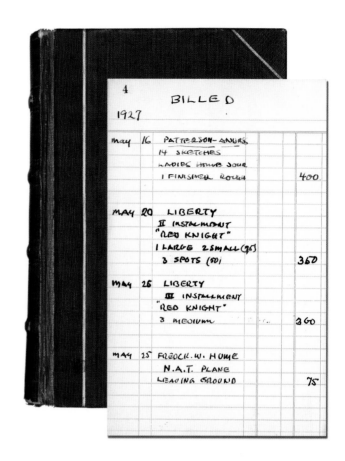

Clayton Knight's log book. The first three entries, all dated May 1927, were for work done for *Ladies Home Journal, Liberty* magazine, and National Air Transport. Knight's drawings for "The Red Knight of Germany" by Floyd Gibbons, serialized in *Liberty* magazine, would solidify his reputation as the premier aviation artist of his time. (Clayton Knight Papers, Archives & Special Collections, University of Connecticut Library)

The AMERICAN LEGION Monthly

Complete Details of The American Legion Monthly -
Houghton Mifflin Company

$25,000 PRIZE WAR NOVEL CONTEST

CHAPTER TWO

William Heaslip:
The Formative Years

William Heaslip, the youngest of six children, was an orphan by the time he was four. The story he passed down to his family about his parents' early deaths was that both parents passed away at the same time, possibly from diphtheria, a common killer of children. But we know that not to be the case, because the ravages of contagious diseases in Canada were meticulously recorded in the early years of the 20th century. Dr. Charles Sheard, Toronto's medical health officer, reported 91 cases of diphtheria in that city, but no deaths in January 1902, the month and year of Heaslip's mother's death.[1] Most likely, the "facts" that William Heaslip believed about his parents' deaths were distorted by his own early childhood trauma.

In truth, Joseph Heaslip, an emigrant from Ireland, married Annie Veitch, another Irish immigrant, in October 1890. By 1898, the city directory of Toronto placed the couple on Waterloo Avenue in Ward 6, in the west end of Toronto. Joseph was a laborer with the Canadian Pacific Railway, and Annie maintained the family dairy business. Disaster struck in 1900 with Joseph's death, listed only as "mitral obstruction."[2] It must have come on suddenly, as no length of illness is stated. According to the family Bible, Annie passed away two years later, on January 22, 1902. There is no official registration of her death, and thus, no way to confirm the actual cause.

Information about William Heaslip's early years is poorly documented. It seems probable that after Annie's death all of the children were taken to London City by Charles Veitch, Annie's brother, who worked as a brakeman with the railway. These six children, when added to a family already five strong, posed a formidable challenge for Charles. At some point, William and Ethel—the two youngest—must have required more of an investment in time and resources than the others, because they were sent to

Opposite: The cover of a colonial soldier by William Heaslip was intended to reinforce the feature "The Stars in the Flag." That month, the focus was on New Hampshire, one of the original thirteen colonies. (American Legion Monthly)

Below: This photo of the Heaslip children dressed in black—Jennette and Anne Irene (back row, left to right) and William, Kate, Ethel, and Joseph (front row, left to right)—was presumably taken soon after the death of Annie, their last surviving parent. This would be the last portrait of the family prior to its breakup. (Allan M. Heaslip)

The Births page from the Heaslip family Bible completely records the immediate family, including William John Heaslip, born on May 16, 1897. The Deaths page neglects to list his passing on July 21, 1970. (Allan M. Heaslip)

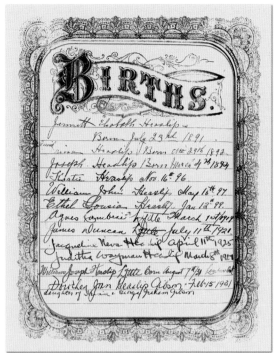
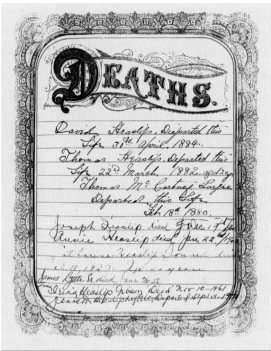

live at the Protestant Home for Orphans on the corner of Cheapside and Richmond streets, next to St. Joseph's Hospital. [3]

In 1911 the Canadian census lists the Veitch household as including Charles, his wife Mary, his brother John, two Veitch children—Elizabeth and Thomas—and two Heaslip children—Joseph Jr. and Katie. Joseph Jr. is listed as an apprentice at the Wright Lithography Company. A year later, two separate entries in the London City

The Protestant Home for Orphans, Aged and Friendless in London City, Ontario, was established in 1874. In the 1890s, the child welfare system took over responsibility for the orphans and focused on families in crisis. (London Free Press Collection of Photographic Negatives, D.F. Weldon Library, Western University, London, Ontario, Canada)

directory indicate that the two older Heaslip sisters, who may have lived with the Veitch family immediately after the deaths of their parents, had by then established themselves professionally: Jennette, the eldest, was forelady at C. R. Sommerville, a manufacturer of paper and fancy boxes; and Anne Irene was a nurse at the Provincial Insane Asylum.

The 1911 census also reveals that William had been adopted by the family of Thomas Snell, a tailor of Irish heritage. The Snell family lived just a few blocks from the Protestant Home for Orphans, where their son Harold taught Sunday school. Harold apparently took a liking to William.[4] Minutes from the March 7, 1910, meeting of the Board of Trustees indicate that of the 32 children living at the Orphan's Home at the time, 14 had chickenpox—and a Mrs. Snell had indicated an interest in adopting one of the children. A board member was assigned to visit the household to see if Mrs. Snell "was a suitable person."[5]

The adoption, a legal agreement classified as an "adoption indenture," took place in March 1910 when William was almost 14.[6] This hybrid denotation was probably typical for an "adoption" of an older child. A document from the Children's Aid Society in New York provides some insight into this arrangement: "Boys between the ages of 12 and 15 are expected to work for their board and clothes till they are 18, but must be sent to school for a part of each year, after which it is expected that they receive wages."[7] Above all, the indenture provision excluded the right of the adoptee to inherit.

The Snell family lived at 419 Oxford Street, not far from the Wolseley Barracks—a building constructed in 1883 specifically for Canadian army troops and home to the Royal Canadian Regiment. It would be a fair assumption that many of Thomas Snell's customers were military officers who had their uniforms made by a custom tailor.[8] Snell's son Harold was still living at home at the age of 22 with a full-time job as a clerk in the local foundry, so we can further conclude that menial shop and home duties fell to young William.

Wolseley Barracks, London, Ont.

The Wolseley Barracks was created as a facility for the training and housing of officers. It included a lecture hall, reading room, and parade grounds for drilling and maneuvers. From a card produced by Red Star News, London City, Ontario, postmarked 1910.

The situation of William's sister Ethel evolved quite differently. She was adopted, took on the name of her adopted family, and graduated from the Toronto Conservatory of Music with honors.

In his later years, William Heaslip did not often talk about his childhood. When he did recall his experiences with the Snell family, he was not kind to the memory of Thomas Snell. He described his adoptive father as self-righteous and domineering. He particularly remembered Snell for requiring him to clean out the backyard chicken coop without the benefit of shoes. And Mrs. Snell was kind, but otherwise deferential to her husband.[9] As a consequence, William's new life was difficult and may not have been much of an improvement over the orphanage. He may also have harbored some deep-seated resentment against his own family members over the proceeds from the sale of the Heaslip dairy farm. These monies were to have gone for the care of the family,[10] but William seems to have been the only one of Joseph and Annie's children left to his own resources.

The lone family member with whom William developed a close association was the youngest Snell offspring, Neva. She was four years older, may have worked with him in the shop for a time, and wrote to him later during his World War I service. Neva became a nurse— and then, a statistic as one of the 50 million people worldwide who succumbed to the influenza epidemic of 1918.[11] Years after leaving the Snell household, Heaslip acknowledged this steadfast relationship by naming one of his daughters after her.

Becoming an Artist/Illustrator

William Heaslip began to display his extraordinary talent early on, overcoming odds that would have discouraged an individual of ordinary gifts. We cannot determine with any accuracy where he received support for the development of his talent. Nor can we be certain where or when his art instruction began.[12] At the orphanage, his education was provided primarily by the public school system—specifically, St. George's Public School.[13] He may also have received some informal instruction and encouragement from his first cousin, Thomas Veitch, who displayed early artistic inclinations in a highly decorative book inscription he created for his aunt Annie, of whom he was very fond, in 1889.[14] Much later, Thomas received recognition as the sculptor of a credible portrait bust of Sir Adam Beck, titled "Spirit of Niagara," which was displayed in the window of Veitch's employer, the Benson-Wilcox Electric Company.[15] For the most part, however, William acted autonomously, often taking his sketchbook into the countryside to draw.

William Heaslip began his formal training in 1912 at the London Industrial and Art School, which had been established through the Industrial Education Act passed in Ontario in 1911. The school, located in a building that formerly housed the old Colbourne Street School, was within walking distance of the Snell home. Its first principal was H. B. Beal, an exemplary educator whose leadership and dedication to his students is remembered today in the school that now bears his name. And one of its teachers, David Wilkie—a practicing artist and landscape painter from England who passed on his classical British training to students—provided Heaslip with formative instruction.

The London Industrial and Art School opened its doors in 1912 and began offering both day and night classes. (Research Collection of Maya Hirschman)

Wilkie's coeducational evening classes precluded the use of nude models; and so, students practiced their draftsmanship by producing repetitive drawings of antique casts.[16] Wilkie offered Heaslip more than a strong classical curriculum: he mentored and encouraged the promising young artist, and later provided a way for Heaslip to continue his studies in New York.[17]

With the confidence that comes from recognition, at age 17, William Heaslip followed his brother into the printing business. In 1913, he joined Lawson & Jones Printers and Lithographers, a job he would continue until he left to support the war effort.

Lawson & Jones, a far-reaching printing enterprise, had been founded in 1882 by Frank Lawson, a reporter with *The London Advertiser*, and Henry James Jones, a printer for the paper. After a short-lived business venture publishing a semi-monthly magazine called *The Family Circle*, the partners became specialty printers and began producing calendars, which were sold with personalized sales messages. By 1903, they had enjoyed enough success to be able to move to larger facilities, expanding their capabilities with more modern equipment and increasing their workforce to 60 employees.

In 1911, Frank died unexpectedly, passing his portion of the partnership to his son Ray. Two years later, Ray purchased Henry James Jones's shares of the company and became president at the age of 27.[18] It was at this time that Heaslip was hired by the firm, along with fellow apprentice Albert Edward "Ab" Templar (1897–1992). Templar later studied with Heaslip in New York, and then returned to London to become one of the area's most renowned artists. Bill Heaslip and Ab Templar maintained a lifelong friendship.[19]

Left: Lawson & Jones apprentices William Heaslip (far right) and Albert Edward "Ab" Templar (far left), *c.* 1913. (Allan M. Heaslip)

Right: William Heaslip at his desk at Lawson & Jones, *c.* 1913. (Allan M. Heaslip)

J. F. CAIRNS LIMITED

SASKATOON, SASK.

THE FINEST RETAIL STORE IN THE PROVINCE

The J. F. Cairns retail store welcomed 12,000 people on opening day on March 17, 1913, and employed 250 people in 25 departments. This steel-engraved illustration, which was featured on the store's stationery, was executed by William Heaslip as an apprentice at Lawson & Jones. (Allan M. Heaslip)

The 1913 city directory lists William Heaslip as an "engineer" with Lawson & Jones. That designation may reflect the department in which he worked, rather than a mechanical position he might have held. Examples of his work from this time indicate that he worked with Ab Templar as an engraver, putting his personal touch on the many promotional calendars produced by the company. This early training as an engraver served Heaslip well in his later work in fine art intaglio printmaking.

The start of the war in Europe led to a downturn in corporate profits. Sales fell, costs increased, and employees left to join the service. As a result, Ray Lawson began to rely heavily on young, inexpensive labor, and Templar and Heaslip were part of that young workforce. They were each paid $.50 a week, with promises of semiannual increases of $.50 cents over a five-year tenure.[20]

In 1914, London City was one of the most important financial and manufacturing centers in Canada, with a population of 55,000. Labatt and Carling Breweries, McCormick and Perrin soda crackers, McClary stoves, Leonard boilers, and Emco pipes—all household names across Canada—provided the city with a strong commercial base. A 94-page promotional booklet published by the newly organized Bureau of Industry, with illustrations of existing companies, municipal buildings, and distinguished homes, aptly reflected the city's prosperity and the pervasive optimism of the time.[21] But much of that would end abruptly on the evening of August 4, 1914, with a declaration of war.

World War I commenced when Germany sent its armies through neutral Belgium to launch a massive attack on France. Honor-bound to protect the neutrality of Belgium as a signatory to the 1839 Treaty of London, Britain declared war against Germany—and the British Empire automatically followed suit.

Late on August 4, the citizens of London, Ontario, received the news bulletin: "Great Britain Declares War: God Save the King!"[22] The next day, the *Free Press* described the scene: "Wild cheers went up when the declaration of

This Indian head engraving done with steel and diamond needles is another example of the highly skilled work of apprentice William Heaslip at the age of 18, c. 1915. (Allan M. Heaslip)

Once enlisted, recruits would often be assigned to the Wolseley Barracks, a training camp for many units formed in southwestern Ontario. This photo was taken *c*. 1915. (Western Archives and Special Collections, Western University, Hines Studio Fonds, AFC 341-S18-I3)

war was announced; and gathering at Richmond and Carling streets, the crowd lustily sang 'God Save the King,' 'Britannia Rules the Waves,' 'The Maple Leaf Forever,' 'O Canada,' and other national and patriotic airs." Few citizens of the Empire—or indeed the world—realized the horror that was to follow.

Becoming an Aviator

Studio photograph of William Heaslip and his brother Joseph (in uniform). Joseph enlisted on September 26, 1917, in the Canadian Overseas Expeditionary Force. (Allan M. Heaslip)

London, Ontario, was already home to major military installations, and the Wolseley Barracks soon became the site of several large "tent cities" where thousands trained for battle. The 7th Fusiliers, 6th Field Battery, and 1st Hussars were all accommodated in the London Armories.

Though there was no military aviation presence in London City at the time, the young Bill Heaslip was surely an eyewitness to the earliest appearance of an airplane in that town. On May 27, 1912, the American pilot Beckwith Havens took off from Carling Farm—located next to the Wolseley Barracks and a few blocks from the Oxford Street home of Thomas Snell—and flew down Dundas Street at 600 feet in a Curtiss E pusher bi-plane.[23] Soon thereafter, the Royal Flying Corps (RFC) invited young men, ages 18–30, to become participants, rather than observers, in the newly developing field of aviation by advertising for "strong, keen, and courageous" men of "fair education and eager for accomplishment." They offered $1.10 per day, certainly an improvement on Heaslip's wages at Lawson & Jones.

Future flying ace Billy Bishop of Owen Sound, Ontario, just 130 miles north of town, was stationed in London City for a short time as a member of the 7th Canadian Mounted Rifles. After an inauspicious introduction to the infantry, Bishop transferred to the air service, which was, in his own words, "the only way to fight a war; up there above the mud and the mist in the everlasting sunshine." He left for England in 1915 and returned to Canada two years later on extended leave, having earned the Military Cross, the Distinguished Service Order, and the Victoria Cross.[24] News of Bishop's exploits must have inspired William Heaslip, the self-possessed young man whose tumultuous life experiences engendered a need for positive male role models and a sense of belonging.[25] On September 21, 1917, Heaslip traveled to Toronto and enlisted in the Royal Flying Corps. Upon his departure from Lawson & Jones, he was presented with a gold signet ring inscribed "to Bill Heaslip from Ray Lawson, 1917." His years as an apprentice were over.

When the United States entered the war in 1917, a number of agreements of reciprocity were inaugurated between the U.S. and Canada to train men for the military. Among them was an agreement between the Aviation Section of the United States Signal Corps (USSC) and the Royal Flying Corps to train 10 squadrons of pilots in two aerodromes in Texas. A portion of a third aerodrome was set aside for an aerial gunnery school, also under the control of the Royal Flying Corps.[26] With a keen eye and adroit athleticism, William Heaslip was perfectly suited for training in ground observation and aerial gunnery.

Studio photograph of William Heaslip in uniform. His attestation form states that he took his oath and was approved and appointed to the Royal Flying Corps on September 21, 1917.
(Allan M. Heaslip)

William J. Heaslip was part of a group of 238 pupils in the fifth course offered under these agreements of reciprocity. Students proceeded from Camp Borden on Kempenfelt Bay north of Toronto, to Hicks Field at Camp Taliaferro west of Fort Worth, Texas. The facilities in Texas were outstanding, and the equipment—which included synchronized gear, camera guns, and turret machines—was more than adequate for training purposes.[27] Aerial instruction was initiated within 24 hours of arrival, with nearby Lake Worth providing an ideal locale for unencumbered target practice.[28]

By April 1918 Heaslip was back in Canada at the newly constructed aerodrome at Beamsville, with its state-of-the-art facilities.[29] Improved training techniques there were

Training Cadre, RFC, Camp Taliaferro, Field #1, Fort Worth, Texas, 1917. William Heaslip is seated front row, sixth from left. (Allan M. Heaslip)

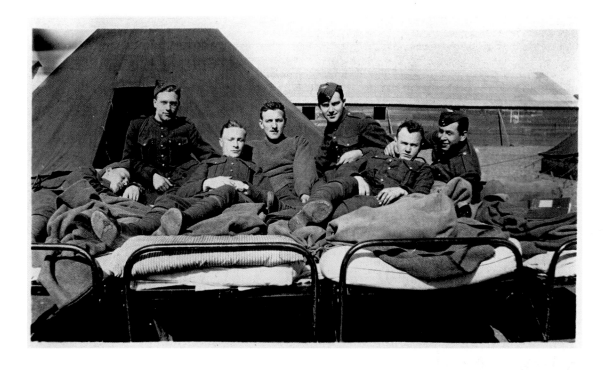

Tent mates, Camp Taliaferro, Fort Worth, Texas. William Heaslip is second from right. (Allan M. Heaslip)

Sgt. C. Saunders with Second Class Air Mechanics William J. Heaslip, George Lundy, and Archie Barr (left to right) in Dallas, Texas, December 1917. (Allan M. Heaslip)

replicating conditions experienced at the front, and by September pupils were regularly passing all proficiency tests. [30] Heaslip became quite popular with the officers, who took advantage of his ability to complete a pencil portrait in less than 20 minutes. [31]

On November 11, 1918, after four years of bloody conflict, the Armistice was signed, and the Great War drew to a close. On December 28, Heaslip was discharged, having served just one year and 99 days, a short period during which his skills of observation became finely honed, and his self-confidence—free from the stigma of being raised an orphan—grew exponentially. This period of service in the military clearly left an indelible mark on the artist.

Prior to leaving Beamsville, Heaslip met his future wife, Clare Wayman, an immigrant from Swansea, Wales, whose father owned a sizable farm in Grimsby, Ontario. Clare Wayman was a member of the Royal Flying Corps Auxiliary and worked in the "dope shop," [32] applying translucent dope and varnish to the fabric that covered the wooden structure of aircraft. Heaslip, who had lost his closest female friend when Neva Snell passed away in October, was typically taciturn in the company of women. Nonetheless, he was receptive to Clare who—family members said—"set her eyes on him immediately." [33]

At one point during this period, Heaslip returned to London City and reestablished contact with David Wilkie. Sensing great potential in his former student, Wilke made financial and administrative arrangements for Heaslip to study at the famed National Academy of Design in New York.

Clockwise from top left:

Clare Wayman, one of 91 civilian female volunteers supporting the School of Aerial Fighting in Beamsville, Ontario, Canada. (Allan M. Heaslip)

William Heaslip and Clare Wayman at her father's farm in Grimsby, Ontario, 1919. Grimsby, on the shores of Lake Ontario in the Niagara region, was approximately six miles from Beamsville. (Allan M. Heaslip)

The Fine Art Society Building displayed exhibitions of the National Academy of Design from 1900 to 1940. This building housed the exhibition that displayed students' work for which Heaslip won the Suydam Silver Medal for Drawing from Life. It also housed the Art Students League, which Heaslip attended.

Regular National Academy of Design classes were held in a nondescript building at the corner of W. 109th Street and Amsterdam Ave. (Wurts Bros., New York, NY/Museum of the City of New York. X2010.7.1.1273)

William Heaslip's enrollment card for the first term at the National Academy of Design in New York. A later notation was added to the card in red ink when he won the Suydam Silver Medal for Drawing from Life. (Historic Archives, National Academy of Design, New York)

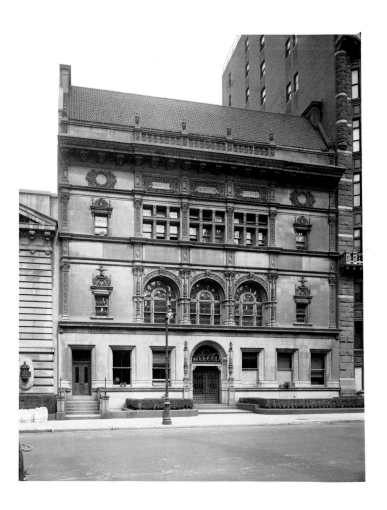

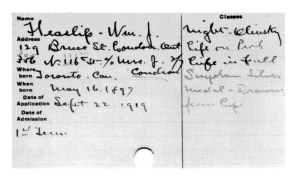

Becoming an Aviation Artist & Illustrator

The National Academy of Design was founded in 1826 with the stated objective of "the cultivation and extension of the arts of design, and its funds shall be employed in promoting that object." Membership included academicians, associates, and honorary members with "premiums" granted for the encouragement of students.[34] Its first president was the esteemed Samuel F. B. Morse (1826–45). During the war years of the early 20th century, American Impressionist painter Julian Alden Weir and sculptor Herbert Adams served as consecutive presidents, shepherding the organization through upheaval and tumult.

Despite the fact that enrollment dropped to 219 students during the Great War, members of the Academy were actively involved in various patriotic gestures, including the establishment of an Art War Relief Fund designed to raise funds for the purchase of clothing and hospital supplies. The Academy even took the extraordinary step of outlawing dissent among its members, with a bulletin declaring: "The National Academy of Design has gone on record as upholding the government of the United States in the present war, and it is requested that all students not in sympathy with this action will resign their membership in our Schools before further action is necessary."[35]

In September 1919, Heaslip enrolled at the National Academy and settled into a rooming house at 356 West 116th Street in Harlem. Then, as if to establish his partisan credentials, he joined the National Guard, Old 7th Regiment in New York, and faithfully served until 1923. This allowed him an opportunity to network with members of New

Left: William Heaslip in the distinctive regimental dress of the 7th Regiment, worn from around 1825 to 1970. The uniform consisted of a grey coatee, with worsted epaulettes and white cross belts, white trousers, and a black leather bell crown shako with white pompom. (Allan M. Heaslip)

Right: This photograph of William Heaslip and a National Guard buddy, dated 1923, is most likely from annual training at Camp Smith, Peekskill or Pine Camp (Fort Drum). (Allan M. Heaslip)

York's political and social elite—and to stay close to military life. The 7th Regiment conducted weekly two-hour drills; offered miscellaneous lectures; and participated in parades, inspections by high-ranking American and foreign military leaders, dinners, dances, garden parties, musicals, shooting competitions, and sporting events.[36] In 1923, Heaslip donated his professional services as an illustrator by designing a new logo for the regiment. Officers were quite pleased with his work and proudly declared: "Hence, we have an artist on our private staff."[37]

Heaslip probably held a day job, as he signed up only for night classes at the Academy. Nonetheless, he developed quickly as an artist, taking life drawing under the watchful eye of the Russian-born Ivan Olinsky, the sought-after painter of portraits, landscapes, and murals; and former assistant to famed muralist John LaFarge. Olinsky, who was represented by the Macbeth Gallery, was able to command up to $2,000 per portrait in the 1920s.[38] Heaslip began by drawing from plaster casts, later advancing to Life in Full with live models, as was standard for students of the day.[39]

Heaslip excelled at his work and was soon recognized for his abilities with the coveted Suydam[40] Medal (Silver) for Drawing from Life.[41] News of this remarkable achievement reached the *The Free Press*, London, Ontario (April 29, 1920) newspaper, which reported: "Londoner Wins Coveted Honor: William Heaslip Awarded Medal for First Year Showing in Art." The article continued:

> In view of the fact that a student is seldom able to capture this primary honor until his second or third term, Mr. Heaslip is to be congratulated. The medal is the highest award outside of the traveling scholarship which can come to an artist student of New York, and Mr. Heaslip's friends are therefore predicting a great future for the young man.[42]

Heaslip left the Academy after only a year and signed up for a course in Life and Pictorial Composition at the Art Students League in October 1920. The course was taught by John Sloan (1871–1951), a member of the "Ash Can School."[43] Heaslip also took a course on Illustration and Composition taught by Wallace Morgan,[44] an alumnus of the National Academy, former newspaper artist at the *New York Herald*, and official artist of the American Expeditionary Forces during World War I. Heaslip was certainly aware of his instructor's war art, which was known to capture "the moment" in his depictions of battle-worn infantry. He found a kindred spirit in Morgan, and he stayed with him for the duration of the academic year. Their personal friendship endured for many years.

Having acquired the essential tools of his trade, Heaslip invited Clare Wayman to join him in New York where they were married at the Church of the Transfiguration (Little Church Around the Corner) on November 5, 1921. They moved to an apartment in Greenwich Village over a lively speakeasy called the Pig & Whistle.

Family members recall that Clare was known for her exquisite penmanship and found employment as a correspondence secretary

Wallace Morgan taught at the Art Students League off and on from 1905 to 1929 and was made an honorary member of that organization, a rare honor bestowed only to the likes of George Bellows, Howard Pyle, and Robert Henri.

FEED a FIGHTER
Eat only what you need —
Waste nothing —
That he and his family
may have enough

UNITED STATES FOOD ADMINISTRATION

for Edith Roosevelt, the widow of President Theodore Roosevelt, possibly from connections made through the 7th Regiment.[45] But it is unknown for whom Heaslip worked at this time. This dearth of information could point to the anonymity that often comes when young illustrators attach themselves to corporate entities. Or Heaslip may have been building his portfolio with samples to submit to art directors for consideration and review.[46]

Nonetheless, Heaslip was soon inducted into the Dutch Treat Club, a society founded in 1905 for creative writers and artists,[47] and a place where Clayton Knight and Elliot White Springs were known habitués. Almost certainly, Heaslip's membership was sponsored by Wallace Morgan, then at the top of his profession.

In 1925, Heaslip and another artist started an art service, but it dissolved after a year of operation.[48] Sometime in 1926 Heaslip opened his own studio at the Holbein Studio Building, 154 West 55th Street in midtown Manhattan, working as a freelance illustrator. That year he began producing illustrations for *American Legion Monthly.* With limited circulation and low pay, the magazine was the perfect venue for a beginning illustrator.[49]

Heaslip's military pedigree and veteran status reinforced his suitability for the association with *American Legion*

As an official World War I combat artist, Captain Wallace Morgan had permission to witness and record life in the trenches. This image from Morgan's "Feed a Fighter" poster is typical of the wartime sketches he made while on duty in 1918.

William Heaslip and Clare Wayman were married at the Church of the Transfiguration, also known as the Little Church Around the Corner, an Episcopal parish church located at 1 East 29th Street, between Madison and Fifth Avenues in Manhattan.

This photograph, by Jesse Tarbox Beals, shows the Pig & Whistle Inn, 175 West 4th Street, New York, where Mr. and Mrs. Heaslip first lived. It is listed in city directories from that time as one of Greenwich Village's many tea rooms, but during Prohibition the establishment also sold alcoholic beverages in the evenings. (Schlesinger Library, Radcliffe Institute, Harvard University)

Monthly. William MacLean, its art director, had served with the American Expeditionary Forces (130th Field Artillery, 35th Division) during the Great War, holding the rank of major when the war ended,[50] and he and Heaslip soon became fast friends. Heaslip contributed work to the magazine from July 1926 to January 1955.

While Heaslip's early illustrations for the magazine were patriotic, they did not portray aviation with any specificity. But that was about to change. In September 1928 Heaslip attended a meeting of the Ancient Order of Quiet Birdmen in New York. Founded by World War I pilots, this exclusive and secretive group was comprised of the most distinguished aviators of the times. The group's social gatherings—famous for serious drinking and camaraderie—often included a ritual aptly named the "short snorter." The ritual included attendees' signing currency, usually a one-dollar bill. On that September night, Heaslip brought home a short snorter that included the signature of Clayton Knight.

Knight was already famous for his illustrations in *War Birds: Diary of an Unknown Aviator,* first serialized in *Liberty Weekly* magazine, and *The Red Knight of Germany* by Floyd Gibbons. Heaslip must have been thrilled when he made Knight's acquaintance, and even more thrilled when Knight presented him with an original, signed and inscribed woodcut from *War Birds* in December 1928.

The Dutch Treat Club was founded in 1905 as a social club for illustrators, writers, and performers based in New York City. This logo was designed by James Montgomery Flagg, one of the 11 founders, of the organization, which is still active today. (Library of Congress, Prints & Photographs Division, LC-DIG-ggbain-11682)

The GENTLEMAN and the SCOUNDREL

By Marquis James

Illustrations by William Heaslip

ON THE night of the nineteenth of September, 1780, Private John Paulding of the First Westchester County Regiment of Militia, a prisoner of war in the hands of the British Army in New York City, escaped from the North Dutch Church, which had been turned into a military prison. He passed the British sentries north of the city and entered the American lines near Tarrytown, in Westchester County, a few miles away.

His Majesty's forces did not bother much about the flight of Private Paulding. It had occurred at a moment when General Sir Henry Clinton was busy with a larger scheme. Sir Henry expected to have the war won for his sovereign in a few days now. He was writing to London about the peace terms which should be offered to the Colonies. He suggested pretty liberal conditions. Sir Henry was not such a bad fellow.

Whilst Private Paulding was making his cautious way northward, another soldier of the Revolution also was saying farewell to New York. Major John André was the guest of Colonel Williams's mess that evening. Colonel Williams commanded the Eightieth Infantry of British Regulars. He was fortunate to have André at his table. Anyone was fortunate to be a host to the adjutant general of the British Army in America and right-hand man of Sir Henry Clinton. André was twenty-nine years old, brave, able, gay and handsome. He was the life of any party. He brought the gathering at Colonel Williams's to a close by standing on a chair and singing a resounding barrack ballad entitled, "How Stands the Glass Around?"

That was in the small hours. After a snatch of sleep Major André embarked on a great adventure.

Sundown next day found him, as well as Private Paulding, safe within the American lines. André was safe in the enemy's country because he was on the British man-of-war Vulture, which was anchored off Teller's Point, thirty miles up the river. Teller's Point is now called Croton Point. It is a state park. But the Vulture dared not venture farther than the Point, beyond which the Hudson gradually narrows from a width of three miles to half a mile. Lofty cliffs look down from both sides of the stream. Those heights were fortified for miles and were vigilantly manned by more than one-fourth of Washington's army.

The loss of the Highlands of the Hudson would have opened a highway for the British from the Atlantic ocean to Canada. It would have cut the Colonies in two. The British held New York City with twelve thousand soldiery and a fleet. The sole remaining link for the passage of American troops between New England and the South was a ferry below West Point. So Washington had to hold the Highlands at all hazard. To this task he had allotted three thousand men. He picked their commander with great care—a general who had no superior as a combat leader in the Continental forces—Benedict Arnold.

The fortunes of the Continentals were low. Washington's army was reduced to 11,400 men. Half of these were militia whose terms would expire in three months. Prospects for re-enlistments were dark. Washington had just attempted a drive for recruits to bring his force up to thirty-five thousand. It had failed dismally. Troops were poorly clad, badly fed and worse paid. Some had drawn no pay for three years. The treasury was empty and credit was poor. Congress was jealous of the army when it won and nagged it when it did not win. At that stage of the game the Continental Congress was pretty small potatoes.

Washington was getting worried. He based his immediate hopes on the French. Rochambeau and Lafayette had five thousand troops encamped in Rhode Island. Whilst Private John Paulding, escaped prisoner of war, and Major John André, win-the-war schemer, their fates curiously joined, were making their separate ways into the American lines along the Hudson, Washington was a few miles away at Hartford, Connecticut. He was talking to the French generals about getting their troops into action.

When Major André boarded the Vulture he must have been pretty well keyed up. A big moment in his life was at hand. Here he was, a kid of twenty-nine, trying to win a war practically single-handed. For fifteen months he had carried one end of the deepest conspiracy ever laid on American soil, and now in fifteen minutes' time he expected to find out the result of these efforts. Aboard the Vulture he was to receive a mysterious stranger, and his hopes were based on the supposition that this caller would turn out to be Benedict Arnold.

Arnold was one of the American generals the British feared most. He had done brilliant work early in the war. But he was a spendthrift and had the bad habit of touching his friends for loans and never paying them back. This weakness and others were widely advertised by Arnold's enemies, who included some high generals who were jealous of their colleague's abilities. Washington, who needed all the good men he could find, rather took Arnold's part, and when the British evacuated Philadelphia he put Arnold in command with a small force. Philadelphia was a soft snap, but Washington figured Arnold had it coming because he had seen some rough usage. Besides, he was just out of the hospital and his wounds still bothered him. Philadelphia would soothe his vanity and give him a chance to rest up and get well.

Arnold was a great lady-killer and the society of Philadelphia was the swellest in the Colonies. Arnold was in the swim in no time, and of course he met Peggy Shippen, the belle of the town. Peggy's father was a Tory. The winter before the British had been in Philadelphia and the Shippen mansion was the scene of many a brilliant entertainment for His Majesty's officers.

Arnold fell in love with Peggy at once, but he did not accomplish much, at first, because Peggy's heart had been half won already by a young gentleman who was fighting on the other side. His name was John André.

But to make a long story short, in a few months the captivating General Arnold and the beautiful

"The Gentleman and the Scoundrel," a story by Marquis James, recounts the treachery of General Benedict Arnold. Following his service as an Army captain in World War I, James served as national director of publicity for the American Legion, and as a member of the staff at the *American Legion Monthly* from 1923 to 1932. (*American Legion Monthly*)

The tradition of the "short snorter" was started by bush pilots in Alaska in the 1920s but soon spread throughout military and commercial aviation. (Allan M. Heaslip)

Just after that initial meeting, Heaslip was selected by *American Boy* magazine to illustrate a series entitled "What Makes it Fly" by Alexander Klemin, director and professor at the Guggenheim School of Aeronautics at New York University. This was the beginning of Heaslip's focus on aviation.

In December 1928, Heaslip joined the Society of Illustrators, and soon thereafter he started to receive assignments with aviation themes. In 1929, he began a brilliantly conceived series of illustrations for paint manufacturer Berryloid (Berry Brothers, Detroit, Michigan), in which finishes of featured airplanes were inspired by the markings of birds. And for the first time beneath his signature there appears an abstract logo of an aircraft. This symbol became inexorably associated with Heaslip's name for the duration of his career.

Rochester, New York, and Toronto, Ontario—birthplaces of Clayton Knight and William Heaslip, respectively—are less than 100 miles apart as the crow flies. Both cities depended on the industrial development of the Great Lakes region for their prosperity; and both were situated within the orbit of Glenn Curtiss's fledgling aviation enterprises at Hammondsport, New York. Moreover, both Knight and Heaslip—separated only by a seven-year age difference—started their training at technological art schools and continued their professional instruction at prestigious art institutions in America. Following the amazing triumph of Charles Lindbergh in 1927, Clayton Knight and William Heaslip would communicate aviation themes with an accuracy and immediacy possible only from artists who had personally experienced flight. Indeed, these two artists seem to have formed an unofficial partnership to engage and educate the American public on that subject. No two artists so devoted their careers to this passion, unquestionably earning them the moniker "champions of flight."

This original hand-painted woodcut from *War Birds* shows a pilot ready for take-off in his Royal Air Force Sopwith Dolphin, while others come in for landing. (Allan M. Heaslip)

What Makes It Fly?

The Eighth Talk on Aerodynamics

By ALEXANDER KLEMIN

DIRECTOR OF DANIEL GUGGENHEIM SCHOOL OF AERONAUTICS
NEW YORK UNIVERSITY
ILLUSTRATIONS BY WILLIAM HEASLIP

THE modern aircraft motor will run for days at a time—you've read of the record made by the Army plane "Question Mark" in staying in the air nearly seven continuous days. You know what the wonderful aircraft engine will do. But do you know why? Do you know what it looks like? How it operates? What it's made of, and why? Professor Klemin gives you the answers to all these questions in this article.

THE modern aircraft engine is the most wonderful source of power ever developed.

The automobile engine must be reliable, but it can be made fairly heavy and it is not expected to operate at nearly full power for many hours at a stretch.

The aircraft engine must be nearly five times as light for a given horse power as the automobile engine, and it is required to deliver nearly its maximum power for several hours continuously.

It is a nuisance, but no worse, for a motorist to have to get out and adjust something in the engine. For the flier, engine failure may mean serious danger.

How It Really Works

THE gasoline engine is generally called an internal combustion engine, because the burning of the gases takes place inside the engine. A steam engine could not be termed an internal combustion engine because the fuel is burned under the boiler and outside the engine itself.

The first problem in the gasoline engine is to supply the fuel and air in the correct proportions. About 14 pounds of air for every pound of fuel is the usual ratio.

For this purpose a carburetor is con-

MASTER CONNECTING ROD WITH 8 LINK RODS

nected to the gasoline tank. In the carburetor there is a float, to which a needle is attached. When gasoline flows in too fast from the tank, the float rises and the float needle cuts down the supply. The drawing illustrating the four stroke cycle principle shows what happens very clearly.

From the float chamber the gasoline passes to a mixing jet. The supply of air passes by this jet, from which the gasoline emerges in a very fine stream and mixes intimately with the air in the

GASOLINE TANK IN WINGS
FUEL LINE TO ENGINE
COWLING

PROJECTING AIR COOLED CYLINDERS INTERFERE to SOME EXTENT WITH PILOT'S VISION

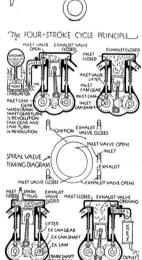
GIPSY AIR COOLED ENGINE WITH CYLINDERS IN LINE GIVES MORE VISION

form of vapor. The vapor then passes along the inlet pipe to the inlet valve. In the pipe is set a throttle or butterfly valve, with which the pilot can regulate the amount of mixture admitted to the engine.

The heart of the engine lies in the cylinder, at the top part of which is the combustion chamber. In the cylinder there is a piston, which because of its piston rings, remains gas tight even when the piston is moving rapidly up and down in the cylinder.

The entire working cycle of the engine takes place in four strokes of the engine piston, down, up, down, and then up again. That is why the gasoline engine of the usual type is called a four cycle engine. The artist has drawn a one cylinder engine as it would look in cross-section at the beginning of each of the four strokes.

Suppose we start with the piston at the top, leaving a comparatively small space vacant at the top of the cylinder. As the piston moves down, the crankshaft turns in the direction shown in the sketches. The up-and-down motion of the piston is called "reciprocating" motion, and it is converted into "rotary" motion by the crankshaft. A man's forearm and hand can be readily made to imitate this conversion of reciprocating motion into rotary motion.

The crankshaft, as shown in our diagram, has a small gear mounted on it. This gear meshes with a gear wheel having twice as many teeth. The gear wheel is mounted on another shaft, which turns accordingly at half the speed of the crankshaft, and which carries a cam. This cam, owing to its peculiar contour, pushes a roller up and down. The roller in turn pushes the inlet valve rod up and down—against the action of a spring, which serves to hold the roller against the cam.

(Continued on page 46)

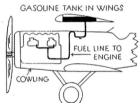
The FOUR-STROKE CYCLE PRINCIPLE

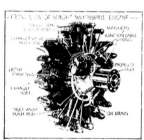
FRONT VIEW OF WRIGHT WHIRLWIND ENGINE

REAR VIEW WRIGHT WHIRLWIND ENGINE

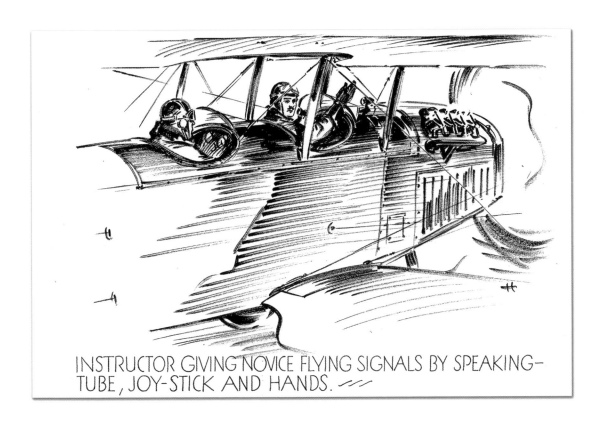

INSTRUCTOR GIVING NOVICE FLYING SIGNALS BY SPEAKING-TUBE, JOY-STICK AND HANDS.

STUDENT FLIER RECEIVES PARTING ADVICE FROM HIS INSTRUCTOR ON FIRST SOLO FLIGHT.

Opposite & this page: Alexander Klemin taught the first aeronautics course at New York University from 1919 to 1925. In 1926 he wrote *If You Want to Fly: The Boy's Book of Aviation*, published by Coward-McCann, New York, and in 1929 he followed with his "What Makes It Fly" series in *American Boy*, which introduced boys to the possibilities of flight. The original illustrations here cover both the technical and the practical. (Allan M. Heaslip)

Overleaf: Heaslip's striking Bald eagle/Eaglerock combination is depicted in this original oil painting, measuring 29 x 21 inches. (Theodore Hamady)

Bald
EAGLE

CHAPTER THREE

Boom, Bust, and Recovery

Left: Charles Lindbergh's *Spirit of St. Louis* is caught in the glare of spotlights as he approaches Le Bourget airport at the end of his epic crossing of the Atlantic Ocean. His feat electrified the world and heralded the true beginning of the Golden Age of Aviation. This illustration by Clayton Knight was for the June 1930 issue of *Redbook* magazine. (Hearst Publications)

Right: This cover for *Popular Aviation and Aeronautics* magazine (February 1929), illustrated by Clayton Knight, was intended to show the public feeling comfortable flying at night.

The deprivations of World War I soon gave way to new freedoms and ushered in the consumer economy known as the Roaring Twenties. America enjoyed robust growth during this decade, with dramatic economic developments especially in the field of transportation. In 1924, a basic Ford Model T roadster sold for an easily affordable $265, which caused passenger rail travel to lose a great deal of its ridership to the ready availability of automobiles.[1]

At the same time, the public began to recognize the importance of flying in both business and recreational endeavors. With the passage of the Air Commerce Act of

May 21st, 1927—*The arrival at Le Bourget. "That black night in Paris, his plane came to a halt on Le Bourget field; but Lindbergh the man kept on going."*

NEW YORK

Herald Tribune

MAGAZINE

Section XIII

Mrs. William Brown Meloney, *Editor*

Sunday, August 5, 1928

Thirty-two Pages

Bigger and Better Airports Are the Need of Cities That Look Toward the Future
Drawn for the Herald Tribune by Clayton Knight

Airports of the Future

By William. P. MacCracken Jr.

Assistant Secretary of Commerce for Aeronautics

NEW YORK

Herald Tribune

MAGAZINE

Section VII

Mrs. William Brown Meloney, *Editor*

Sunday, August 7, 1927

Thirty-two Pages

The Pony Express of the Air
Drawn for the Herald Tribune by Clayton Knight

Columbia—Gem of the Airways

By Herbert Hoover

United States Secretary of Commerce

Above: *New York Herald Tribune* articles of August 7, 1927, and August 8, 1928, both of which were illustrated by Clayton Knight, proclaimed respectively: "Airports grew in greater numbers with active support from the cities they served, flying clubs were organized, and aviation was adopted as a subject taught in public schools, flying meets, air races," and "aeronautical expositions increased in number and attendance."

Right: The new aviation industry required substantial capital to sustain its growth—and American investors, in the spirit of the 1920s, were ready to participate. This Aviation Securities advert was offered in *Aero Digest* (May 1929).

1926, the government took responsibility for expanding the country's networks of airports and route systems. Air mail and air cargo quickly increased, and the public's interest in private and recreational flying flourished.

1929 was a year of tremendous growth for airlines. They doubled their mileage and carried three times the quantity of airmail and four times the number of passengers compared to the previous year. During the same period, the number of licensed pilots grew from 1,500 to more than 11,000, and over 4,500 airplanes were put to use in a variety of commercial endeavors. Many engine manufacturers, finding more orders for commercial planes than for military aircraft, launched commercial aviation divisions.[2]

Clayton Knight's Career Takes Off

With the dramatic upswing in aviation activities, Clayton Knight's backload of projects greatly increased, propelling him into a frenetic work schedule. The preponderance of his illustrative work between 1926 to 1930 focused on aerial combat that had taken place in World War I and were published in *Liberty* magazine. Introduced to the public in 1924, *Liberty* was a collaborative effort of Col. Robert McCormick of the *Chicago Tribune* and Capt. Joseph Medill Patterson of the *New York Daily News*. In contrast to *Saturday Evening Post*'s more sedate readership, *Liberty* targeted what *Time* magazine referred to as the "more jazz-loving level of the public." Each weekly issue of the magazine cost five cents.[3]

Liberty magazine published the first segment of "The Red Knight of Germany" by Floyd Gibbons in its issue dated June 18, 1927—a serial that ended with the November 19 issue. Knight's artwork, interspersed with numerous contemporary photographs

This illustration by Clayton Knight appeared in the second episode of "The Red Knight of Germany" in *Liberty* magazine (July 2, 1927). It depicts Baron Manfred von Richthofen as an observer pointing out an enemy fighter to his pilot. Baron von Richthofen entered the war in 1914 as a Uhlan (light cavalry) officer and transferred to aviation in 1915. After serving as an observer, he became a pilot, scoring his first victory on September 16, 1916. At the time of his death in combat on April 20, 1918, he had scored 80 victories. Baron Manfred von Richthofen was the Ace of Aces of the Great War. (Liberty Library Corporation, 2018. All rights reserved.)

wonderfully illustrated the story. Gibbons's story, which commanded a separate exhibit in the former World War I Gallery at the Smithsonian Institution's National Air and Space Museum in Washington, DC, helped establish the myth of the World War I combat pilot and rekindled America's interest in Great War military aviation. The museum exhibit label read:

> In his bestselling book *The Red Knight of Germany*, Floyd Gibbons portrayed Manfred von Richthofen's life as the romantic saga of a modern-day hero. Although he based the book on official sources, Gibbons interpreted the facts in a highly fictionalized manner. Many youths of the 1920s and 1930s learned about the Red Baron and the war in the air from these exaggerated accounts.[4]

Knight shared honors with two other artists—Harold von Schmidt and John Thomason, Jr.—for illustrating Norman S. Hall's serialized story "The Balloon Buster: Frank Luke of Arizona." The other artists did most of the illustrative work for the serial, but Knight's contributions were superior in quality.

Knight then produced several illustrations for the serial "Leaves from My War Diary," written by former Brigadier General William Mitchell, U.S. Air Service, and published in May 1928. Mitchell, who was known for his prescience concerning future wars, had resigned from the service on February 1, 1926, following his court martial for "insubordination and conduct of a nature to bring discredit upon the military service." His rank and allowances were restored after his death; and Congress, awarded him the Congressional Gold Medal in 1946.

Left: This original painting from "The Red Knight of Germany" (*Liberty*, October 1, 1927) by Clayton Knight shows Baron Manfred von Richthofen emerging from his Albatross D. V with a severe head wound on July 6, 1917. He had scored a total of 57 victories at that point. (Theodore Hamady)

Right: Kaiser Wilhelm II is seen talking to the injured Baron—note the bandage under his cap. Baron von Richthofen returned to combat in mid-August, after his brief and incomplete convalescence. He was killed in action on April 21, 1918.

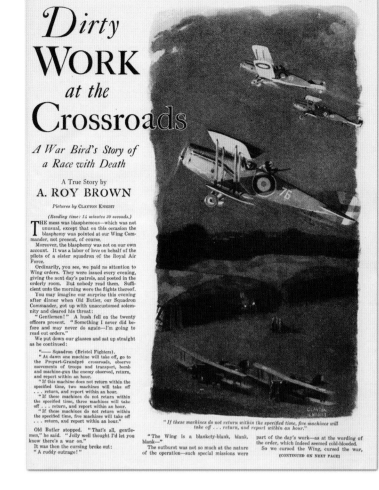

Clayton Knight illustrated this *Liberty* article (December 10, 1927) by A. Roy Brown, a Canadian pilot who was initially credited with having downed Baron von Richthofen. Later research would show that von Richthofen had been shot down by an Australian machine gun unit on the ground as he was passing overhead.

Knight illustrated another *Liberty* article (December 24, 1927) by A. Roy Brown relating the true story of an RAF pilot's perilous aerial intelligence mission.

Frank Luke, nicknamed "the Balloon Buster," was a highly successful, but insubordinate pilot who excelled at destroying well-defended observation balloons. Disliked by his squadron mates, he was ultimately shot down and killed by the enemy. He was one of four U.S. Air Service personnel awarded the Medal of Honor for exemplary gallantry and bravery in combat during World War I. Had he lived, he might have surpassed Eddie Rickenbacker's record, becoming America's Ace of Aces.

And, as referenced in Chapter 1, *Liberty* magazine published the serialization of John McGavock Grider's diary "War Birds: The Uncensored Diary of an American Aviator in France," which led to the important book *War Birds: Diary of an Unknown Aviator*, published by the George H. Doran Company. *Liberty* magazine would remain one of Clayton Knight's most important clients for the next 10 years.

In 1929, Clayton Knight gathered his best illustrations from recently published books—including *War Birds: Diary of an Unknown Aviator* (1926), *Nocturne Militaire* (1927), *Balloon Buster* (1928), and *Above the Bright Blue Sky* (1928); and with the kind permission of *Liberty* magazine and Doubleday Doran, published them in *Pilot's Luck*. Elliott White Springs provided a lengthy foreword and Floyd Gibbons wrote the introduction. Knight explained the book's rationale in the preface:

There were multiple illustrators for the "War Birds" serialization, including Will Foster and Frank Hoffman, but Clayton Knight provided the illustrations for aerial combat. The series concluded in the November 20, 1926 issue of *Liberty* magazine. (Liberty Library Corporation, 2018. All rights reserved)

Opposite: The book *War Birds: Diary of an Unknown Aviator*, containing splendid illustrations by Clayton Knight, was published by the George H. Doran Company in 1926. This colorized version of a dog fight on the book cover described a harrowing aerial battle in July of 1918. A black-and-white version of this same image, which had previously been used in the November 6, 1926 issue of *Liberty* magazine as part of the serialization, appears on the interior, opposite page 44. (George H. Doran Company an imprint of Penguin Random House)

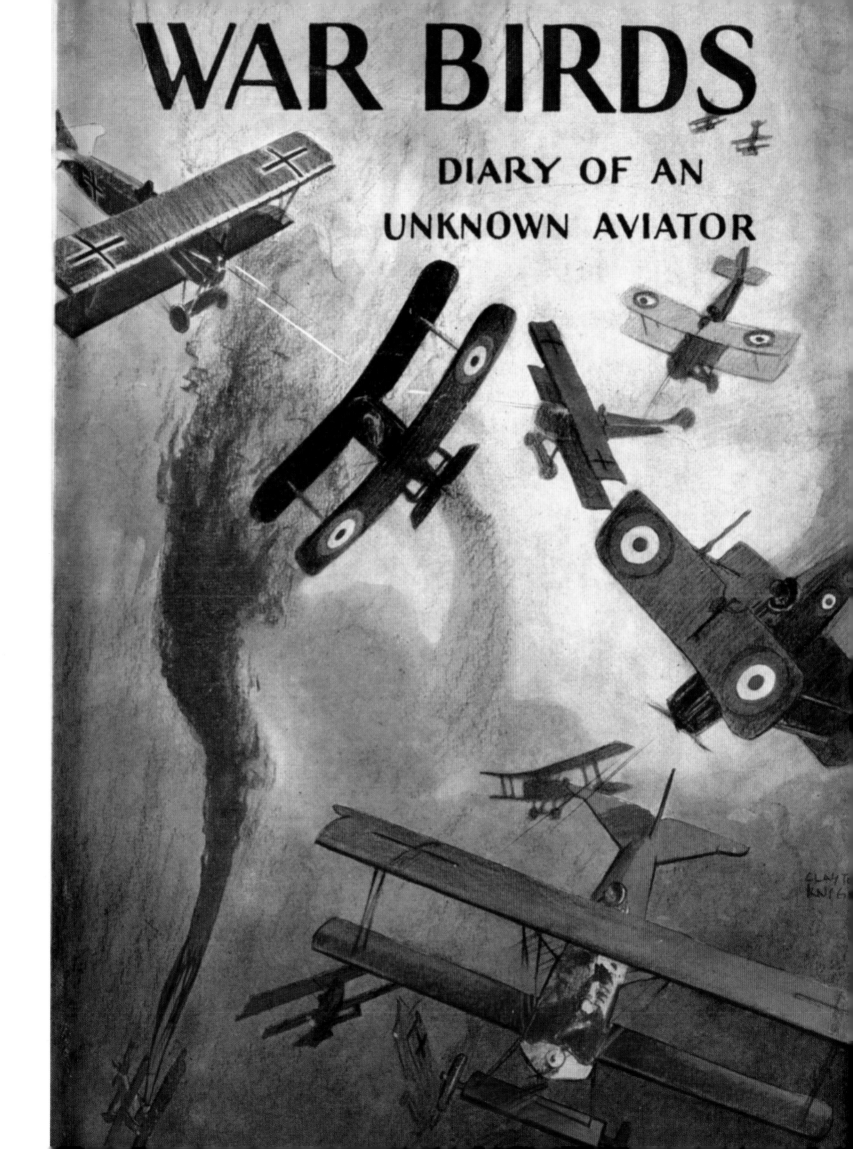

Nocturne Militaire, written by Elliot White Springs and illustrated by Clayton Knight, was published by the George H. Doran Company in 1927. Each of the eight stories in the book was dedicated to a fellow aviator, including Billy Bishop and Larry Callahan, fellow members of No. 85 Squadron. (George H. Doran Company an imprint of Penguin Random House)

Elliot White Springs' *Above the Bright Blue Sky* was published by Doubleday, Doran in 1928, completing Springs' trifecta of Great War aviation books illustrated by Clayton Knight. Doubleday had purchased the George H. Doran Company the previous year. (Elliot White Springs)

In these pictures I have tried to show in an accurate, but not too technical fashion those movable platforms going about their work—a work much more impersonal than the ground war. The pilots of those platforms were invariably young and had expressed a definite preference for that way of making war. They trusted to their skill and personal luck to bring them through. Some escaped with no outward scratch. Others, not so fortunate, came to know the same sufferings as the men who, making war on the ground, had looked up and envied and cursed the flyers.[5]

World War I illustrations such as those produced by Knight began to garner wider interest after the war. At the same time, the advertising business was burgeoning. Overall, total advertising volume in the United States grew from about $200 million in 1880 to nearly $3 billion in 1920.[6] In describing the decade of the 1920s, Norman Rockwell noted that advertising agencies became the new patrons of illustrators.[7]

Clayton Knight, along with other talented illustrators, took advantage of the beneficence of big corporate budgets and accepted numerous assignments to advertise such consumer goods as Ipana toothpaste, Baker's coconut, Campbell's vegetable soup, Heinz baked beans, Benrus wristwatches, and Coca-Cola, among others.[8] But Knight's specialty was aviation art—and advertisers for products even tangentially related to aviation sought him out, determined to connect their ads with this popular topic. Examples of Knight's work include ads for Western Electric, Texaco, and Scripps-Howard newspapers.

Left: Clayton Knight excerpted stories by and about combat pilots in the lavishly illustrated book *Pilot's Luck*, published by David McKay publishers in 1929. (Clayton Christopher Knight)

Right: This original drawing from *Pilots' Luck*, titled "The Dog Fight," had been previously used in the serialization as well as the book of *War Birds: Diary of an Unknown Aviator*. (Clayton Christopher Knight)

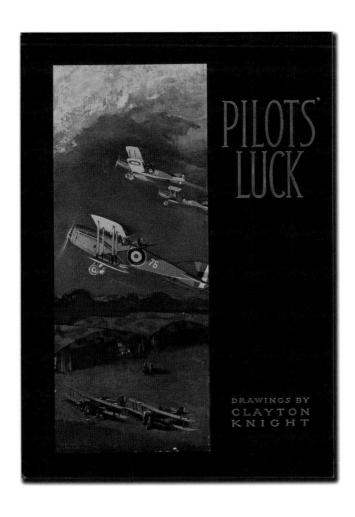

AMONG THE SHELL HOLES

Clockwise from top left:

Knight's illustration in *Pilot's Luck* features Grid Caldwell crawling out onto the wing of his S.E.5 Fighter to try to get his plane out of a spin. (Clayton Christopher Knight)

This original drawing from *Pilot's Luck*, titled "The Crash," illustrates Norman S. Hall's recounting of a crash landing by American Ace Frank Luke—a crash from which he escaped fairly unscathed. (Allen Airways Flying Museum)

Knight's illustration of a tethered observation balloon erupting in flames and plummeting to the ground comes from the section titled "The Balloon Buster at Work" in *Pilot's Luck*. (Clayton Christopher Knight)

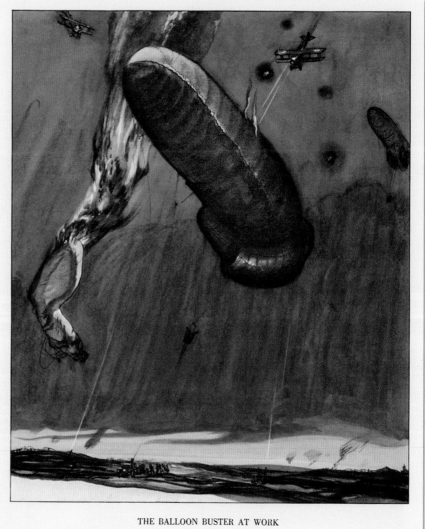

THE BALLOON BUSTER AT WORK

Clayton Knight at his easel in his studio, ca. 1930. (Clayton Christopher Knight)

Clayton Knight's illustration of a car body for Hayes-Hunt Bodies. This ad appeared in the April 10, 1926, issue of *Saturday Evening Post*. (Theodore Hamady)

Clayton Knight did this stunning original charcoal drawing of an Air Mail pilot jumping from his airplane at night and releasing a flare as he prepares to deploy his chute.. The date is likely sometime in 1934 as the Air Mail Scandal was then underway. Air Mail contracts had been removed from the airlines because of collusion among the larger airlines and was subsequently given to the Air Corps until new regulations could be put in place. Major General Benjamin Foulois, then chief of the Air Corps, assured the President that the Air Corps could do the job. However, Foulois' judgement was flawed as Air Corps pilots were ill-trained to fly at night in aircraft that were ill-equipped to navigate at night or in inclement weather.
(Allen Airways Flying Museum)

Out of the storm

— *by telephone*

WITH his Western Electric radio telephone the pilot talks with the airport and receives directions for avoiding the storm.

He also hears Government weather reports and directional radio beacon signals which guide him through darkness, clouds or fog.

This equipment, keeping plane and ground in constant touch, marks a great step ahead in flying. It helps to put the new mode of travel on a dependable, efficient basis—doing for air transportation what telegraph, telephone and wire-

less have done for railroads and steamship lines.

The airplane telephone is backed by more than 50 years' experience with problems of voice transmission.

It was designed by Bell Telephone Laboratories and tested under actual flying conditions in their own planes. It is made with the same care and skill as all the Western Electric apparatus used by the Bell System.

When you travel or ship goods by air, ask whether the plane is equipped with Western Electric Airplane Telephone.

MADE BY
THE MAKERS OF
BELL TELEPHONES

Western Electric

Aviation Communication Systems

A well-equipped pilot communicates with the ground via Western Electric telephone. (Theodore Hamady)

This signed, original artwork by Clayton Knight was produced for Airport Lighting, Inc. One of the company officers who signed the piece is Harold Hartney, former C.O. of the First Pursuit Group, U.S.A.S. (Theodore Hamady)

William Heaslip's Career is Launched

Working in the shadow of Clayton Knight, William Heaslip was ready to take advantage of the public's aviation craze after the Lindbergh flight. Heaslip had not experienced aerial combat during the war as Knight had, but he trained as an RFC observer/gunner and knew how to accurately and dramatically portray an aircraft in flight. Heaslip established himself as a freelance artist and remained an artist-entrepreneur for most of his career, with much of his work coming from ad agencies.

William Heaslip appeared on the national scene in 1929 as an accomplished and highly innovative illustrator. His reputation seemingly had been made overnight with the publication of striking advertisements he designed and painted for the Berry Brothers company of Detroit, Michigan, which produced varnishes, enamels, and lacquers.

William Heaslip illustrated this foldout brochure introducing the Columbia Convertible Amphibion. The aircraft might have been a success, but the Depression was just months away, and only two aircraft were produced. This brochure was among the earliest aviation-related works that Heaslip undertook. (Theodore Hamady)

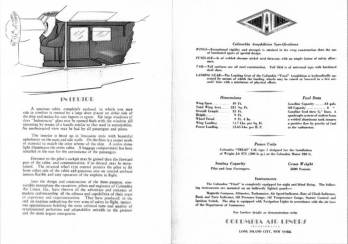

The Berry Brothers had directed their New York-based advertising agency Snyder & Black to devise a campaign to promote a new product line to the aviation industry, and Snyder & Black commissioned Heaslip to do the illustrations. Heaslip later explained in an interview that the inspiration to paint popular civil aircraft of the day with colorful bird plumage came from spotting a scarlet tanager in his yard. He parlayed this inspiration into a national sensation.[9]

Heaslip produced 14 colorful paintings—12 of which were published—for use in advertisements that appeared monthly during 1929 and 1930 in all the major aviation magazines, including *Aero Digest* and *Western Flying*. The ads were also published as a promotional calendar in 1930.

Right: This Berryloid ad heralded the series of colorful and innovative ads that appeared in *Aero Digest* and *Western Flying*. The series was lauded by art directors, advertising agencies, and the aviation industry. (Barry Martin)

Opposite: Heaslip produced an oil study of a red-winged blackbird with plumage, which he copied to a biplane. It would later appear in print in a revised composition adapted to the Monocoupe aircraft. (Allan M. Heaslip)

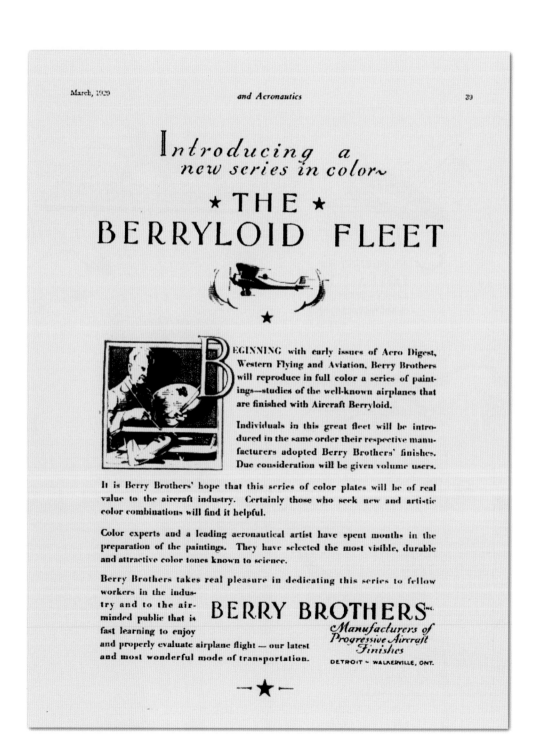

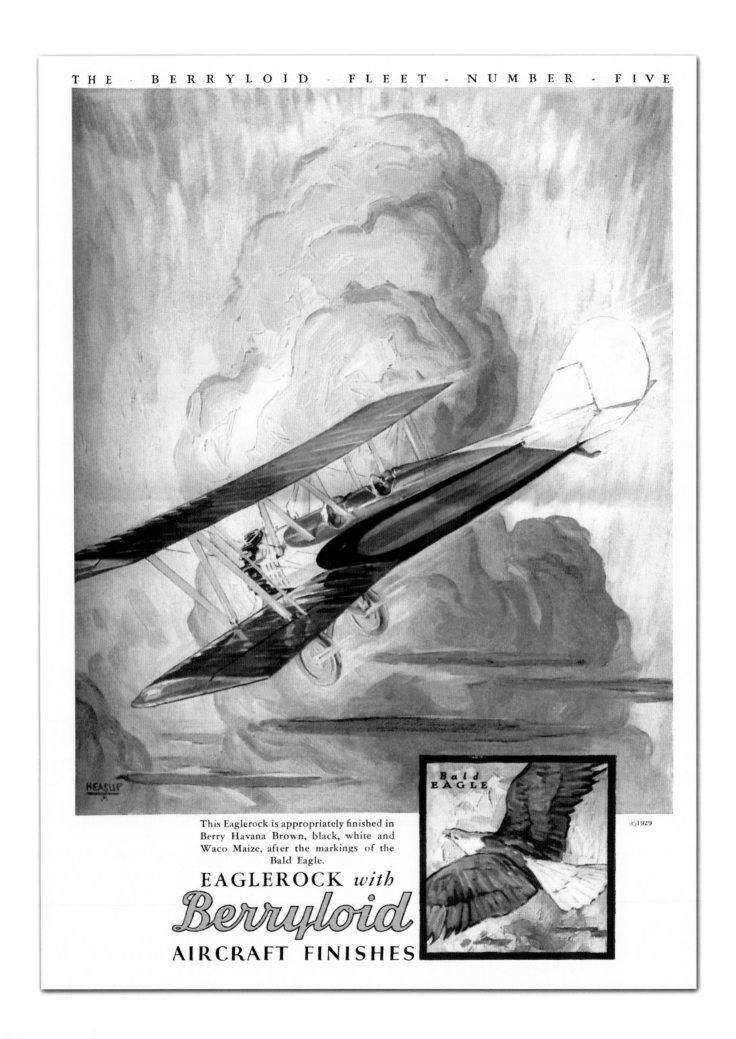

This Eaglerock is appropriately finished in Berry Havana Brown, black, white and Waco Maize, after the markings of the Bald Eagle.

EAGLEROCK *with*

Berryloid

AIRCRAFT FINISHES

Heaslip's perfection of detail and use of resplendent colors were responsible for the blossoming of brilliantly colored planes at airports all over the nation. His work also promoted the use of full-color advertisements in magazines. These stunning and colorful advertisements are still remembered as milestones in the field of aviation art.

Cyril Cassidy (Cy) Caldwell, former Royal Flying Corps and commercial pilot, and by 1930 a highly respected writer and associate editor at *Aero Digest*, briefly summarized the impact of Clayton Knight and William Heaslip as the premier aviation artists of the time:

> So far as I know, there are only two artists in America who can draw an airplane as it actually is—Bill Heaslip and Clayton Knight. Heaslip's excellent flying illustrations in various well-known publications, with Knight's spirited sketches in *Liberty* and other magazines, form the entire worthwhile contribution to aeronautical art.[10]

Opposite: The Bald eagle/Eaglerock painting appeared in a Berryloid ad measuring 12 x 8 inches. (Barry Martin). The original painting is shown at the beginning of this chapter.

Below: Berry Brothers published William Heaslip's entire bird plumage/aircraft series in a 1930 calendar. (Theodore Hamady)

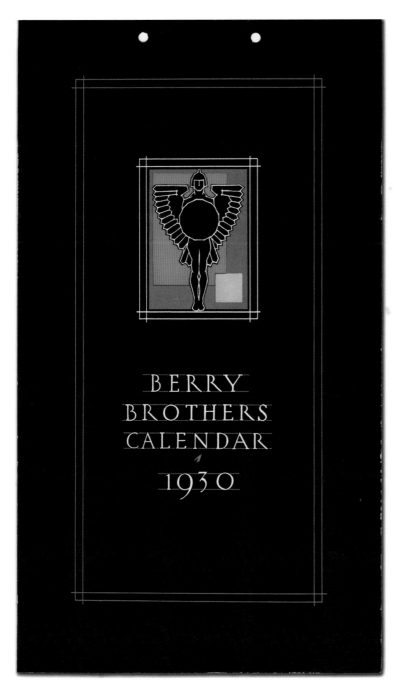

Clockwise from top left:
Condor/Fokker Super Trimotor; Bald eagle/Eaglerock; Yellow-shouldered parrot/Boeing Transport; Hooded tanager/Keystone Patrician. (Theodore Hamady)

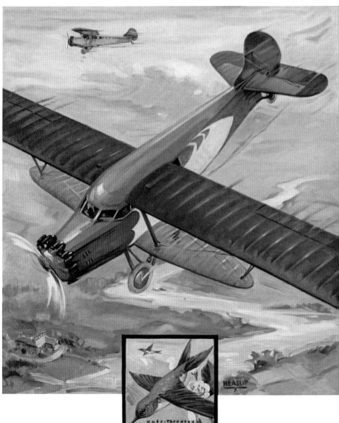

Clockwise from top left:
Scarlet rump tanager/Commandaire; Macaw/Travelair; Cardinal/Great Lakes Sport Trainer; Ruby-throated hummingbird/Buhl Airsedan. (Theodore Hamady)

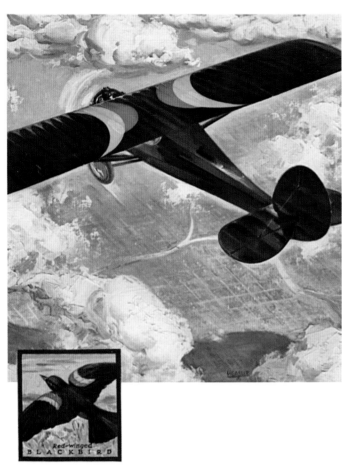

Clockwise from top left:
Red-winged blackbird/Monocoupe; European goldfinch/DeHavilland Gypsy Moth; Golden paroquet/Fairchild "71"; Redstart/Stinson. (Theodore Hamady)

Knight in the Tumultuous 1930s

Few observers would challenge that these two artists were the most successful at channeling the enthusiasm of a public crazy for airplanes, but the good times were soon to come to an end.

After less than three years of unbridled growth, the aviation industry took a severe tumble as the Great Depression took hold of the economy in late 1929. Between 1929 and 1932, commercial and military aviation production dropped over 50 percent in total units, and over 35 percent in total value. The commercial aviation market took the brunt of the crash, literally collapsing. But military production was aided by an enlightened Federal government policy that awarded small, but life-sustaining contracts designed to retain skilled workers and maintain some stability in the industry.

Advertising dollars spent on newspapers, magazines, and radio ads fell from a peak in 1929 to a low in 1933, regaining 1929 levels only in 1943.[11] We have no income figures for William Heaslip during this period, but an examination of Clayton Knight's personal account log book reveals a direct correlation between his income levels and the precipitous drop in advertising expenditures in the United States during that period. Knight's billings for 1932 was roughly 44 percent of his reported billings for 1929, rising slightly in 1935, and finally exceeding 1929 figures in 1936.[12] He did benefit from established relationships with the publishers of *Liberty* and *Cosmopolitan* magazines: both "air-minded" publications contributed significantly to his income between 1932 and 1936.[13]

In October 1929, newspapers across the country announced the onset of what became the most devastating economic depression in U.S. history. Few Americans imagined the Depression would last 10 years. (*Brooklyn Daily Eagle*, Brooklyn Public Library, Brooklyn Collection)

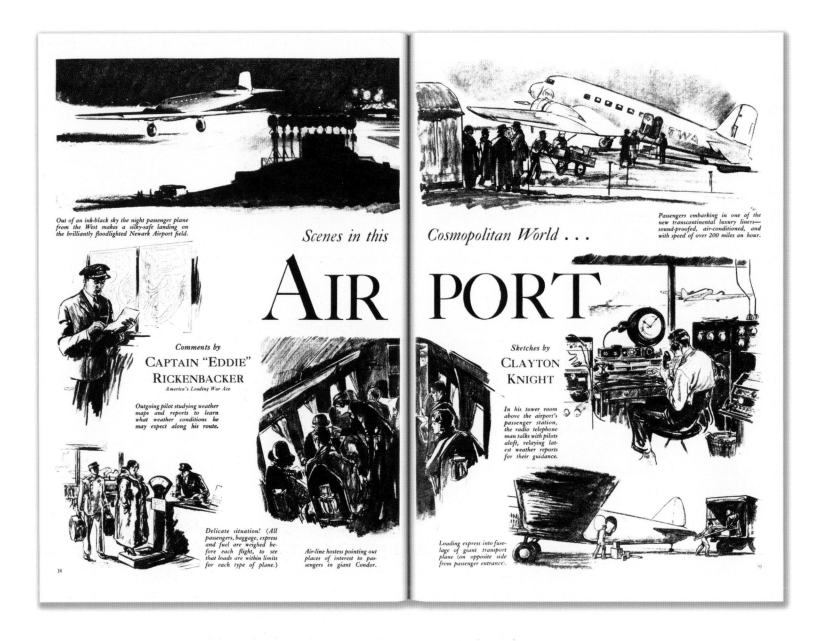

Out of an ink-black sky the night passenger plane from the West makes a silky-safe landing on the brilliantly floodlighted Newark Airport field.

Passengers embarking in one of the new transcontinental luxury liners—sound-proofed, air-conditioned, and with speed of over 200 miles an hour.

Scenes in this *Cosmopolitan World* . . .

AIR PORT

Comments by
CAPTAIN "EDDIE" RICKENBACKER
America's Leading War Ace

Outgoing pilot studying weather maps and reports to learn what weather conditions he may expect along his route.

Sketches by
CLAYTON KNIGHT

In his tower room above the airport's passenger station, the radio telephone man talks with pilots aloft, relaying latest weather reports for their guidance.

Delicate situation! (All passengers, baggage, express and fuel are weighed before each flight, to see that loads are within limits for each type of plane.)

Air-line hostess pointing out places of interest to passengers in giant Condor.

Loading express into fuselage of giant transport plane (on opposite side from passenger entrance).

In this spread from the June 1934 issue of *Cosmopolitan* magazine, Knight captures details in the day of a typical 1930s airport. The transport aircraft in the background is a modern Douglas DC-2. (Hearst Communications)

Despite the Depression, domestic and international air travel became increasingly accepted by the American public as a reliable mode of travel during the early 1930s. Pan American, founded and managed by the brilliant and aggressive visionary Juan Trippe, led the way with the establishment of a route system throughout South America, soon to be followed by a trans-Pacific route from California to China, with stops in Hawaii, Midway, Guam, and Manila. Aircraft manufacturers Sikorsky and Martin designed and built massive "flying boats" to maximize passenger comfort on long flights; and before the end of the decade, Pan Am was offering trans-Atlantic flights aboard its luxurious Boeing 314 Flying Boat.

In 1933, Clayton Knight journeyed to South America to record aeronautical events for *Cosmopolitan* magazine. Accompanying him was Forrest Wilson, playwright, short-story writer, and *Cosmopolitan*'s air-travel editor on a "20,000-mile flight around far-flung South America, and back again to Florida's shores." Wilson and Knight produced a series of articles reflecting "an air-minded account of our great sister continent—modern, but still jungle-clad and darkly mysterious." The articles focused on the trail-blazing efforts of Charles A. Lindbergh, then chairman of Pan American's technical committee and responsible for charting a 26,652-mile system of air routes linking North, Central, and South America. The objective was to capture "one of the most important markets in the world for foreign trade."[14]

Clayton Knight lavishly illustrated another article by Forrest Wilson, titled "Let's Dine in Europe Tomorrow Night!" The article proclaimed, "Regular transatlantic passenger and mail service by dirigible airships—American dirigibles among them—is almost at hand. Within four years, it is safe to say, tourists will be crossing the ocean in great, silvery air-mail packets on schedules as undeviating as those of surface liners."[15] Wilson and Knight let readers experience a fictional flight aboard an American dirigible of the near future. Tragically, Wilson's predictions proved faulty, for the loss of several U.S. Navy dirigibles and the fiery destruction of the Hindenburg in 1937 brought a sudden end to both the military and commercial use of dirigibles.

In 1934, Knight began a five-year collaboration with Edward "Eddie" Rickenbacker, America's Ace of Aces, on a comic strip entitled *Ace Drummond*, loosely based on Rickenbacker's wartime experiences. Rickenbacker provided the continuity (the logical progression of the plot and characters), while Knight illustrated the strip. *Ace Drummond* began appearing in Sunday newspapers in early 1935. Knight's journal reveals that he completed an average of one strip per week, billing the distributor, King Features Syndicate, $100 per strip.[16]

Another joint effort of Rickenbacker and Knight followed. The comic strip *Hall of Fame of the Air* featured brief cartoon bios of outstanding combat pilots of the Great War (and the planes they flew), along with pioneering male and female pilots of the 1920s and 1930s who had captured the public's eye. These two strips ran together, usually on the first page of the comic section, with *Hall of Fame of the Air* appearing on top.

At their peak, *Ace Drummond* and *Hall of Fame of the Air* were featured in 135 newspapers. A review of Knight's journal reveals that both strips provided a steady stream of income for him in the latter half of the 1930s, a distinct benefit not shared by other illustrators and artists at the time. Shortly after the strips ceased publication, Eddie Rickenbacker and Clayton Knight became fully involved in new war work.

Clayton Knight sold the movie serial rights for *Ace Drummond* to Universal Pictures, and in 1936 Universal produced a 13-episode serial.[17] It starred John King as Ace Drummond; Noah Berry, Jr., as sidekick Jerry; and Lon Chaney, Jr., as the bad guy.

Pity the woman being weighed on a baggage scale prior to flight in this original drawing. Weight and balance considerations were as critical to safe flight then as now. (Clayton Christopher Knight)

William Heaslip illustrated this lovely cover for the June 1934 issue of the *American Legion Monthly*. A Pan American Sikorsky S-40 Flying Boat is seen flying by the coastline of Miami, Florida, the site of the American Legion's national convention in 1933. (*American Legion Monthly*)

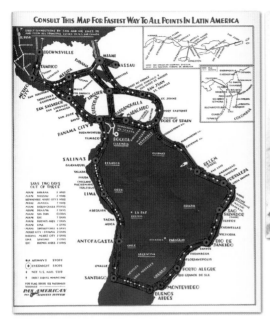

8. Clayton Knight, illustrator, Richard E. Berlin, vice president and general manager, Hearst International Magazine Corporation, and Forrest Wilson, writer, at Miami before Knight and Wilson started their 20,000 mile cruise to gather material for the series on Pan American for Cosmopolitan Magazine.

Left: Clayton Knight (left), together with Forrest Wilson (right) and Richard Berlin, vice president of *Hearst's International* magazine, in Miami, before embarking on a 20,000-mile flight to explore the new Pan American route shown on the route map. (*Pan American News*, New York City, New York, 1933)

Below: Forrest Wilson's article, beautifully illustrated by Clayton Knight, appeared in *Cosmopolitan* magazine in 1934. (Hearst Communications; courtesy Peter Kilduff)

EAGLE WINGS *under the Southern Cross*

Gigantic sea eagles provide quick communication and transportation to Central and South America.

Part marked in red shows the 15,802-mile route being flown by the author and artist of this series of articles.

Eagle drawn by Carl Burger

Do you realize that giant 4-engined, 44-passenger clipper ships of the air sail away every day from here—to Mexico, to Haiti, to Guatemala, to Brazil, to Argentina, to Chile and Peru—carrying men, mail and merchandise and now link the three Americas with the constantly strengthening bonds of trade and goodwill? Here is the first of a notable series of articles presenting vivid word and pen pictures of the impressions and adventures of two men who are making the 15,800-mile flight over all the airways of Central and South America in these great American clipper airships of ours.

by
FORREST WILSON
Drawings by Clayton Knight

FOREWORD

COLONEL CHARLES A. LINDBERGH, chairman of the Technical Committee of Pan American Airways System, made the four trail-blazing flights upon which was established the present amazing 26,652-mile system of air lines linking North, Central and South America.

Why were these airways connecting the Americas established, at great labor and an investment of $20,000,000? Here's the reason:

South America is one of the most important markets in the world for foreign trade. We are in continual competition with European firms for this rich trade, and an advantage in the faster transportation of mail and of samples and shipments of merchandise is of utmost importance to us. By means of it, we are in a position to beat other nations in the strenuous race for clients and contracts in Latin America.

Here are a few dramatic figures and facts about this airway system:

Pan American's operating airway mileage comprises a 26,652-mile network of coordinated air lines . . . Its fleet of 139 modern planes carry mail, men and merchandise as far south as Patagonia (see map on preceding page) . . . A corps of 2,000 employees mans its 147 airports, 72 ground radio-control and weather-forecasting stations in 32 countries . . . Pan American has a four-year record of 99.67 percent of all flights completed on schedule (U. S. Post Office rating) . . . To date, Pan American has carried 203,000 passengers over 61,000,000 miles, and transported 12,000,000 pounds of mail and cargo . . . Its giant 4-engined, 44-passenger "Clipper Ships" are the largest aircraft in service in the world.

The man who conceived this international air-transport system and is chiefly responsible for establishing this merchant marine of the air is Juan T. Trippe, president of Pan American Airways, Inc. He got his first flight training as ensign in naval air service during the war.

THIS DELICATE WING, reaching out over the terminal pier at Miami like a high white awning, becomes at one hundred miles an hour a rock of buoyancy in the air, firm as the arm of a Titan. It is the wing of a Pan American Airways "Commodore" seaplane about to set forth on the regular weekly voyage to Brazil with passengers, mail and express.

Everything about this great plane is mechanical. It is pulled by twin Pratt & Whitney Hornet engines whirling three-bladed propellers and developing 575 horse-power each. More than once, if you go on this voyage, you will feel and exult in the might of these eleven hundred and fifty horses dragging you upward out of some tight position for a take-off. It is mechanical, the whole thing—though surely it was a happy coincidence that from the engineering calculations of streamlines emerged a hull as low and long and rakish as that of this flying boat. A fit craft in which to fly the ancient Spanish Main!

No such thought, however, was in the minds of the designers when they built this huge dragon fly. The window slots along its sides might be dark scales. Its high, absurd double tail makes it a monster unknown in nature. Hull and engines are articulated by stout

24   25

FLYING ARTIST AT WORK

Cosmopolitan artist, Clayton Knight, sketches the picturesque Rio de Janeiro from the top of Sugar Loaf Mountain. Mr. Knight, in company with Forrest Wilson, playwright and author, recently completed a 20,000 mile trip around South America "via Pan American," writing and illustrating a series of stories for Cosmopolitan magazine.

Clayton Knight at work overlooking Sugar Loaf Mountain in Rio de Janeiro, Brazil. This photo was published in *Pan American News*, 1933. (*Pan American News*, New York City, New York, 1933)

Clayton Knight (left) and Captain Eddie Rickenbacker collaborated on the *Ace Drummond* and *Hall of Fame of the Air* Sunday comic strips during the mid-1930s. They are seen here reviewing an exhibit of Knight's work. (Clayton Christopher Knight)

Jean Rogers played Ace's love interest, Peggy Trainor. The story—which includes a villain named "Dragon"—was set in Mongolia, but filmed in the San Fernando Valley. The popularity of pilot-as-hero comic strips and serial adventures, particularly in the 1930s, was evidenced by the success of the Rickenbacker-Knight joint venture, as well as by the comic strips *Tailspin Tommy* (1928–1942), drawn by Hal Forrest, and *The Adventures of Smilin' Jack* (1933–1973), drawn by Zack Mosely.

This front page of a Sunday newspaper comic section displays Clayton Knight's illustrations for *Hall of Fame of the Air* and *Ace Drummond*. (*Ace Drummond* ©1935, King Features Syndicate, Inc.)

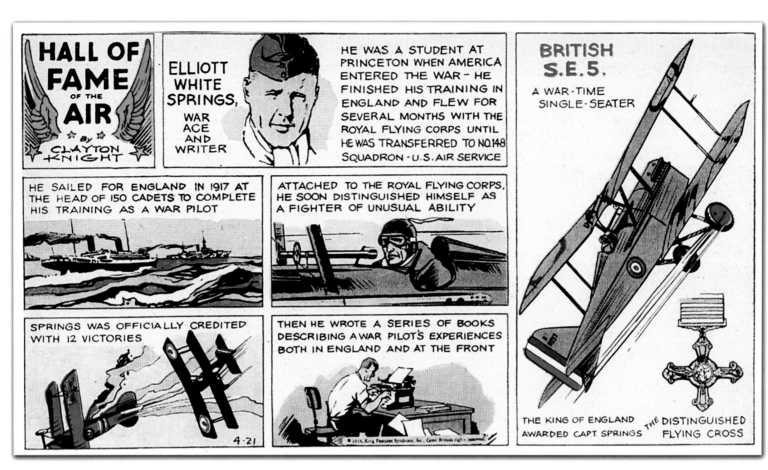

Hall of Fame of the Air featured the wartime and post-war feats of famous pilots. As part of this project, Knight illustrated a brief visual bio of his friend Elliott White Springs. (*Hall of Fame of the Air* ©1935, King Features Syndicate, Inc.)

Amelia Earhart, the first woman to pilot an aircraft across the Atlantic ocean, with her bright red Lockheed Vega 5B aircraft. The Vega is presently on exhibit at Smithsonian's National Air and Space Museum in Washington, DC. (*Hall of Fame of the Air* ©1935, King Features Syndicate, Inc.)

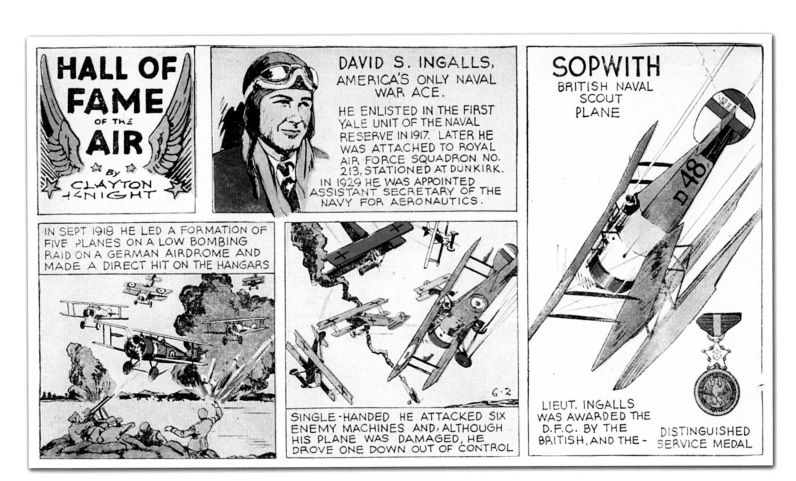

David Sinton Ingalls became the first and only U.S. Navy Ace in World War I while flying the Sopwith Camel. Ingalls later became the first Assistant Secretary of the Navy for Air under the Hoover Administration. (*Hall of Fame of the Air* ©1935, King Features Syndicate, Inc.)

Jimmy Doolittle, air racer extraordinaire, test pilot, MIT PH.D. in Aeronautics, scientist, and later, Medal of Honor recipient and commanding officer of the Mighty Eighth U.S. Army Air Force. (*Hall of Fame of the Air* ©1935, King Features Syndicate, Inc.)

UNIVERSAL
presents
"THE SIGN IN THE SKY"
CHAPTER number 8 of
Captain Eddie Rickenbacker's
(AMERICA'S GREATEST WAR PILOT)
"ACE DRUMMOND"
with
JOHN KING, JEAN ROGERS, NOAH BEERY, JR., GUY BATES POST, LON CHANEY, JR., JACKIE MORROW, ROBERT WARWICK, ED COBB, CHESTER GAN, JAMES LEONG
FROM THE POPULAR KING FEATURES' NEWSPAPER STRIP

Heaslip Weathers the Depression

William Heaslip was among those who enjoyed steady income and an enhanced professional reputation as a result of his involvement with the *Sportsman Pilot* magazine, perhaps the most elegant periodical ever produced for the "air-minded" American public. Conceived in 1928 for yachtsmen and pilots, *The Sportsman Pilot* was shortly thereafter refocused almost exclusively on sport aviation and enlarged to appeal to those wealthy American men and women who could afford to purchase, fly, and maintain private aircraft.

Monthly issues of the *Sportsman Pilot* contained articles about current civil and military aviation topics, adventure stories, new aircraft and aircraft systems. It showcased aviation art and the increasing acceptance and utility of private aviation. The magazine reported faithfully on the doings of the aviation social set and the activities of members of exclusive aviation country clubs.

An abundance of adverts appeared in the early issues of the *Sportsman Pilot* for an ever-wider range of private aircraft, and for airplane brokers offering financial services and aviation securities. However, with the onset of the Depression, advertising revenues dwindled and ads for aviation securities disappeared entirely. An article titled "Unsold Airplanes," published in May 1930, provided a sobering account of the overproduction of private aircraft. The magazine foundered as its market shrank.

Fortunately, the *Sportsman Pilot* was resuscitated when Frank A. Tichenor, publisher of the authoritative and well-established *Aero Digest*, became publisher in 1930. In a letter published in the December issue of the magazine, Tichenor assured readers that the "publishing policy [would] remain unchanged." He described an exciting selection of articles to be published each month, he noted "short story writers and humorists will enliven the magazine," and he promised that "America's foremost etchers, artists and photographers will illustrate." Tichenor already had in mind William Heaslip as the magazine's foremost artist and etcher.[18]

William Heaslip owed his good fortune in this period to his friend and supporter Cy Caldwell, associate editor of *Aero Digest*. Canadian-born Caldwell had joined the Royal Flying Corps in 1916 and flew night bombers over Germany during the war. He was active in U.S. commercial aviation for 10 years after the war before deciding to devote himself to a writing career. Beholden to Heaslip because Heaslip had illustrated several of his articles and columns in *Aero Digest*, Caldwell extolled the artist's virtues to his boss, Frank Tichenor. He believed that Heaslip's art had improved his articles "by 50 percent."

William Heaslip became officially involved with the *Sportsman Pilot* in the early 1930s, appearing as consulting art director on the magazine's masthead in February 1931. His impact on the magazine was immediate and apparent. He began modernizing the magazine cover and interior by incorporating many of his own illustrations—including small silhouettes of famous aviators, sprinkled randomly; sketches of men and women who were active in aviation circles; intricate treasure-hunt maps for venturesome weekend flyers; and numerous advertising illustrations.

Under Heaslip's artistic tutelage, the magazine's illustrative content evolved—and by the mid-1930s, both cover and interior articles were illustrated with stunning black-and-white

Opposite: Clayton Knight sold the movie serial rights for *Ace Drummond* to Universal Studios in 1936. This poster, titled "The Sign in the Sky," was produced for episode 8 of the series.

The panache of the "sportsman pilot" was very much in evidence in the *Sportsman Pilot*'s early issues, as is apparent in this cartoon, which appeared in the July 1929 issue. (Theodore Hamady)

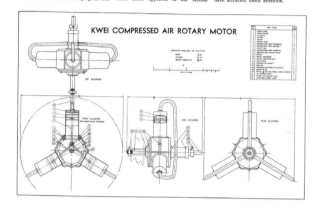

William Heaslip produced several gratis drawings for his friend and patron Cyril "Cy" Caldwell, associate editor of the prestigious *Aero Digest*. (Allan M. Heaslip)

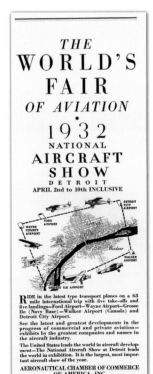

Heaslip produced this illustration for the World's Fair of Aviation held in Detroit, Michigan, in 1932. It was also used as a heading for Cy Caldwell's report on the Fair. (Allan M. Heaslip)

May, 1929   35 Cents

The Sportsman Pilot

Published in the Interests of Aviation Country Clubs
By THE SPORTSMAN PILOT, Inc.

photographs. Heaslip amassed a substantial photo archive, and every issue contained a series of carefully selected and composed photographs.

While aviation celebrities and the accompanying social scene continued to be widely covered in the *Sportsman Pilot*, Heaslip turned readers' attention to airplanes. This is evident in the following illustrations in which Heaslip has clearly portrayed affection for, and even veneration of, the airplane itself.

Heaslip's name disappeared from the *Sportsman Pilot* masthead in early 1938 as he moved on to other projects. By then, it was apparent that the nature of private aviation was rapidly changing: more pilots were being licensed and catered to with safer and more affordable aircraft, such as the Taylor J-2 Cub, later rebranded the Piper J-2 Cub. And as the exclusivity of the pilot's world slipped, the cachet of the magazine was lost. Moreover, private aviation, which had flourished between 1938 to 1941, ceased abruptly when U.S. industry converted to full wartime production after the attack on Pearl Harbor brought the United States into World War II. The magazine, which had been renamed *Sportsman Pilot at War*, ceased publication in 1943.

Above: Early *Sportsman Pilot* covers were drab and held little appeal for readers. The failing magazine would gain new life after William Heaslip became consulting art director in 1931. This example is from May 1929. (Allan M. Heaslip)

Below: Heaslip's newly designed covers portrayed privately owned aircraft in use for events in all seasons, including August vacations, November football games, and the Christmas holidays. (*Sportsman Pilot*, June, November, and December 1932 respectively) (Theodore Hamady)

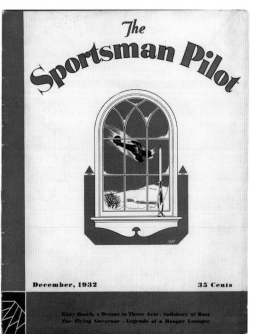

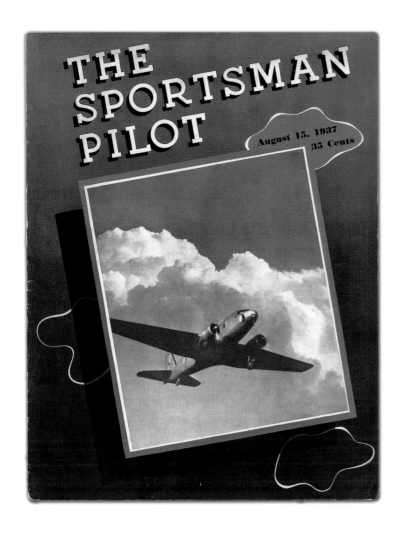

Lady Hay Drummond-Hay whose Waco Cabin is creating a great deal of interest in England by virtue of its performance and lines. (Pencil portrait by Heaslip)

Top left: Heaslip finally settled on the use of photographs of aircraft in flight to grace the covers of *Sportsman Pilot*. The dramatic cloud bank background reveals his love of cloud patterns in the sky. (Theodore Hamady)

Top right: Men and women sport pilots, those whose fortunes survived the Depression era, were avid readers of *Sportsman Pilot*. Their aviation interests and activities were featured monthly. Lady Hay Drummond-Hay, an English journalist who wrote about her flying adventure as a passenger, was a particular favorite of William Heaslip's. (Allan M. Heaslip)

Left: This photograph of a pontoon airplane taking off, with a lovely cloud formation in the background, is from *Sportsman Pilot*, September 15, 1935. (Allan M. Heaslip)

Left: Heaslip's son Allan plays with his model of a Martin 130 Flying Boat in this etching. (Allan M. Heaslip)

Right: Heaslip's wife, Clare, is portrayed dressed in flying togs in this original drawing. (Allan M. Heaslip)

Below: This photograph of a well-attended Aerial Country Club event and Rally Map for an Aerial Fox Hunt were featured in *Sportsman Pilot* magazine. (Allan M. Heaslip)

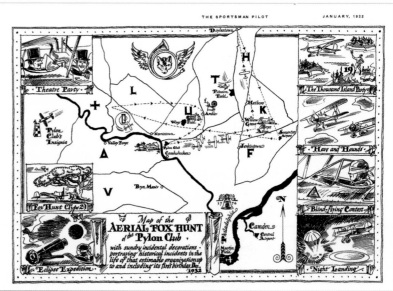

Private Aircraft Insignia

THE

FLYING COLORS

of those

WHO FLY FOR SPORT

Their colors are reproduced
on the following pages

31

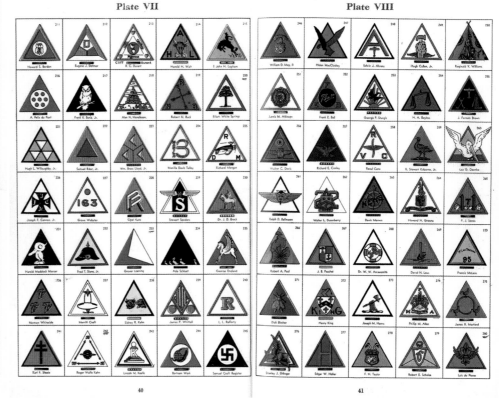

Above: Heaslip solicited commissions from owners of private aircraft for the design of personalized insignia for their aircraft. These examples are from *Air Pilots Register*, published in 1935. (Theodore Hamady)

Left: Cowboy Will James hugs his private airplane and Indian chief gestures upwards as a giant DC-4 transport flies overhead. (Theodore Hamady)

A Distant Friendship

Inevitably, Clayton Knight and William Heaslip competed during the 1930s for the same potential clients. They covered the same or similar aviation events, subjects, and personalities then in the public eye. Here are several examples of their work done.

While artists Clayton Knight and William Heaslip also traveled in many of the same social and professional circles and respected each other's talents. They were not close friends. Rather, they maintained a guarded, but respectful professional relationship, a likely outcome given that they were strong competitors during the difficult years of the Depression. However, when economic conditions began to improve at the end of the 1930s, both artists' careers began moving in different directions.

Left: Clayton Knight illustrated this ad for the highly innovative and reliable Franklin Model 145 Coupe. The Franklin Car Company, which began production in 1902, enjoyed success until plummeting sales forced it to close in 1934 at the height of the Depression. (Theodore Hamady)

Right: William Heaslip illustrated this ad for the Packard Motor Car Company, managing to tie it in with aviation. Packard's prestigious and pricey brand survived the Depression era by producing a less expensive six-cylinder line. (Allan M. Heaslip)

Clayton Knight illustrated this image of a bright-red Texaco Lockheed Vega against a brilliant sky, while William Heaslip illustrated another aircraft from Texaco's stable of airplanes, a Travel Air Model R Mystery Ship. (Theodore Hamady)

Knight's leather-tooled program cover features an SE-5 Fighter for the premiere of the 1930 film *Hell's Angels*. Heaslip's ad for *Hell's Angels'* London premiere appears on the right. (Theodore Hamady)

Above: Heaslip produced illustrations of the Douglas DC-3, the Martin 130 China Clipper, and the RMS *Queen Mary*, all of which entered service in 1935, a banner year for travel by air and sea. (Allan M. Heaslip)

Right: Passengers aboard a Douglas 14 Passenger DC-2, the predecessor to the magnificent DC-3 that equipped many of the world's airlines for three decades. (American Aviation Historical Society—Robert Stanley photographer)

Above: William Heaslip at his easel, with a finished painting of the Martin 130 Flying Boat. (Allan M. Heaslip)

Left: The Martin 130 China Clipper in flight over a yet-to-be-completed Golden Gate Bridge. (National Air and Space Museum)

FIFTEEN DAYS around the world! Tickets on sale . . . regularly scheduled service by Spring 1937! Flights that made aviators world-famous . . . transformed into regular routes of commercial travelers. London . . . Paris . . . Bombay . . . Honolulu . . . San Francisco . . . New York . . . linked by air! The take-off of the first plane will undoubtedly be broadcast by short-wave. Even though you cannot be a passenger . . . you can follow each day's flight . . . via short-wave and Philco! And this very day Philco will carry you to the four points of the compass! Set the dial for London and hear a momentous address by a Cabinet Minister. Turn it slightly . . . and Paris broadcasts the stirring strains of the "Marseillaise." Honolulu strums "Aloha Oe." Now back to America to finish your trip! Complete operas from the Metropolitan . . . comedy by Phil Baker . . . the dramatic offerings of Leslie Howard . . . all reach you with unparalleled realism through Philco!

The most important step forward in radio this year — the Philco *built-in* Aerial-Tuning System, which *automatically* tunes the aerial as you tune the set. A Philco discovery that doubles the number of foreign stations you can get and enjoy. *Built-in* . . . not an extra . . . not even in price. *And only Philco has it!* . . . See your classified telephone directory for your nearest dealer and have a demonstration. Sold on the Philco Commercial Credit Time Payment Plan.

A MUSICAL INSTRUMENT OF QUALITY

FORTY-THREE MODELS $20 TO $600

THE NEW PHILCO 116X

A true High-Fidelity instrument bringing you the overtones that identify and distinguish the many and varied musical instruments. Exclusive Acoustic Clarifiers prevent "boom". The famous Inclined Sounding Board projects every note up to your ear level. Five wave bands bring you every broadcast service in the air . . . Foreign, American, Police, Weather, Aircraft, Ship, Amateur. With exclusive, automatic *built-in* Aerial-Tuning System, $180

PHILCO
A Musical Instrument of Quality

PHILCO REPLACEMENT TUBES IMPROVE THE PERFORMANCE OF ANY RADIO . . . SPECIFY A PHILCO FOR YOUR AUTOMOBILE

Wherever you find this symbol *turn to page 8 to find WHO SELLS IT*

Clayton Knight featured the Martin 130 in this ad for Philco. (Theodore Hamady)

Left: Heaslip's study of a young lady dressed in flying pants sitting on an airplane's wheel later appeared on the cover of an *American Legion Monthly*. (*American Legion Monthly*)

Below: Clayton Knight and William Heaslip each painted striking aviation covers for the popular *Saturday Evening Post*. Knight's illustration is on the left; Heaslip's is on the right. (Illustrations © SEPS licensed by Curtis Licensing Indianapolis, IN. All rights reserved)

CHAPTER FOUR

Aviation Fine Art

By its very nature, illustration is transitory. It is generally intended to be a visual representation of the text appearing in advertisements, magazines, or books—and the original illustration is often fundamentally influenced by an art director working with the illustrator. Although well-articulated oil paintings were often created for major projects such as book jackets or magazine covers in the 1920s and 1930s, the vast majority of illustrations were produced for printers' eyes only. As such, illustrations were often painted on inexpensive particle board, their margins filled with crop marks and printer's notes. And many original illustrations ended up in the trash heap of ad agencies.

Fine art has a different purpose. Artists who produce fine art expect to communicate directly with their audiences without intermediaries; and if the artwork is a commission from a client, the artist expects to control the interpretation of his or her subject.

Both Clayton Knight and William Heaslip studied at some of the finest and most respected art institutions in the country—the School of the Art Institute of Chicago, the National Academy of Design, and the Art Students League—all of which offered impressive lists of instructors. For this reason, both artists were able to move between the two worlds of illustration and fine art.

Fine Art Supplements the Commercial Artist

Interestingly, Clayton Knight's course of study at the School of the Art Institute prepared him primarily for a career in illustration. The source of the skill set that Knight exhibited with such masterful dexterity in his woodcut prints for *War Birds: Diary of an Unknown Aviator* (1926) and paintings for *Pilot's Luck* (1929) lies further back in his training—at the Mechanics Institute in Rochester. His acumen for fine arts derived from the necessarily multifarious courses of a more general education.

Knight's first teacher and mentor at the Mechanics Institute was Frank von der Lancken, who had been recruited from the Pratt Institute in Brooklyn to bring progressive art education to the Mechanics Institute.[1] Von der Lancken restructured the Arts and Crafts program there, promoting both technical and traditional instruction as equal parts in the creative process. He was well-equipped to do so since he himself had attended the

Opposite: Attack from the Sun oil on canvas by Clayton Knight appears to illustrate an incident described by Knight himself, rather than one of his guest-storytellers in *Pilot's Luck*. As he recounts, "Up in the sun was the danger spot! What appeared at one second as a group of specks might develop an unbelievably few seconds later into enemy planes, dropping out of the sky with engines full on and machine-guns spitting bullets with a staccato pup-pup-pup!" (USAF Art Collection)

Frank von der Lancken was hired by the Mechanics Institute as part of the effort to restructure the Arts and Crafts program into an autonomous department—the School of Applied and Fine Arts, *c.* 1910. (Julie von der Lancken Kurtz)

Pratt Institute, the Art Students League, and the Académie Julien in Paris.[2]

Von der Lancken imparted to Knight a working knowledge of linear techniques utilized in illustration, together with a painterly style often observed in von der Lancken's own landscapes. With proficiency in both, Knight was able to carve out a career as both a commercial and fine artist, affording him alternate forms of artistic expression, and more practically, two distinct sources of revenue.

Knight's initial foray into the world of fine arts began with the renewal of his friendship with Elliot White Springs, and their collaboration on *War Birds: Diary of an Unknown Aviator* (see Chapter 1). That project led to the publication by the George H. Doran Company of a separate, large-format portfolio edition of *War Birds*, limited to 210 copies of 6 original woodcuts, each of which was intended to be framed and hung on the wall. In the 1951 paperback edition of *War Birds,* Springs notes that Doran had offered to make prints of the woodcuts for distribution to survivors and families of the 210 men who enlisted in the Aviation Section of the Signal Corps and were sent to England to fly for the Royal Flying Corps in 1917.[3] These woodcuts, which were influenced by both Japanese printmaking and by the Arts and Crafts movement, were designed to stand separately from the *War Birds* manuscript, and appreciated on their own merits.

Illustrator Curtiss Sprague recognized Knight's technical abilities and included one of the *War Birds* woodcuts in *How to Make Linoleum Blocks*, a 1928 handbook for "teachers, art students, letterers, and engravers."[4]

As a result of the success of *War Birds, Pilot's Luck* was picked up by the David McKay Company and marketed to a broad audience, including all age groups. The primary focus of the book was Clayton Knight's artwork, with text playing a subordinate role. Scattered throughout the action-packed drawings and accompanying text are four oil paintings that reveal the strong influence of von der Lancken's painterly style on an artist looking for ways to convey the dynamism of aviation. The paintings served to showcase the virtuosity and versatility of Knight as a fine artist.

In 1927, Clayton Knight began a long-term relationship with the New York department store R. H. Macy with an assignment to design a furniture poster.[5] The following year, he designed an aviation poster, most probably for the Macy's Boys Club annual spring party, often attended by as many as two thousand boys from chapters nationwide.[6]

In April 1928, the department store allocated the northwest corner of its fourth floor at 34th and Broadway for what was billed as New York's first aviation exhibition. Alongside a flight simulator and a bevy of model airplanes was "one of the most interesting exhibits,"[7] a display of World War I paintings by Clayton Knight, incorrectly identified as a British aviator. For Macy's Christmas catalogue 1929, the book *Pilot's Luck* was prominently featured on a page offering adventure and sports books for boys.[8] This early promotion of aviation was followed by a succession of other specialized exhibitions.

In 1931, the publisher G. P. Putnam's Sons and the *New York Times* sponsored the First

Woodcut: The primary relief technique in which the design is carved into a fairly soft wooden block with gouges, chisels, and knives. A woodcut is distinguished from a wood-engraving in that the carving is generally with the grain rather than against it.

Clockwise from bottom left:

Cover page of a special edition of *War Birds* with the signatures of several commanding officers and the artist. This is copy number 2 out of an edition of 210. (Springs Close Family Archives)

An original woodcut print from the special edition of *War Birds*, signed by Clayton Knight, shows a desperate attempt by those on the ground to alert a pilot landing his Sopwith Camel that he is missing a wheel. (Clayton Christopher Knight)

The frontispiece of a special edition of *War Birds*, with the inscription from Clayton Knight "to Elliot Springs." (Springs Close Family Archives)

Left: *Off to the Lines at Dawn* oil on canvas by Clayton Knight complements a story titled "Dirty Work at the Crossroads," by Captain A. Roy Brown, excerpted in *Pilot's Luck*. To quote Captain Brown, "At dawn, one machine will take off, go to the Proyart-Grand-Pre crossroads, observe movements of troops and transport, bomb and machine-gun the enemy observed, return, and report within an hour." (Clayton Christopher Knight)

Below & opposite page:
Details from the painting *Off to the Lines at Dawn* by Clayton Knight. (Clayton Christopher Knight)

Top Man Wins oil on canvas by Clayton Knight complements the story "Fed Up," by Elliot White Springs, excerpted in *Pilot's Luck.* Springs describes a fight to the finish: "He was watching the Fokker—an ugly square plane with a white nose and a black-and-white checkerboard fuselage and tail. He made out a skull-and-crossbones on it. … He was upside down now, both guns playing on that white nose." (Springs Close Family Archives)

International Exhibit of Famous Aviation Prints and Photographs to include the now-discredited faked Cockburn-Lange Collection of World War I air combat photographs.[9] Among the paintings were "six gorgeously colored canvases of war planes in action by Clayton Knight" and paintings and etchings by William Heaslip, who by now had established his *bona fides* in the field.[10]

In 1932, an exhibit of paintings and drawings by Clayton Knight was displayed at the thirteenth annual Aviators Ball, held at the Ritz-Carlton ballroom in New York City;[11] and later that year, his work was included in a survey of American Sports in Art at the Cronyn & Lowndes Galleries, also in New York City.[12] Group exhibitions of artists from the Society of Illustrators,[13] including Clayton Knight, continued to be popular with the public looking for a respite from "recent ultra-modern spasms" in the art world.[14]

This oil on canvas by Clayton Knight was based on a drawing from a *Liberty* magazine article titled "Billy Barker, Deadliest Ace of All" by Lieutenant Colonel William A. Bishop (August 29, 1931). The magazine caption reads "The Albatros was slow. Barker came out behind his opponent and with one burst, destroyed him." (Springs Close Family Archives)

Depression Era Mural Revival

With the advent of the Great Depression in October 1929, the art world found itself in freefall. Despite the fact that interest in aviation-related subject matter remained high, most artists struggled.

In 1933, Franklin D. Roosevelt created the Public Works of Art Project (PWAP), the first of several initiatives to provide economic relief for suffering artists. Hundreds of thousands of paintings and sculptures were commissioned by the government to enhance newly constructed courthouses and federal buildings throughout the country—and mural projects became widespread.[15] Both Clayton Knight and William Heaslip were actively engaged in the mural revival.

In 1933, Heaslip was awarded a prestigious commission by the Franklin Institute in Philadelphia to commemorate the 30th anniversary of the Wright brothers' first controlled flight in a powered, heavier-than-air craft. The painting he created is an artistic interpretation of the photograph *The First Flight of 17 December 1903*, part of the *Papers of Wilbur and Orville Wright* donated to the Library of Congress by the estate. In the painting, the plane—with its whirling propellers lifting from the sands at Kill Devil Hills, North Carolina—is the focus of the composition.[16] Wilbur runs alongside the plane, while the pilot, Orville, is almost indistinguishable from the engine. The artist compressed the space to include John T. Daniels, the photographer of the historic image, along with a group of spectators. A caption at the bottom reads "conceived by genius, achieved by dauntless resolution and unconquerable faith." Validation of authenticity is printed on the back with the words "personally approved by Orville Wright on the anniversary (30th) of the first flight, December 13th, 1933."[17]

In the case of Clayton Knight, we know of two major mural commissions from payment notations in his log book.[18] The first was for New York's Hotel Gotham, which had long been headquarters for aviators in the metropolitan area. Hotel management set aside a club room for their exclusive use in early 1934 and opened the facility with four murals by Knight depicting the history of aviation. There appear to be no extant photographs of the works, but a contemporaneous news article vividly describes the quartet of paintings as a chronological narrative starting with the Wright brothers' first flight, continuing with a scene of World War I aerial combat, another of the barnstorming era, and ending with an image of modern transport planes guided by huge beacons to a safe landing.[19]

A few months later, Knight was commissioned to produce four murals for the Blackstone Hotel in Chicago, perhaps in conjunction with the 1933–34 Century of Progress Exposition (Chicago World's Fair) that focused on the technology of train and air transportation. While at the fair, visitors could view exhibits of modern aviation at the Travel and Transport complex and observe aviation in action through demonstrations at surrounding airfields.[20]

Left: John T. Daniels' photograph *The First Flight of 17 December 1903* is a silver gelatin print from a glass negative. Daniels, a member of the Kill Devil Hills lifesaving station, had never seen a camera before being recruited to document the event. The camera was owned by the Wright brothers. (Library of Congress, Prints & Photographs Division [LC-DIG-ppprs-00626])

Below: This is the preliminary pen-and-ink drawing with watercolor on which the mural painting *The First Flight* was based. Note that the space is divided by a grid, a common technique used by artists to scale up a drawing to mural size. (Allan M. Heaslip)

CONCEIVED by GENIUS · ACHIEVED by DAUNTLESS RESOLUTION and UNCONQUERABLE FAITH

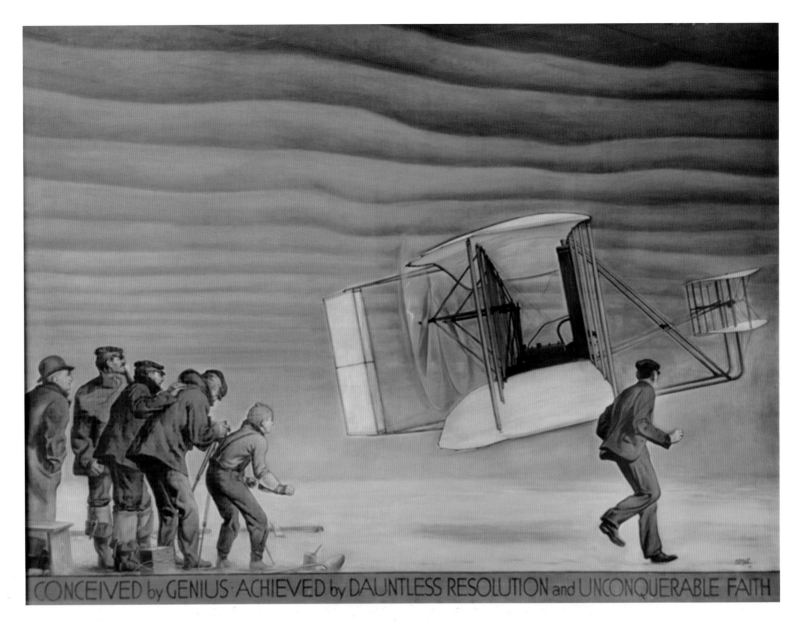

CONCEIVED by GENIUS · ACHIEVED by DAUNTLESS RESOLUTION and UNCONQUERABLE FAITH

Above: The painting *The First Flight* was commissioned by C. T. Ludington for the Hall of Aviation at the Franklin Institute in 1933. The original registration card describes the painting as the "historic first flight made by the Wright Brothers at Kitty Hawk, NC, on December 13, 1903. Orville Wright is flying the plane; Wilbur Wright is at the wing tip. The spectators are: John T. Daniels; W. S. Dough; A. D. Etheridge of the Life Saving Station; W. D. Brinkley, a lumber buyer of Manteo; and John Moore of Nags Head, a 16 year old boy." The card also notes that Ludington paid the expenses of Heaslip, who donated his time. (From the Historical and Interpretive Collections of The Franklin Institute, Philadelphia, PA)

Right: This etching by William Heaslip may be unique, as we know of no other extant examples of this print. Based on the date of the painting *The First Flight* on which the print was based (1933), this may also be one of Heaslip's earliest prints, done while he was studying with master etcher Frank Nankivell. Note the addition of seagulls. (Allan M. Heaslip)

This photograph dated March 24, 1934 was circulated with the story "Commemorating an American Epic." It describes the future disposition of the painting: hanging "above a model of the original airplane—the first motor-driven plane" at the Franklin Institute. (Associated Press)

SOME 'BIRD' LIFE

Clayton Knight, noted aviation artist and illustrator for the Cosmopolitan Magazine, puts the finishing touches on one of four murals for the aviators' clubrooms at the Blackstone Hotel, while Alice Joy of the radio offers him two small bird figures symbolic of his interest in flight. Knight flew in France, was wounded and taken prisoner. Last year he flew 30,000 miles in South America, making sketches. (Chicago American photo.)

In this newspaper photo, Clayton Knight paints one of the murals for the Blackstone Hotel in Chicago. (Tribune Content Agency, LLC; ©2018, all rights reserved)

This photograph of the unveiling of the mural in December 1933 shows Orville Wright and William Heaslip admiring the work. Not pictured, but in attendance, was Amelia Earhart. (Allan M. Heaslip)

Democratization of Fine Art through Printmaking

The pervasiveness of mural-making and printmaking during the Great Depression increased the accessibility of fine art among the populace. While a painting in a museum required an individual's attendance in order to be appreciated, the creation of a mural in an unrestricted space engaged the public as a community. Printmaking allowed distribution of multiple impressions of an image from a single matrix. And the public's universal interest in aviation exponentially expanded accessibility.

Consider the dramatic, but short-lived career of Scottish born artist/architect/aviator John MacGilchrist (1893–1977). MacGilchrist left home to study architecture at the Carnegie Institute of Technology in Pittsburgh before returning to serve in the British Royal Flying Forces as a gunner, machinist, and kite balloon observer during World War I. He returned to the United States in 1920, first practicing architecture, and in 1927 taking up the art of etching.[21] It took MacGilchrist a year to excel in that medium, but at the end of the learning process, he was able to render action-filled vignettes with remarkable clarity. While art critics were reviewing contemporary etchings in derisive terms—for lacking "new, compelling ideas," for example—they were hailing the work of MacGilchrist for "his dramatic visions of aviation."[22]

An article in the *Brooklyn Daily Eagle* (February 24, 1929) points out the uniqueness of MacGilchrist's memorable images. Printmakers such as John Taylor Arms and Joseph Pennell had occasionally depicted airplanes in their work, but no artist working in etchings had focused on the subject of airplanes until John MacGilchrist. (*Brooklyn Daily Eagle*, Brooklyn Public Library, Brooklyn Collection)

Spirit of St. Louis (Lindy's Plane) 1st B ©1929   John MacGilchrist

As a balloon-pilot observer during World War I, MacGilchrist spent long hours in his stationary hydrogen-filled balloon sketching aerial battle scenes. The average life of a pilot observer in this hazardous duty was 50 hours in combat. MacGilchrist was in combat for 200 hours and ended the war as a captain, the only pilot observer in his company to survive. Several of his etchings were purchased by Charles Lindbergh in 1929 for his personal collection. (Patrick Coffey)

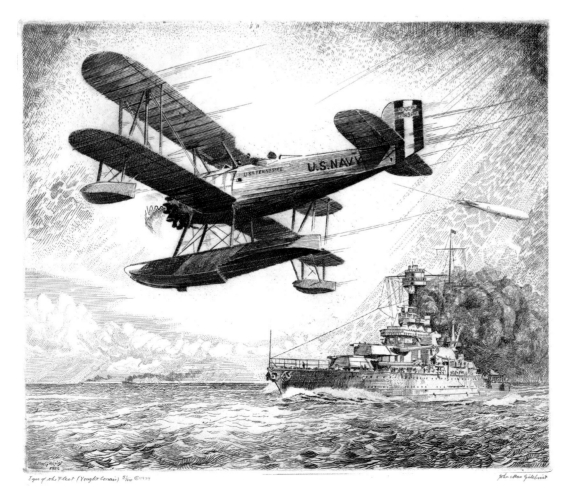

Eyes of the Fleet (Vought Corsair) 3/100 ©1929   John MacGilchrist

Here McGilchrist portrays a Chance Vought O2U Corsair with a Navy battleship and dirigible in the background. (Patrick Coffey)

A photo of Frank Nankivell with an inscription to Bill Heaslip, dated December 1936. Early in his career, Nankivell illustrated for daily newspapers and served as a cartoonist and caricaturist for *Puck*, the humor magazine. In 1910, he produced a cartoon that depicted New York City's skies filled with aircraft by 1960. (Allan M. Heaslip)

In a 1929 article, MacGilchrist correctly analyzed the source of his achievement: having both technical knowledge of planes and an etcher's training.[23] That article caught the attention of William Heaslip, who was familiar with intaglio techniques from his days as an apprentice at Lawson & Jones in London, Ontario. Like many artists of the day, he was attracted to the financial promise of etching and printmaking during a time of severe economic contraction.

In April 1930, MacGilchrist exhibited his etchings at Kennedy & Company, one of the most successful galleries in New York City, and self-promoted his etchings for $25 each in the December 1930 issue of *Sportsman Pilot*, a magazine targeted to the wealthy who flew for pleasure, rather than just for business. Then, in 1931, at the height of his success, MacGilchrist abandoned printmaking and retreated to the security of architecture, which had become a more reliable source of income.

With MacGilchrist's departure, William Heaslip seized an opportunity in the printmaking market—and sought out the best instructor to help him learn the most advanced etching techniques. Frank Nankivell was one of the few printmakers exhibited at the groundbreaking Armory Show of 1913.[24] He was a master printer who printed, and sometimes even countersigned, the works of other well-known artists, such as Arthur B. Davies,[25] and occasionally, he took on private students.[26] Heaslip studied with Nankivell for three years.[27] He referred to Nankivell as "the old master" of etching, and credited him with providing the critical training he needed to etch a metal plate and to produce images comparable in quality to those found in his aviation paintings and illustrations.[28]

William Heaslip was producing prints as early as 1931.[29] In 1932, he followed the lead of John MacGilchrist and started marketing his prints in *Sportsman Pilot* magazine. An etching titled *Solo,* which recorded the epic flight of Amelia Earhart, was offered as a limited edition.[30] This simple offer of an individual print by a single artist to a targeted audience was a harbinger of a much larger trend.

In 1933, six of America's most famous printmakers formed the Contemporary Print Group and began to sell a series of six prints for $15 as mail-order subscriptions. In 1934, a more aggressive campaign was initiated by gallerist Reeves Lewenthal, who began soliciting works not just from printmakers, but also from painters who were encouraged to try their hand at printmaking. To that end, he founded the Associated American Artists (AAA) and began employing mass-marketing techniques to sell prints at department stores and universities, and through mail order. In January 1935, the first presentation of "40 original etchings by 36 distinguished American artists" was advertised for purchase singly or collectively at $5 each.[31]

Soon Heaslip found himself on equal footing with such American luminaries as Thomas Hart Benton, John Steuart Curry, and Frank Nankivell. The print *Propeller* served as

Propeller (1934) by William Heaslip is an etching measuring 10 7/8″ x by 8″ (plate size). Heaslip's first print for Associated American Artists is in the collection of numerous museums, including the National Gallery of Art, Washington, DC; the Smithsonian American Art Museum, Washington, DC; and the Albright-Knox Art Gallery, Buffalo, NY. (Allan M. Heaslip)

Old Timer of the Air Mail may have originally been a commission for the Omega Watch Company. Heaslip produced a painting and later this aquatint (*c.* 1935). Both were used as the basis for Omega ads domestically and internationally. (Allan M. Heaslip)

Heaslip's introduction to a general audience: it did not emphasize the airplane; rather, it focused on a centrally placed mechanic carrying a propeller. This subject was more in keeping with the depictions of laborers in the industrial age that had become a common theme of artists during the Depression years. (It might be noted that the mechanic in *Propeller* bears an uncanny resemblance to Heaslip himself.)

By 1936, the AAA had been so successful in its emphasis on representational art that the organization's headquarters was moved to a more spacious location on Madison Avenue. There, with well-appointed exhibition galleries, the organization was able to better serve a growing cadre of collectors eager to own a piece of original art for a modest price.[32]

Heaslip's frequent focus on the human component of aviation, as seen in *Propeller*, was a departure from the genre established by John MacGilchrist—and that same focus would later distinguish Heaslip from the oeuvres of Clayton Knight, who gave equal standing to individuals who operated in the world of aviation and the machines themselves. Heaslip's divergent approach can be explained through an understanding of his upbringing: shaped by the vagaries of circumstance at a young age, he developed both a steely resolve and an outgoing personality capable of connecting on a personal level with his subjects.

Heaslip's *Old Timer of the Air Mail* is an excellent case in point. World War I pilot and author Captain Burr W. Leyson became the model[33] for the dramatically lit figure emerging from the darkness in this aquatint, while the airplane is relegated to the background. In other prints from this same period, the airplane isn't even visible, while the pilots, in full flight gear, are shown engaged in various tasks in preparation for flight. (Clayton Knight, having looked into the face of death during World War I, was always in awe of the machine.)

As Heaslip continued to improve as a printmaker, he gained recognition for creating increasingly complex works. In February 1937, the International Aeronautical Art Exhibition, sponsored by Women's International Association of Aeronautics and Women Painters of the West, opened at the Los Angeles Museum with over 200 pieces of art. The sheer scale of this exhibit, with its lofty theme "Man's Mastery of the Air," attracted a variety of impressive organizations, many of which donated prizes.[34] Heaslip submitted five prints for consideration and handily won the J. W. Robinson trophy.[35]

J. W. Robinson Company represented a chain of department stores with its headquarters in Los Angeles. It was one of several organizations and companies to offer trophies and prizes for the finest entries in the exhibition. (Allan M. Heaslip)

Defined by spotlights at a nighttime Newark airport, *Airport* would bring enduring fame for the printmaking skills of William Heaslip when it was selected by Thomas Craven in 1939 for inclusion in *A Treasury of American Prints: A Selection of*

Heaslip's *Magic Carpet* won the J. W. Robinson Trophy at the International Aeronautical Art Exhibition at the Los Angeles Museum, February 5–19, 1937. (Allan M. Heaslip)

In this etching, Heaslip paid homage to the "Three Musketeers" aerobatic team, the first precision flying team for the Army Air Corps. Their first major event was the National Air Races in September 1928 in Los Angeles, where they performed stunts and battle formations. When one of the three, Lt. John J. Williams, crashed on September 10 and died the next day, Col. Charles A. Lindbergh replaced him for the remainder of the Air Race shows. The group typically flew PW-9 fighters, but these appear to be the later P-12s. A contemporaneous account of the event reports a military pursuit race in which "a new Boeing single-seater fighter, which recently underwent its acceptance tests but which is not yet in production, averaged 180.2 mph for 60 miles." (Allan M. Heaslip)

Heaslip's *Spilling the Chute* was part of the International Aeronautical Art Exhibition and was published in *Fine Prints of the Year 1936*. (Allan M. Heaslip)

Another of Heaslip's etchings on display at the International Aeronautical Art Exhibit was *Caribbean Mail*, depicting one of three Sikorsky S-40 aircraft put into operation by Pan American Airways in 1931. Pursuant to passage of the Foreign Airmail Act of 1928, Pan Am was awarded contracts to operate routes that would eventually encircle the Caribbean. For the inaugural two-day flight from Miami to Cartagena, Colombia, the S-40—named "American Clipper"—was flown by Charles A. Lindbergh, who had served as a technical advisor to Pan Am since 1929. (Allan M. Heaslip)

- AIRPORT. Newark New Jersey . Air Mail taking off.

One Hundred Etchings and Lithographs by the Foremost Living American Artists.[36] Craven provided context for the piece by explaining that Heaslip "went out to the Newark Airport and made some night flights as the guest of the superintendent, both taking off and landing in the floodlights." That same year, *Airport* was exhibited at the annual exhibition of the Society of American Etchers, an esteemed national organization re-organized from the Brooklyn Society of Etchers under the leadership of renowned printmaker John Taylor Arms.[37] It was also part of the Artists for Victory exhibition at the New York Metropolitan Museum of Art in 1942.

Arms recognized Heaslip's mastery of the technique and called upon him to demonstrate the process of etching and aquatint at the New York World's Fair of 1939–40.[38] William Heaslip would continue his affiliation with this organization for the duration of his printmaking career.

Clayton Knight followed Heaslip to Associated American Artists in 1938. His printmaking technique of choice was not etching, but lithography. Just as Heaslip became

Lithography: A planographic technique in which an image is drawn or painted with a greasy medium on a flat surface, usually fine-grained limestone, but also on zinc or aluminum plates. The stone is treated with nitric acid and gum Arabic to set the image, then dampened, inked, and printed, traditionally using a press with a bar that scrapes across the back of the paper laid face down on the stone.

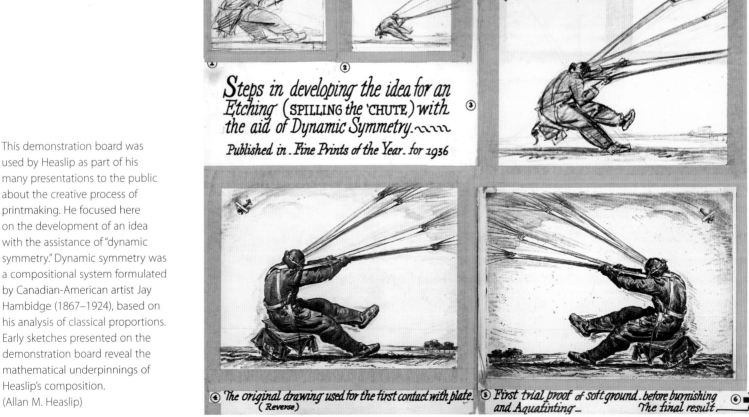

Around the World commemorates Howard Hughes record-breaking flight around the world on July 14, 1938. There were 25,000 wildly excited spectators to greet Hughes and crew flying a Lockheed 14 Super Electra into Floyd Bennett Field, New York City's first municipal airport. A ticker-tape parade down the city's "Canyon of Heroes" followed the next day. With this feat, Hughes had successfully demonstrated that safe, long-distance air travel was possible. (Allan M. Heaslip)

This demonstration board was used by Heaslip as part of his many presentations to the public about the creative process of printmaking. He focused here on the development of an idea with the assistance of "dynamic symmetry." Dynamic symmetry was a compositional system formulated by Canadian-American artist Jay Hambidge (1867–1924), based on his analysis of classical proportions. Early sketches presented on the demonstration board reveal the mathematical underpinnings of Heaslip's composition. (Allan M. Heaslip)

Above: An exhibition and members' dinner of the Society of American Etchers on December 5, 1940. William Heaslip is seated (center), flanked by Dr. Benjamin F. Morrow (to his right) and Robert Benney (to his left). Morrow was an artist and writer who'd profiled Heaslip in an article "Highlights of Copper (William Heaslip)" in *Prints* magazine in January 1935. Artist and illustrator Robert Benney, not known as a printmaker, might have been in attendance due to his personal friendship with Heaslip. (Allan M. Heaslip)

Left: This publicity shot shows Clayton Knight discussing his lithograph *Wings Aloft* with Reeves Lewenthal of Associated American Artists (AAA) in 1942. The accompanying newspaper caption describes the AAA business model as organizing "a group of artists to sell paintings and etchings to Mr. and Mrs. Joe Public at a reasonable price … $5."

AVIATION FINE ART   **129**

Clayton Knight's *Wings Aloft*, a lithograph measuring 10" x 13", was offered in the 1939 Associated American Artists catalogue.

Opposite: Knight's *The Last Lap*, a lithograph measuring 9 5/8" x 12 ¾", was offered in the 1939 Associated American Artists catalogue. (Reba and Dave Williams Collection, National Gallery of Art, Washington, DC)

familiar with intaglio techniques during his days as an apprentice, Knight became familiar with commercial lithography from his days at as an apprentice lithographic designer at the Mechanics Institute.

Knight's first print *Wings Aloft* illustrated the DC-4E, a design later downsized and standardized as the DC-4. In the print, the plane is difficult to identify, but that may not have been as important to the artist as communicating the spiritual component of the miracle of flight. The subject emerges from the clouds on rays of light into an open sky of unlimited potential.

Clayton Knight understood the power of words and generally imbued his titles with special meaning. *The Last Lap* detailed the critical moment when flamboyant barnstormer Roscoe Turner secured his third Thompson Trophy at the Cleveland Air Races in 1939. After that event, Turner announced his retirement. The competitive racing circuit, which needed celebrities, danger, and large cash prizes to thrive, soon began to suffer, as the military, heretofore a reliable source of revenue, withdrew its monetary support to reallocate resources in preparation for a new war effort.

Both Artists Refocus their Efforts on the Future

For Clayton Knight, *The Last Lap* signaled the end of an era. He would no longer look to the past for inspiration; rather, he would look to the future. This transition was facilitated by developing hostilities in Europe, which produced for Knight a lucrative commercial contract with Pratt & Whitney, a company at the forefront of aviation technologies. From 1937–44, Knight produced a series of eight stone lithographs depicting various applications of Pratt & Whitney engines as they advanced in power from peacetime to wartime. Knight's technical abilities matured through the process of pulling each different Pratt & Whitney print, culminating in a final Associated American Artist publication *Flying Fortresses at Work* in 1943.

For some time, Heaslip—who was sole provider for a wife and three young children—had been interested in etching portraits as a way of increasing his income. Joseph Margulies (1896–1984), the highly regarded Vienna-born American painter and printmaker, was both a friend and close colleague of Heaslip through the Society of American Etchers

Knight's *Flying Fortresses at Work* depicts the B-17 heavy bomber used by the United States Army Air Forces in the strategic bombing campaigns of World War II against German targets. Knight saw the B-17s in action during his trip to England in mid-1942 as a special correspondent for the Associated Press.

"OLD TIMER"

A comparison of the drawing and etching *Old Timer* reveals Heaslip's creative process. (Allan M. Heaslip)

and Associated American Artists. [39] He was known for his etched portraits commissioned by prominent New Yorkers, including politicians, entertainers, and writers. [40] Heaslip, who'd had some early experience with portrait drawings during his stint in the RFC and RAF when he spent evenings sketching likenesses of the officers, [41] recognized that he may have his own target market. He began advertising his skills in etched portraits in *The Sportsman Pilot* for the purpose of "permanence, individuality, and distinctiveness." [42]

It's impossible to overestimate the role of printmaking in creating the legacies of Knight and Heaslip. During the Great Depression, when fine artists turned to commercial illustration to supplement their income, commercial illustrators turned to printmaking to do the same. Through the encouragement of entrepreneurial individuals such as Reeves Lewenthal, and the democratization of art through organizations such as Associated American Artists, many artists who might have been lost to history are instead recognized for their considerable contributions. Today, the reputations of Clayton Knight and William Heaslip are solid, and their works in intaglio and lithography are appreciated by a wide audience.

CHAPTER FIVE

Aviation Art for America's Youth

Words and illustrations have always had the power to inspire. This was especially true when the world was simpler and freer from the distractions of modern-day technology. Starting in the early 20th century, books about aviation began to appear, capturing the imagination of young boys. And by the 1930s, both Clayton Knight and William Heaslip were directing a large portion of their professional energies to America's youth. They brought to life the stories of both imaginary characters and real-life aviators throughout the golden age of aviation, stories that deeply influenced their target audience of adolescent boys.

Aviation Art in Juvenile Literature

Too young to join the military while the battles of World War I raged, Charles A. Lindbergh—a solitary young man from a distinguished, but dysfunctional family—found solace and subsequently a path to greatness by following the exploits of both real and fictional aviators. The young Lindbergh was particularly riveted by the fictional adventures in *Tam o' the Scoots,* written by that most prolific of early 20th-century authors Edgar Wallace. *Tam o' the Scoots* is the story of a reluctant Scottish automobile mechanic turned ace pursuit pilot and highly decorated officer.[1] The story was serialized in nineteen episodes of *Everybody's Magazine,*[2] starting with the November 1917 issue. For Lindbergh, the spark of ambition to make the first solo nonstop flight across the Atlantic may have been ignited by this story and similar literature. And his singular act of courage in making that flight would generate reams of additional stories about aviation for generations of young people eager to learn more about the future of aviation.

Before Lindbergh and the national euphoria that followed his exploits, aviation in literature did exist, but it was of a different nature. The genesis of many of the popular books for young people in the 20th century evolved from formulaic series books published in the mid-19th century. Of note were those created by "Oliver Optic," a pseudonym of William Taylor Adams; and those of Horatio Alger, Jr., which promulgated the virtues of courage and moral fortitude to achieve the American Dream.[3]

Opposite: Original illustration by Heaslip for *American Boy.*
(Allan M. Heaslip)

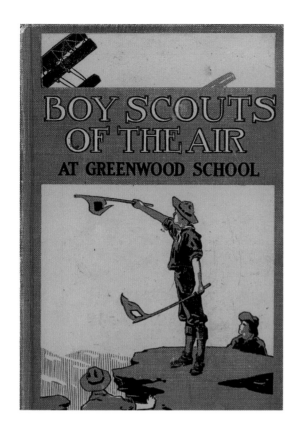

This cloth cover from *Boy Scouts of the Air at Greenwood School* (1912) was illustrated by Norman P. Hall. Although ostensibly about "aeroplanes," the book is mostly about the adventures of a group of boys at a rather isolated private boarding school who study and learn about the Boy Scout movement, and after 109 pages are introduced to an "airship"—in this case, an experimental helicopter.

This dust jacket for *Boy Scouts of the Air in Indian Land* (1912), a sequel to the title set at Greenwood School, was also illustrated by Norman P. Hall. Each book in the series was a standalone title with a different cast of characters in various settings. *Indian Land* takes place in New Mexico. The cover image does not even bother to depict the "aeroplane," but instead focuses on an encounter with a mysterious Indian as the boys seek out the monster Thunderbird of legend. The featured biplane, which was assembled by a resident aviator together with the scouts, was not incorporated into the storyline until page 161.

But it was Harry Lincoln Saylor, a journalist with the City Press Association in Chicago, who was credited with establishing the aviation series as a genre.[4] Saylor's early series *Aeroplane Boys* (1910–13, eight titles), authored under the pseudonym "Ashton Lamar," often involved older mentors backing the adventures of adolescent boys with technical information or financial assistance, with aviation experimentation secondary to the story line. Saylor's third series, *The Boy Scouts of the Air* (1912–22, fourteen titles), issued under the authorship of "Gordon Stuart," was advertised only as "stirring stories of adventure in which real boys, clean-cut and wide-awake, do the things other wide-awake boys like to read about."[5]

The emphasis of adventure over aviation held true in boys' literature of the period even after Saylor's death in 1913, when G. N. Madison and Henry Bedford-Jones took over the franchise and carried the series into wartime.[6] The cloth cases for books published during this period occasionally featured aviation imagery, but the dust jackets and interior illustrations supported the overall story line, with protagonists positioned center stage and aircraft relegated to the background, if present at all.

Other series books for youth had gained popularity when entrepreneur Edward Stratemeyer began publishing in 1890. After some early promotional success, the Stratemeyer Syndicate started to hire writers to flesh out its plot outlines, producing books in approximately 70 different series—among them the 40-title *Tom Swift* series, which debuted in 1910.[7] Thought to be based on the life of aviation pioneer Glenn Curtiss, Tom Swift was a technologically savvy backyard inventor with little formal education. In the third book of the series, Tom invents a fanciful airship—half dirigible/half airplane—which can travel up to 80 miles per hour and stay in the air for two weeks.

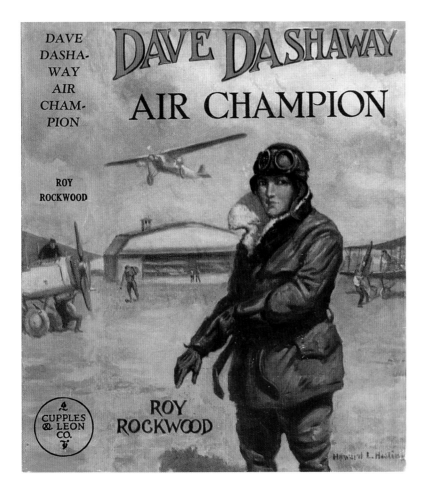

Subsequently, Stratemeyer created the fittingly named *Dave Dashaway* series (1913–15, five titles) by "Roy Rockwood," which features a young, record-breaking aviator;[8] and the *Air Service Boys* series (1918–20, six titles) by "Charles Armory Beach," featuring two young aviators on the front line. But he was initially timid about the aviation series market, and these series were soon upstaged by the New York publisher A. L. Burt Company in the most notable aviation series of World War I: *Our Young Aeroplane Scouts* (1915–19, twelve titles) by Horace Porter. This series, which offered a more realistic portrayal of the perils of war and aerial combat, together with Lindbergh's Atlantic flight in 1927, eventually spurred Stratemeyer to create the *Ted Scott* series (1927–43, twenty titles) entirely devoted to aviation.[9]

There was certainly an effort by various authors at the time to be technologically accurate and up to date in their stories. In his comprehensive studies of boys' and girls' aviation books (1910–50), Fred Erisman, the Lorraine Sherley Professor of Literature Emeritus at Texas Christian University in Fort Worth, sourced the incorporation of relevant information on aviation milestones in boys' literature to Victor Lougheed's *Vehicles of the Air* (1909) and to the popular science magazine *Scientific American*. However, the illustrations accompanying these titles were often artistically unremarkable and mechanically inaccurate: they were produced by illustrators who specialized in series books and were accustomed to the assembly-line pace of publication which did not allow sufficient time for research. And of the dozen or so publishers of boys' aviation books created pre-Lindbergh, Stratemeyer devoted fewer resources than most to the visual support of the aviation narrative.

Left: *Dave Dashaway: Air Champion* (1915) by "Roy Rockwood," a Stratemeyer Syndicate house name, included a color dust jacket, cloth binding, and black-and-white frontispiece illustrated by Howard L. Hastings, known for his animal and outdoor sports subject matter. It was published by Cupples & Leon Company, New York, which advertised the good character of its books as being "clean, interesting, inspiring and educational."

Right: "Charles Armory Beach" was another Stratemeyer Syndicate house name. Books with this author's name were actually penned by two respected writers—St. George Rathborne and Howard R. Garis. Robert Gaston Herbert illustrated most of the *Air Service Boys* series, but he is not specifically listed for this one. A rather primitively drawn sketch of a Curtiss JN-4 appears on the frontispiece. The book was published by the George Sully Company in 1920.

It must have been very frustrating for someone with the background of Clayton Knight to see illustrations executed in such a slapdash manner. Knight's wife, Katherine Sturges, had illustrated a number of books for Gordon Volland Publications, known for high-quality non-series children's books illustrated by well-known artists; and in 1928, he himself wrote and lavishly illustrated *The Non-Stop Stowaway: The Story of Long-Distance Flight* for the Buzza Company/Gordon Volland in Minneapolis. In that story, Captain Malcolm McBride, his co-pilot, and the captain's stowaway son, Jack, fail in their challenging long-distance flight from New York to India. As a result, they find a "safe landing" in "that place beyond the clouds which is home to departed heroes who have sacrificed their lives to further the progress of aviation." Once there, Jack is instructed by famed World War I pilot Captain Armbruster on all the great airplanes of the past. This fanciful story, designed to connect a youthful audience with the future of flight, features illustrations of airplanes that appear to be moving, rather than statically suspended in air.

Perhaps this was Knight's creative way of transitioning from the kind of fiction published in pre-Lindbergh books to adventure stories that featured content that was both entertaining and more educational. From that time forward, better options existed for authors and illustrators to reveal to a younger generation the possibilities and career opportunities in aviation.

Clayton Knight was not the only illustrator setting new standards in boys' aviation illustration. William Heaslip entered the world of publishing through popular magazines for boys. In January 1911, George S. Barton of Somerville, Massachusetts, an official in one of three competing scouting organizations, published the first issue of *Boys' Life* magazine, targeted at the Boy Scouts of America, the American Boy Scouts, and the New England Boy Scouts. The magazine was an immediate success: by the end of its first year of publication, circulation had increased to 65,000. In July 1912, Barton learned that the most successful of the three groups—the Boy Scouts of America—intended to start its own magazine. Faced with that possibility, Barton sold *Boys' Life* to the Boy Scouts of America.[10]

After Lindbergh's transatlantic flight in May 1927, aviation fiction in *Boys' Life* proliferated. The June 1927 issue published a story titled "The Air Mail Flies," by former silent-film star, pulp fiction writer, and World War I aviator Raoul F. Whitfield.[11] The illustrations in that three-part story, which include a cover by Jerome Rozen, were capably rendered, but uninspired. In November of the same year, Heaslip received his first assignment from *Boys' Life*: he was asked to produce illustrations for "Barking Water Hunts Wolf," a story about Lewis and Clark, by Constance Lindsay Skinner. Heaslip's

The cover design for *Non-Stop Stowaway* (1928), written and illustrated by Clayton Knight, shows the Dauntless traveling through a full circle rainbow—a rare phenomenon only visible under certain atmospheric conditions. In the story the pilot interprets the rainbow as a good omen for a successful flight, but instead it becomes the gateway to a deadly, turbulent storm.
(Clayton Christopher Knight)

This interior illustration from *Non-Stop Stowaway* (page 92) by Clayton Knight features what appears to be a variant of a Travel Air Type 6000 plane. In the story, the captain and his son Kiwi take every precaution prior to takeoff, but even so, Kiwi must perform a very risky action to stop a fuel leak. The underlying moral of the story is that long, ocean flights are inherently dangerous, given the vagaries of both the machine and the weather. (Clayton Christopher Knight)

illustrations for that story, which communicated a wide range of human emotions, caught the attention of art director Francis Rigney, who saw Heaslip's style as perfectly suited to the depiction of aviation.

That same month, a six-issue series titled "*The Flying Patrol*" was first advertised in the magazine. Designed as a marketing tool for subscriptions to *Boys' Life*, the series was to be written by frequent contributor—and later managing editor—J. Irving Crump. And while the announcement did not list an illustrator, the project would join Crump and William Heaslip for the first time from December 1927 through May 1928. When the series debuted, the aviators in Heaslip's illustrations appeared not as idealized characters, but as real men who openly express anger, fear, and triumph. Through these distinctive illustrations, *Boys' Life* readers were better able to connect with the characters, and by extension felt more like participants in the action. As a result, the act of flying became more tangible to the magazine's audience.

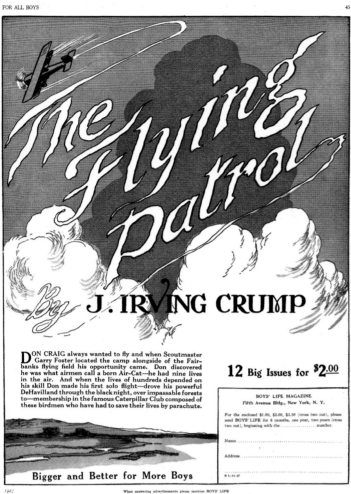

The Flying Patrol

By J. IRVING CRUMP

DON CRAIG always wanted to fly and when Scoutmaster Garry Foster located the camp alongside of the Fairbanks flying field his opportunity came. Don discovered he was what airmen call a born Air-Cat—he had nine lives in the air. And when the lives of hundreds depended on his skill Don made his first solo flight—drove his powerful DeHavilland through the black night, over impassable forests to—membership in the famous Caterpillar Club composed of these birdmen who have had to save their lives by parachute.

12 Big Issues for $2.00

BOYS' LIFE MAGAZINE
Fifth Avenue Bldg., New York, N. Y.

For me enclosed $1.00, $2.00, $3.50 (cross two out), please send BOYS' LIFE for 6 months, one year, two years (cross two out), beginning with the ....number.

Name..

Address...

Bigger and Better for More Boys

1927 When answering advertisements please mention BOYS' LIFE

Above Left: "The Cloud Patrol" was first introduced to *Boys' Life* readers as "The Flying Patrol" in the November 1927 issue. (*Boys' Life* magazine)

Above Right: In the December 1927 issue of *Boys' Life*, we are introduced to Boy Scout pilot Don Craig, flying with forest ranger Garry Foster near the Snake river. William Heaslip's original illustration shows the duo after an emergency landing coming across a rather threatening man armed with a rifle and a "big, black-butted Colt six-gun." (Allan M. Heaslip)

This illustration for the 1929 book *The Cloud Patrol* conveys the moment when Don Craig realizes he must jump from his burning De Havilland to survive. Through dramatic contrasts of light and dark and skillful draftsmanship, Heaslip pulls the viewer in to share the pilot's panic as his plane begins its downward trajectory. (Allan M. Heaslip)

HE BRACED HIS LEFT FOOT, LET GO HIS HOLD AND KICKED
HIMSELF OUTWARD.

The Cloud Patrol. *Frontispiece (Page 130)*

THE CLOUD PATROL

BY
IRVING CRUMP

ILLUSTRATED BY
WILLIAM HEASLIP

GROSSET & DUNLAP
PUBLISHERS   NEW YORK

Heaslip's original illustration for "*The Cloud Patrol: Part IV*" depicts Don Craig, who, at this point in his aviation career, has just over 20 hours of flight time and has never flown solo or at night. He is approached by two allies portrayed as ominous shadows. The image appears on page 19 of the March 1928 issue of *Boys' Life* and in Chapter Four of the 1929 book *Cloud Patrol* by Irving Crump. (Allan M. Heaslip)

This original artwork by William Heaslip was created for an ad for the second story in the "*Cloud Patrol*" series, titled "The Pilot of the Cloud Patrol." The ad appeared in the November 1928 issue of *Boys' Life*. The story follows Boy Scout Don Craig as he takes a summer job at the Fullerton airplane factory in New Jersey. The illustration depicts a Black Hawk as it loses power because thieves have siphoned off the gasoline. The illustration and story highlight the dangers of aviation and emphasize the importance of air safety. (Allan M. Heaslip)

For the last half of 1928, Heaslip remained busy with *Boys' Life*. He also provided illustrations for a second Constance Lindsay Skinner series on Lewis and Clark, this one a six-issue serial; a cover for a story about Captain John Smith; and illustrations for three Raoul Whitfield adventure stories on aviation. In November, his name appeared prominently in advertisements for a new serial by Irving Crump called "*The Pilot of the Cloud Patrol*". When you compare the ads for "*The Pilot of the Cloud Patrol*" with those for "*The Flying Patrol*" one year earlier, you begin to appreciate the growing influence of this young artist, who was not yet 30 years of age.

Though the circulation of *Boys' Life* had grown to 179,503[12], Heaslip's work was exposed to an even wider audience when *Cloud Patrol* was picked up by Grosset & Dunlap for its Buddy Books for Boys series in 1929. Heaslip provided both illustrations and cover art for the third installment of the series, "Craig of the Cloud Patrol," in *Boys' Life* (February 1930), and soon thereafter in the *Buddy Books for Boys* series.

BOYS' LIFE

For all Boys — Published by the Boy Scouts of America

FEBRUARY 1930   PRICE 20 CENTS

Beginning *Craig of the Cloud Patrol*—by Irving Crump

This cover features a standalone illustration by William Heaslip intended to express the "admiration and faith in Commander, now Admiral, Richard E. Byrd, Honorary Scout and occasional contributor to *Boys' Life*." It also focuses attention on the contribution of Paul Siple, Eagle Scout and Sea Scout, who assisted in Commander Byrd's conquest of the South Pole. The original painting for this cover is in the Norman Rockwell Museum in Stockbridge, Massachusetts. Note the beginning of the six-episode *"Craig of the Cloud Patrol"* series in this issue. (Allan M. Heaslip)

From 1927 to 1943, William Heaslip provided illustrations for over 70 issues of *Boys' Life*, of which 12 were covers. Among the more notable were illustrations for authors with whom he had connections, including Burr Leyson, Lawrence Guyer, and (Harold) Blaine Miller. Captain Burr Leyson was a World War I aviator,[13] a test pilot,[14] and a rum-runner during prohibition.[15] He became the model for the quintessential pilot on the humorous cover of the November 1935 issue of *Boys' Life*. Lawrence Guyer attended West Point and became a brigadier general in the United States Air Force. And Blaine Miller was an aviation pioneer who launched planes from dirigibles in the mid-1930s; he was promoted to rear admiral at the age of 42, the youngest person to hold that rank at that time.[16] Despite their divergent paths, these aviator-authors all wrote similar stories about wondrous adventures in aviation, stories to which Heaslip gave befitting visualization.

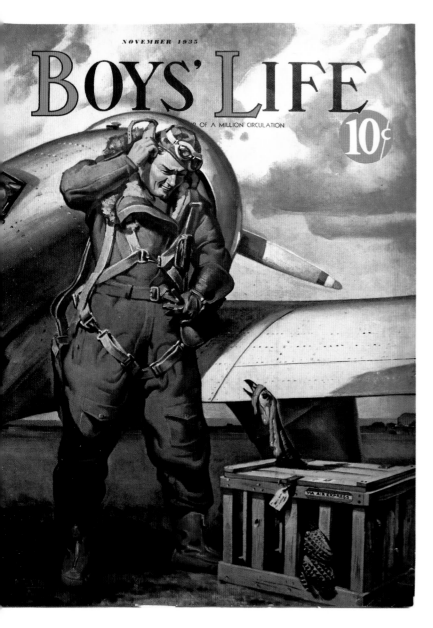

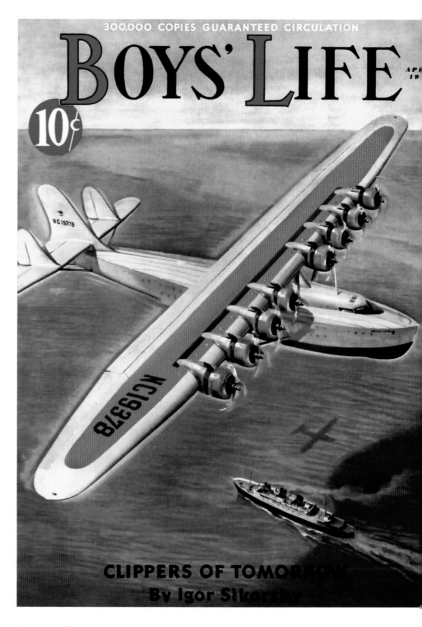

This cover for *Boys' Life* (November 1935) features another standalone illustration by William Heaslip. The magazine contains an article in which the editors take pride in the real-life experiences of their authors who are active commercial and military flyers. The issue also provides a small bio of Heaslip whom they credit with increasing "distinctly the popularity of *Boys' Life* aviation stories." Heaslip is quoted: "Went to camp for a couple of summers with a flock of scouts and a scoutmaster brother." (Allan M. Heaslip)

This cover illustration by William Heaslip highlights "Clippers of Tomorrow" (April 1936), a special article by Igor Sikorsky, as told to Capt. Burr Leyson. Sikorsky , who designed the Pan American Clipper, states that there should be no limit within reason to the size of "flying boats" and predicts the new Clippers will feature "staterooms, showers, a two-story dining room, observation gallery, refreshment counter, and, for diversion in the afternoons and evening, a roomy dance floor." The Clipper, as illustrated by Heaslip, has eight engines, which was Sikorsky's plane imagined. (Allan M. Heaslip)

In October 1935, the series *Airmarks of Aviation* was announced in the magazine. Billed as "the biggest feature in the history of boy magazines," the 12-issue series was to feature "thrilling adventures in the air, written by America's most popular authors of startling aviation tales."[17] It was also to include colorful, full-page illustrations from original paintings, and bimonthly aviation contests. A preview of the *Famous Planes and Pilots* series appeared in that issue. It featured James H. "Jack" Frye, "one of the best-known transport pilots of commercial aviation," together with a painting of a United

JAMES H. "JACK" KNIGHT, one of the best known transport pilots of commercial aviation who flies the Chicago-Omaha run for United Air Lines, is the second ranking pilot of the air mail in the point of service. Only E. Hamilton Lee, another United Air Lines pilot ranks him, both having the stupendous total of over 14,000 hours officially logged in their log books; that time in the air represents nearly 2,000,000 miles each has flown! They are two of United's famous "Million mile pilots," the Line having 45 out of a total of 240 pilots with that distinction.

Two Million Miles Flown!

The Boeing Ten Passenger Transport

UNITED AIR LINES' famous Boeing 247's are the first twin-engined low wing transports and the first of the modern air liners to use a retractable undercarriage. These speedy planes have a top speed of 202 miles an hour at 8,000 feet, carry ten passengers, baggage, mail and express as well as a crew of three,—pilot, co-pilot and stewardess. Yet with this load they cruise over the airways at better than three miles a minute!

The ships are made entirely of metal and possess an unusual degree of strength, far above the limit demanded by the Department of Commerce, Bureau of Aeronautics. The advent of the Boeing saw the first real high speed coast-to-coast service on our air lines. With six intermediate stops they fly from ocean to ocean in 17 hours. Thirty-seven million miles have been flown by these ships in the last two years and at the present time planes of this type fly 1,500,000 miles a month—equivalent to six times around the world!

BOYS' LIFE FAMOUS PLANES AND PILOTS SERIES
Airmarks of Aviation

This illustration of a Boeing 10-Passenger Transport, produced by Clayton Knight for the October 1935 issue of *Boys' Life*, accompanied a photograph of James H. "Jack" Knight, who accomplished much more than the abbreviated description in that issue. Specifically, Jack Knight was part of a relay team of seasoned pilots assembled on February 22–23, 1921, to make a 2,629-mile journey across the country to prove to the U.S. Congress that airmail could be carried both day and night. He volunteered to complete the most dangerous leg of the flight—between Omaha and Chicago in the dead of night during inclement weather. (Clayton Christopher Knight)

Airlines Boeing 247. The painting was produced by Clayton Knight, who—like Burr Leyson—had trained in England as an Oxford Cadet and had been a prisoner of war in Germany.[18]

This series brought together Knight and Heaslip in a convergence of sorts: in all, Knight contributed three paintings to the series, and William Heaslip contributed two. The contests, which revolved around the stories written by Captain Burr Leyson, were also illustrated by Heaslip. For these contests, winners' names were not just drawn from

Riding the Top! Following the "Rainbow Trail"!

CUTTING his way through the clear cold air, bathed in brilliant sunshine and below—a carpet of billowing white clouds that is the roof of a storm which blankets the countryside, wraps it in darkness, whips it with wind and rain, blinds vision with fog. AIRMARKS brings you the scene as a pilot of the Air Mail "rides the top" while to every side stretches the glorious panorama of cloudland, and, like an omen of good luck, dancing from one crest of fleecy cloud to the other, the circular "Pilot's Rainbow" follows the fleeting shadow of his plane.

Finding their way blocked by storm yet knowing from their radio reports that their destination is clear, pilots of the air mail often take-off and, flying blind, climb through the storm clouds to emerge from the murk and darkness into the sun above. Due to the radio beam and the fact that they can orient themselves by the "cone of silence" —the area directly over the transmitters where no signals are received—these pilots can unerringly follow their course without sight of the earth below them.

The Northrop "Gamma" AIRMARKS features is one of this series first flown by Capt. Frank Hawks. Lincoln Ellsworth made his famous trans-Antarctic flight in a Northrop and Howard Hughes spanned the country in record time with another. It is all-metal, low wing, fast and rugged yet lands at low speed. Designed primarily as a mail carrier, it is capable of carrying a tremendous load for its size.

DEAN SMITH—American Airlines veteran—pioneer of the Night Air Mail, pilot with the first Byrd Expedition to Antarctica, winner of the Distinguished Flying Cross, the Congressional Gold Medal and now—awarded the highly prized Harmon Trophy "for his consistent performance of the highest standard over a period of eighteen years in aviation"!
Smith gained a splendid reputation as a mail pilot. Before the advent of radio and the modern instruments that have simplified "blind flight" he possessed an uncanny ability to make his way over the New York-Cleveland route of the pioneer night air mail. This stretch of airway, running over the stormy Allegheny Mountains, was known as the "Pilots' Graveyard" from the number of fatalities due to its treacherous weather.
This year he was awarded the coveted Harmon Trophy by the Ligue Internationale des Aviateurs.

ON THE TOP

BOYS' LIFE FAMOUS PLANES AND PILOTS SERIES
Airmarks of Aviation

Riding the Top! Following the "Rainbow Trail"! by William Heaslip accompanied a photograph of veteran airmail pilot Dean Cullom Smith, which ran in the May 1936 issue of *Boys' Life.* Smith was chosen, along with pilots Bernt Balchen and Harold I. June, to accompany Commander Richard E. Byrd on his Antarctic expedition of 1928–30. For his assistance to Byrd, Smith received the Distinguished Flying Cross in 1930. (Allan M. Heaslip)

a hat: readers had to find the 10 mistakes in aviation fact or practice incorporated into the narrative, and to submit their findings along with 25-word statements on "who my favorite pilot is, and why." The esteemed panel of judges included Captain Eddie Rickenbacker, "American Ace of Aces"; Major Jimmie Doolittle, "famous Army pilot" and later aviation sales manager for Shell Petroleum Products Company; and Tommy Tomlinson, "famed Navy pilot" and "holder of 19 world and American records."[19] Prizes included model kits, pilot radios, outboard motors, bicycles, and cameras. Scattered

William Heaslip's illustration for "I Don't Like Chimneys," written by his friend Captain Burr W. Leyson (*Boys' Life*, August 1936) shows a Bristol monoplane flown by a down-on-his-luck pilot named "Dishes." He barely misses a tall factory chimney as he tries to reach Boston in the dark of night. If readers accurately answered three questions about the story, they would have fulfilled the second of three steps to win a chance for a Graflex or Kodak Camera. (Allan M. Heaslip)

throughout the issues in this year-long campaign were additional aviation stories, mostly by the husband and wife team Blaine and Jean Dupont Miller, all illustrated by Heaslip.

In the same period, *American Boy,* the oldest and largest magazine for youth at the time, began publishing aviation stories that were just as important as those featured in *Boys' Life. American Boy* was managed by Griffith Ogden Ellis, former senior vice-president of the Bank of Detroit and president of the Detroit Street Railway Commission. As head of Sprague Publishing Company, Ellis had been editor and publisher of *American Boy*

FLIGHT QUARTERS

By Blaine and Jean Dupont Miller

ILLUSTRATED BY
WILLIAM HEASLIP

IN MAJESTIC column formation the United States Fleet steamed toward the Canal Zone and anchorage at Coco Solo. Officers and men anticipated several days of rest before the next tactical exercises. Aboard the U. S. S. *Denver*, the senior aviator, Bob Wakefield, had come up on deck. Even after all his years in the Navy this sight of the battle-line ploughing relentlessly through the seas thrilled him as nothing else could.

Presently, he was aware that Captain Rumble was on deck. He turned and saluted.

"An outfit to be proud of, eh, Wakefield?"

"Yes, sir," agreed Bob heartily.

The *Denver* had done her part well during the past week, and the Captain, known to the Navy at large as "Old Ramrod," was in a mellow mood. As a matter of fact, it was hard for Bob to remember that he had, at one time, disliked nothing so much as the idea of serving under his Commanding Officer.

"When do you pick up the new pilot for the unit?"

"Today, sir. He should report aboard as soon as we drop anchor at Coco Solo."

"Fine. Then you will have assistance in your flying schedule next week."

"You know, sir, he's going to be green," replied Bob in a troubled voice, "he's just out of Pensacola."

Captain Rumble chuckled, "Well, you break him into the ways of the air, and I'll see that he gets his sea legs. Nobody stays green on *my* ship for very long."

"If there's anything in blood, Captain," replied Bob, "our new pilot will work out all right. He is a brother of Steve Parker who flew DH's with the Navy's Northern Bombing Squadron during the war."

"Is that so?" asked the Captain with interest.

"You remember, sir, he's the pilot who shoved off alone and sank three German subs at the dock in Bruges. Another time he held up German operations for two weeks by sinking a cargo ship in the channel. He was an ace when he was lost flying a Camel over the front lines."

"Yes," pondered the Skipper, "I remember those stories about him. Let's hope his younger brother has caught his flying ability."

Upon anchoring, Bob took a motor launch and went over to the Air Station for some spare engine parts. Returning, the Officer-of-the-Deck informed him, "Your new pilot is aboard."

"Good!" exclaimed Bob. After delivering the engine spares to Ajax, Bob went down to look over his junior.

In answer to a knock on the door of his room, a voice called, "Come in."

Bob entered to see a tall, freckle-faced, red-headed youth. A trunk stood yawning open, and suitcases were scattered about the small space. Uniforms were strewn about on chairs while shoes were all over the deck.

"I'm Wakefield," said Bob, offering his hand.

"I'm mighty glad to know you—I'm Happy Parker," said the youth, shaking hands and smiling widely. "I've already been up to look over the crates. They seem to be in pretty good shape—and they'd better be, for I'm going to fly their tails off."

Bob was rather irked at Happy's cocky remark about the condition of his planes. But he couldn't help smiling at the youngster's enthusiasm.

"Oh, they're in good shape," he assured Parker.

LOOKING around the room, Bob gave a low whistle. The bulkheads had been decorated with photographs of wartime planes—Spads, Camels, Strutter-and-a-half's, Nieuports. On the desk was a clock mounted in the hub of an old wooden propeller. Above the bunk had been hung a piece of fabric upon which was painted an iron cross. Over beyond, was fabric carrying the colcord of France, the tri-color dotted with tiny, black iron crosses painted over holes pierced by bullets.

Happy followed Bob's eyes.

"Steve sent all these to me when I was a kid," he said proudly, "and, look here!"

He picked up a package of old letters, obviously worn with much handling.

"Here's all the letters Steve wrote home when he was overseas. He tells all about flying, how to dog fight, and how to maneuver. I've been studying them. Watch me do my stuff in the Fleet!"

Bob was dismayed. He realized that Happy's attitude toward flying was colored by memories of his heroic brother. There was nothing he could do about it at the moment, so he merely said, "You'll be wanting to get squared away. I'll see you after dinner."

As he went to his own room, Bob was very much worried. Parker might have been instructed in modern flying at Pensacola, but his worship of his brother's memory had given him the reckless, devil-may-care attitude of wartime flyers. He didn't seem to realize that the day of the heroic ace was over.

After dinner, when they were talking in Bob's room, he attempted to convey something of this idea.

"You realize that out here we don't think in terms of individual pilots any more. Now, it is all formation work. The pilot who loses his squadron today is apt to find himself in trouble."

This possibility did not seem to worry Happy greatly. He argued, "Those letters Steve wrote are a big help to me, and they used to call him 'The Lone Hawk,' you know."

"You will find," persisted Bob, "that different type squadrons have different missions. For instance, we are here to scout and not to do any spectacular maneuvers. You will be of most value by sticking to your mission."

"Maybe," agreed Happy nonchalantly, "but Steve always said to keep your eyes open and perhaps you would be able to do something extra besides your mission."

Bob didn't sleep well that night. What was he going to do about his new pilot? How was he going to steady him down before he broke his neck? He wished fervently that Steve Parker had lived. He would be a Commander by now, and no doubt the first to take Happy in hand and make him see the folly of his attitude toward flying.

THE Fleet was to be in port only four days and Bob worked overtime to indoctrinate Happy into the complex duties of shipboard aviation. He managed to give him a couple of catapult shots in preparation for the work to come. Though Happy had received instruction in formation flying at Pensacola, it was necessary to explain to him the intricacies of squadron work as it was done in the Fleet.

Bob had to admit that Happy handled his plane well in the air, but he found it necessary to caution him several times. He did nothing seriously wrong but his self-confidence kept surging to the fore. He would land too close to the ship headed towards the vessel, so that if he ever found it necessary to take off in an emergency, he could not have flown clear. He would taxi up to the crane too fast. All of this was fine as long as everything went right, but as Bob pointed out to the younger pilot, some day there might be a slip-up.

November

Heaslip's illustration for "Flight Quarters" by Blaine and Jean Dupont Miller (*Boys' Life*, November 1936) captures the moment senior aviator Bob Wakefield tried to free his mechanic Ajax who has gotten trapped beneath a crippled Albatross seaplane while trying to assist the recovery of a cocky, but inexperienced pilot. Blaine Miller was a career naval officer who collaborated with his wife on three Bob Wakefield naval aviation books for Dodd, Mead between 1936 and 1943. (Allan M. Heaslip)

since 1908. In August 1929, just two months shy of the stock market crash, he purchased the rival publication *Youth's Companion,* which had started as a Sunday school weekly in 1827 and he merged it with *American Boy.* The merger was thought to double *American Boy's* circulation, which at that time was estimated at 300,000.[20]

William Heaslip got his foot in the door at *American Boy* by providing small sketches for the monthly column "What Makes It Fly?" by Alexander Klemin. Later he worked on illustrations for "The Spirit of Seventy-Seven" by Laine York Erskine (June 1929) and "The Green Eye" by Benge Atlee (October 1929). These were followed by a fantastical cover for "Haunted Airways," and a three-part serial by Thomson Burtis (beginning in November 1929). The series was billed as an "air mystery of 1985." The artist's dramatic

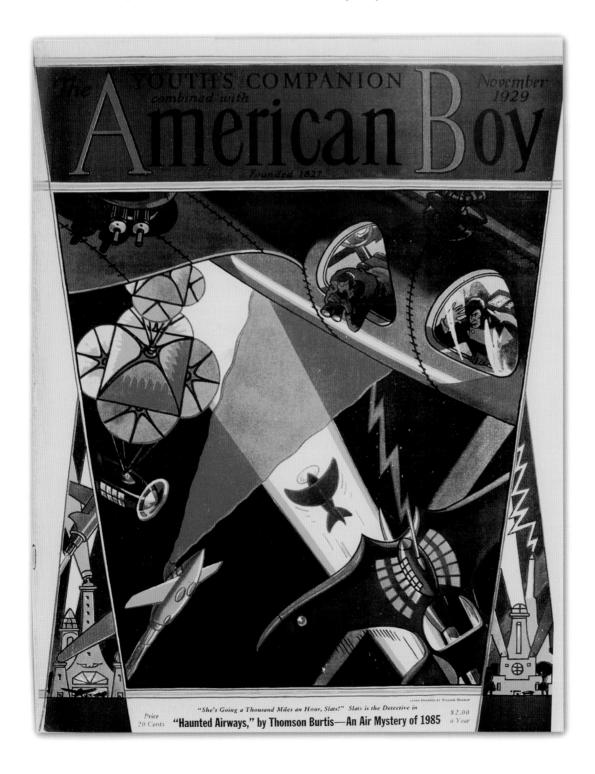

"Haunted Airways: An Air Mystery of 1985" (*American Boy,* November 1929), illustrated by Heaslip, is a story about aviation sabotage in a futuristic world. In 1985, the transcontinental sky is filled with an abundance of large planes, each with a 300-foot wingspan, and each holding up to 500 passengers. The planes are fueled by wireless rays transmitted from a central station on the ground. The story also features smaller rocket ships flying at 600 miles per hour, propelled by rocket fuel provided by service dirigibles in the air. All this came from the imagination of Thomson Burtis, an army-trained pilot turned writer who was a frequent contributor to *American Boy.*
(Allan M. Heaslip)

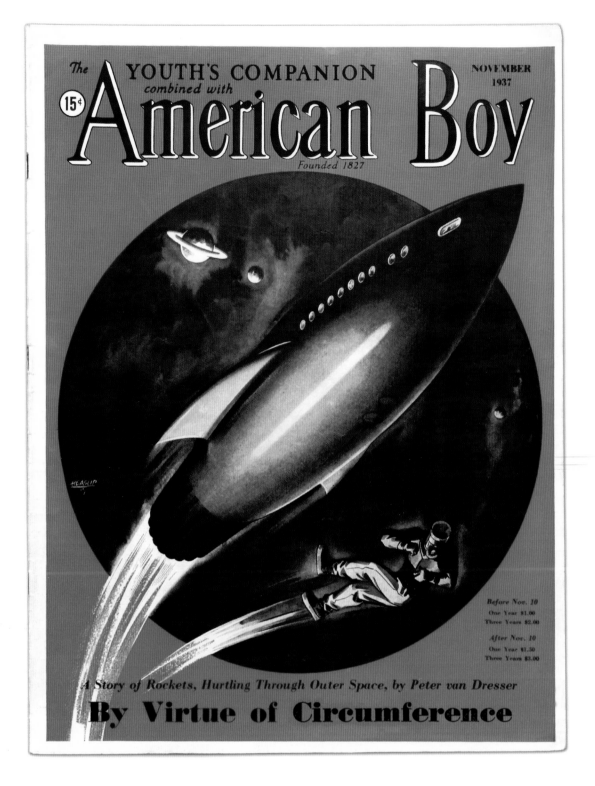

"By Virtue of Circumference" (November 1937) is a lighthearted story, illustrated by Heaslip, about Space Cook Timothy Hawkins who gets stuck in the main exhaust nozzle of a rocket transport because of his 49 ¾-inch circumference. His dramatic extraction through the quick thinking of a young apprentice Alvin Prescott is transformative for all involved. During the 1930s, author Peter van Dresser wrote eight science fiction stories and worked on research related to rocket propulsion with the American Rocket Society's Experiment Committee. (Allan M. Heaslip)

Art Deco design, with its highly structured composition of rockets and "airdromes," was astonishing. Some of the basic motifs were carried over to the dust jacket of the book *Haunted Airways,* published the following year as part of the Young Moderns Bookshelf series, but Heaslip was not credited in the book.

The significance of Heaslip's rockets-and-airdrome illustration to future science fiction illustrators was acknowledged in a December 2000 article by artist David A. Kyle, who credited the piece for his own evolution as "a rabid science fiction fan."[21] Heaslip went on to provide *American Boy* covers for stories by Carl H. Claudy and rocket engine

Heaslip illustrated the serialized story "Return to Mars" by Carl M. Claudy in the September 1939 issue of *American Boy*. The story's protagonist is Dr. Alan Kane, a scientist who has discovered a way to keep metal from melting. He wants to use that invention to fly to Mars to rescue his mentor Professor Isaac Lutyens, who had been captured by bug-like Martians. Claudy, a Washington correspondent for *Scientific American*, wrote 18 science fiction stories for *American Boy* from 1931 to 1939. (Allan M. Heaslip)

pioneer Peter Van Dresser, and illustrations for stories by Franklin M. Reck and Henry Thomson.

As Heaslip was emerging as a leader in rendering aviation of the future, Clayton Knight continued to be a good choice for authors of stories about military aviation. Frederic Nelson Litten, assistant editor of *American Boy*, was a prolific writer of adventure stories for boys. One of his most enduring characters was Jimmie Rhodes, who was introduced to *American Boy* readers in the November 1928 issue when he enrolled in the U.S. Air Corp flying school at Kelly Field in San Antonio. The artist selected to illustrate that

This original painting and the subsequent *American Boy* cover by Clayton Knight depict James "Jimmie" Rhodes, now Second Lieutenant in the Air Corps, in flight gear standing in front of a Curtiss P-6 against a backdrop of what appears to be radial engine variants of the Curtiss P-1 in takeoff. Both pursuit planes pictured were in use at Selfridge Field during this timeframe. This painting is in the collection of the Society of Illustrators Museum of Illustration, New York, NY. (Clayton Christopher Knight)

Knight's magazine illustration was reduced to three colors for the dust jacket of Litten's book *Rhodes of the 94th*. The book, published by Sears Publishing Company, New York, in 1933, included four interior illustrations depicting aerial adventure and predictable mishaps. (Clayton Christopher Knight)

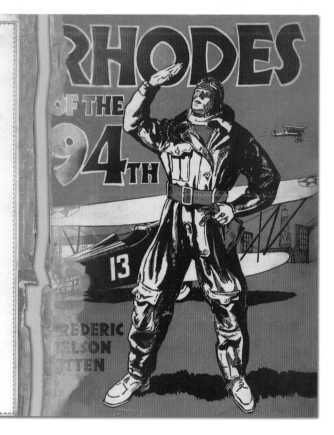

Heaslip distinguished his illustrations by eschewing idealized figures in favor of individual characters appropriate for each story. Typically, he would use models in flight gear to enhance the realism of his work. This original illustration is an excellent example of his skill. Note how much Adam's personality shows through as he is told by Jimmie Rhodes, "Cadet, you will never make a pilot." (Gift of Allan M. Heaslip, Art Collection, National Museum of the Marine Corps, Triangle, VA)

story was Ernest Fuhr (1874–1933), best known for his convincing portrayals of ordinary people.[22] But aviators are anything but ordinary—and while Fuhr's illustrations were competent, they lacked any emotive strength.

Litten selected Clayton Knight to illustrate the second Jimmie Rhodes serial. In this series, Jimmie was now a skilled fighter pilot attached to the 94th Squadron out of Selfridge Field in Michigan. Litten produced a gripping, human interest story through the missions, maneuvers, and adventures of Lieutenant Rhodes in the Army Air Corps in peacetime. The illustration of Jimmie Rhodes on the cover of the April 1931 issue of *American Boy* captured the character's leadership, confidence, and courage—just the attributes one would expect of an officer who saved the day on more than one occasion. A version of the cover was used on the dust jacket of the book *Rhodes of the 94th,* published in 1933.

For the third installment in the Jimmie Rhodes chronicle, Litten chose William Heaslip as his illustrator. By now, Heaslip enjoyed a solid reputation at *American Boy* for his "*Cloud Patrol*" series of stories and books. In "Jimmie Breaks a Rule" (December 1933), Jimmie takes on his first

This original illustration and the one on the chapter frontispiece by Heaslip for *American Boy* accompanied two stories written by Benge Atlee: "The Green Eye" (October 1929) and "Wings Over Bulgaria" (November 1930). Atlee, who enlisted in the Royal Army Medical Corps in 1914, was awarded the Military Cross for gallantry in World War I. During the decade 1928–38, he was a prolific writer under both his own name and the pseudonym Ian Hope. He also became a highly respected professor and physician of obstetrics and gynecology at Dalhousie University in Halifax, Nova Scotia. (Allan M. Heaslip)

command—to build a fighting unit of trained pilots at Bowen Field, Haiti, to combat revolutionaries destabilizing the country. The first illustration in this story is a triptych, with a center panel showing Jimmie reprimanding his cadet Adam, who would later prove himself a hero. The space is shallow and the figures are large in scale, allowing the viewer to feel close enough to hear the conversation. Carrier pigeons, which play an important role in the storyline, are depicted against a solid red background on the decorative side panels. (*American Boy* routinely used spot color to highlight its black-and-white illustrations.) But when the book version—*Rhodes of the Leathernecks*—was published by Dodd, Mead & Company in 1935, the only illustration was a frontispiece. And surprisingly, William Heaslip was not acknowledged.

Aviation Art in the Advertising World

American Boy was published out of Detroit, rather than from New York where *Boys' Life* was headquartered. This is significant because Detroit was home to the automobile industry, and Henry Ford was an early enthusiast who helped shape the future of aviation. Ford's interest in aviation dates to 1910 when an employee of his automobile manufacturing company asked him to invest in a Bleriot-type plane powered by a Ford Model T engine. [23] That engine would prove insufficient to the task, but a government contract during WWI led Ford and other automobile manufacturers to develop the Liberty airplane engine used to power the De Havilland DH4 and one variant of the Curtiss H-16 Flying Boat. [24]

Henry's son Edsel was also an early enthusiast. A director of the Detroit Aviation Society and the Aircraft Development Corporation, Edsel advanced the future of aviation by championing the production of an all-metal airplane at a time when most aircraft were constructed with fabric over wooden frames. After Edsel personally invested in the Stout Metal Airplane Company, Henry committed to building an airport on 719 acres of land in nearby Dearborn to support the Stout enterprise. Upon its completion, the eponymous Ford airport was touted by both civil and military aviation authorities as "America's best." [25] In April 1925, Henry Ford announced the formation of an Air Transportation Service, and by August he had purchased the Stout Metal Airplane Company outright. [26]

As might be expected, the editors of *American Boy* and the executives at the Ford Motor Company saw the benefits of forging a close relationship to promote the future of transportation in general, and the potential of aviation in particular. In 1928 the magazine sponsored an Air Marking campaign, in which readers were enlisted to "mark the roofs of your city so that the aviator flying high above you will be readily able to read the name of your town and check his course." [27] And soon after *American Boy* declared advertising to be the "herald of progress," the Ford Motor Company began a series of expansive advertisements publicizing the growth of commercial aviation and the role of the Ford Motor Company in those advancements.

William Bushnell Stout, who founded the Stout Metal Airplane Company in 1922, built America's first all-metal commercial airplane. That plane evolved into the eight-passenger Stout Air Pullman (2-AT), which featured a corrugated metal exterior and a Liberty engine. The company became a division of the Ford Motor Company in 1925. (Library of Congress, Prints & Photographs Division [LC-DIG-npcc-27223])

THE AIR LIMITED . . . IN 11 SECTIONS

ON TIME! . . . At 5.15, as scheduled, the Chicago air limited appeared high over Detroit, winging at a hundred miles an hour towards the Ford Airport. Following it in close formation were ten additional sections . . . eleven tri-motored, all-metal Ford planes, carrying one hundred and eighteen customers of the Gambill Motor Company, Hupmobile distributors of Chicago. . . .

What would you have thought if you had read this paragraph in a reputable magazine only a few years ago? Pure fiction, of course! Yet this true bit of significant news is no longer startling. For the Stout Air Services have been operating giant Ford planes on passenger flights between Chicago, Detroit and Cleveland on a daily schedule for years. And during 1928 American transport planes flew 10,472,024 miles on established routes, carrying 52,934 passengers!

There was an actual increase in passenger traffic of 420% over the preceding year, and over 100% in distance flown!

Last year was signalized by the great increase in the transport of air mail. This year

is already signalized by the general acceptance of the new vehicle by travelers. Several great new air lines have gone into operation this year, and their success indicates that America has definitely accepted this new form of swift transportation.

Perhaps the most important factor in the development and prosperity of America has been the improvement of its transportation facilities. When you view the United States from the air, this fact becomes manifest. For fleets of ships, streaking across the water, converge towards sheltered harbors where cities have become focal points from which railroad lines and trunk highways extend towards other cities. Along these routes of steel and concrete and water, cities have risen, communities flourish, the land is rich with growing crops and grazing herds and the plentiful products of mines and oil wells. But beyond the traveled roads that bind the nation together there is unproductive stillness, a desert emptiness.

You well know what the coming of the railroad meant to inland places. You know

what the deepening of river channels and ocean harbors has done for commerce and navigation. Doesn't your imagination spark at the significance of this new form of transportation that can carry passengers and cargo faster than the wind, in safety and comfortable relaxation?

Is it not of the utmost importance to the commerce and industry of the nation that it is already perfectly feasible for a business man to leave New York at the same time his partner leaves Los Angeles, and meet for a conference in Kansas City in a matter of hours rather than of days?

Even while you are reading this, great fleets of Ford tri-motored, all-metal planes are winging across the skies, up and down the Atlantic Coast, up and down the Pacific Coast, from ocean to ocean, from nation to nation, from metropolises to fields of production and back again. . . . The American people have this year gone beyond mere speculation as to the future of aviation. They are actually employing the transport plane to speed up the business of the nation!

FORD MOTOR COMPANY

By far, the most significant of *American Boy*'s activities promoting aviation was the creation of the Detroit-based Airplane Model League of America (AMLA), under the auspices of the National Aeronautic Association. The second National AMLA meeting in June 1929 celebrated the winners of a model airplane competition by featuring William B. Stout of Stout Air Services and *American Boy* publisher Griffith Ogden Ellis in the receiving line, and Edsel Ford entertaining contestants at a dinner at Ford airport.[28] Winners were flown to Washington, DC, in a Ford all-metal tri-motor air transport to meet with President Herbert Hoover.[29] William Heaslip was there to document the three-day event.[30] In 1929, it is estimated that the AMLA had 300,000 members,[31] but sometime after 1932, the organization disbanded, most likely another victim of tight money during the Great Depression.[32]

In 1936, Clayton Knight co-authored with Harold Platt a brilliantly colored construction book for future flyers, titled *Ships Aloft*. While working in a two-dimensional board-book format, the authors designed an ambitious, educational, and engaging

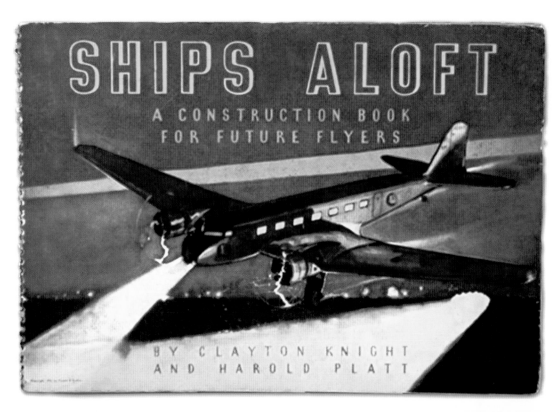

Ships Aloft: A Construction Book for Future Flyers, and one of its interior pages featuring the Boeing Bomber, were the work of Clayton Knight and co-author Harold Platt. Platt, who had also worked with noted maritime artist Gordon Grant on a similar book—*Ship Ahoy: A Construction Book for Fireside Sailors*—had no particular expertise in aviation. (©1936 by Harper & Brothers. Reprinted by permission of HarperCollins Publishers)

publication loosely based on the model airplane genre and focused on four of the era's most publicized flying machines: the Douglas Airliner, the China Clipper, the Boeing Bomber, and the Shipboard Fighter. Each airplane was accompanied by a general explanation as well as specific data. There were even instructions on how to build a picture frame so the final product could be hung on the wall for "air-minded youth," to whom the book is dedicated.

In the November 1936 issues of both *American Boy* and *Boys' Life* magazines, the H. J. Heinz Company announced a far-reaching promotional campaign, one that offered free aviation trading cards in every package of Heinz Rice Flakes and Heinz Breakfast Wheat cereals. By sending in three "57" trademarks from product boxes, young people would receive a 16-page "airplane album" that could accommodate 25 collectible cards with "maps of the routes of famous flights, famous dates in aviation history, and a description of each plane in the Heinz set."

It should be noted that this campaign targeted both boys *and* girls, which may reflect the influence of Joan Diehl, who married H. J. Heinz II in 1935. At the age of 17, Diehl was the 12th woman in the nation to receive her pilot's license; and in the years prior to World War II, she served as a lieutenant in the Civil Air Patrol.[33]

The origin of this campaign, devised by ad agency Maxon of Detroit, is not entirely clear, but it seems to have stemmed from the Heinz company's relationship with celebrated

aviator Colonel Roscoe Turner. On Sunday, May 27, 1934, the Heinz company launched a series of full-color comics through the Bell Syndicate, a distributor of newspaper fiction, feature articles, and comic strips. The comics, which presented *Col. Roscoe Turner's Flying Adventures*, offered "red-blooded American boys and girls from New York to California" the opportunity to become charter members of the Colonel's Flying Corps.[34] During the summer of 1935, the program was expanded to include "Col. Roscoe Turner's Big Prize Contest." First prize was a box seat at the Cleveland National Air Races, and every boy and girl who entered received a set of five brightly-colored aviation trading cards.

Adhering to a general corporate policy, Heinz did not publicly acknowledge the artists with whom they contracted for the illustrations on these trading cards; they apparently considered such information to be a needless distraction from the promotion itself. And any internal documentation at corporate headquarters in Pittsburgh that might have revealed the artists involved is thought to have been destroyed in the St. Patrick's Day Flood of 1936.[35]

For many years, the artists behind the cards remained in question for collectors. However, a careful examination of Clayton Knight's log book in the collection of the Thomas J. Dodd Research Center at the University of Connecticut, strongly suggests that Knight was involved in the production of the first set of trading cards. In that log book, a June 1934 entry lists a $100 payment from the "Bell Syndicate, Heinz Layout," an entry date that neatly follows the May 27, 1934, publication of the comic *Col. Roscoe Turner's Flying Adventures*. Logically, Knight would have been the artist to

Left: This advertisement was placed in the November 1936 issue of *Boy's Life* by the Maxon advertising agency. Founded in Detroit by Lou Maxon in 1927, the agency won the H. J. Heinz Company account in 1928 and held it for 36 years. These strategically placed ads from Maxon's carefully managed campaign provided the lead-up to what would become the successful Heinz "Modern Aviation" and "Famous Air Pilots" trading card albums for boys and girls. (Kraft Heinz Foods Company; courtesy of *Boys' Life* magazine)

Right: (Roscoe Turner Papers, American Heritage Center, University of Wyoming)

Heinz aviation card: Roscoe Turner's 57 Racer, No. 1, Modern Aviation Series, Set One. (Kraft Heinz Food Company; courtesy of Mark Finn)

Heinz aviation card: Bellanca Aircruiser No. 22, Modern Aviation Series, Set One. The back of each card in this series (first and second printing) includes this text: "Colonel Turner wants you to join his nationwide Flying Corps! Just write your name and address on a piece of paper and send it with one big "57" trademark from the side of a package of Heinz Rice Flakes or Heinz Breakfast Wheat, to Colonel Roscoe Turner, c/o H.J. Heinz Company, Pittsburgh, PA. You will receive a certificate of membership, rank, insignia, passwords and all other information." By the third printing, Roscoe Turner's name had been removed. (Kraft Heinz Foods Company; courtesy of Mark Finn)

whom the Bell Syndicate turned for convincing scenes of aviation adventures for this comic. Bell Syndicate's founder John Neville Wheeler certainly knew Clayton Knight from Wheeler's past affiliation with *Liberty* magazine, a publication to which Knight frequently contributed.[36] Moreover, the panel depicting the Thompson Trophy Race of 1933 points to the participation of an artist who specialized in aviation illustration. And considering that Knight was visibly collaborating during this period with Captain Eddie Rickenbacker on the serialized comic strips *Ace Drummond* and *Hall of Fame of the Air* for the King Syndicate, it becomes even more probable that Bell Syndicate would have chosen Knight to produce the illustrations for this comic.

Heinz aviation card: Curtis Wright Condor Transport No. 18, Modern Aviation Series, Set One. (Kraft Heinz Foods Company; courtesy of Mark Finn)

A photograph of an Eastern Air Lines Curtiss-Wright Condor passenger plane in flight. (American Aviation Historical Society, R. Hufford photographer)

As to the Heinz aviation trading cards, a May 1935 entry in Knight's log book lists a payment of $125 from Snyder-Black, a lithography/printing company, for "Preliminary, Heinz—Planes and Booklet." This entry is intriguing, considering that the first set of trading cards reveals some stylistic parallels to Knight's work—especially in the depiction of contexts and backgrounds such as the landscapes and the occasional appearance of people in the illustrations. Several mechanical processes were used in the production of the Series One cards, including photolithography—a process based on photographs.[37] As clearly seen in these illustrations, Knight could have worked with existing photographs to produce illustrations that were then assembled by a printer into complete pictures.

Heinz aviation card: Vultee Transport Monoplane No. 21, Modern Aviation Series, Set One. (Kraft Heinz Foods Company; courtesy of Mark Finn)

This photograph enjoyed wide distribution as a postcard from American Airlines with the description: "World's Fastest Transport Plane, The Vultee, cruising speed 215 miles per hour! One of American Airlines' new fleet." (American Airlines C. R. Smith Museum)

This would explain the similarities between the illustrations and Knight's work, as well as the lack of fine-tuning characteristic of these illustrations. It would also explain why Knight was paid by a printing company, which dealt with the technical aspects of the undertaking.

Why Heinz would not have taken full advantage of the skills of one of the foremost illustrators of aviation could be simple: the company may have considered the first series of trading cards a "trial run," and restricted its budget for the project. Indeed, according to correspondence in the Roscoe Turner archives, the Heinz Company even considered the services of Turner himself to be a trial run.[38] In any case, the project was produced very inexpensively, and the illustrations for Series One were credited only to the "Official Artist of the American Aeronautical Association"—an attribution that may have been the invention of the copywriting department at Maxon, Heinz's advertising agency.

The booklet designed to hold the trading cards, which predates the introduction of Modern Aviation Series Two cards, is also likely Knight's work. Its creation is noted in Knight's log book. Moreover, its cover features the Pan American Clipper NR823M. Between May and August 1933, Clayton Knight had traveled as a passenger over the "routes of the Flying Clipper Ships" of the Pan American Airways System through the Caribbean and around the South American continent on assignment for *Cosmopolitan* magazine.[39] Based on his personal experience, Knight may have considered the luxury airliner a symbol of the promise of passenger travel in the future, and he may have played a part in the selection of that particular airplane for the cover. The cover is photolithography, an accurate reproduction of a painting. And the compositional use of sun rays to focus the eye on the airplane is an artistic device that Knight often used.

The booklet designed to hold the Modern Aviation trading cards, which was distributed by the H. J. Heinz Company from 1935–39, featured a Sikorsky S-42. Three Sikorsky S-42s were built on order from Pan Am on October 1, 1932, each designed to accommodate 32 passengers for daytime flights. The planes were an improvement over the S-40 and cut down travel time from Miami to Buenos Aires from eight to five days. The second S-42 (NC-823M), pictured here, surveyed long-range flights over the Pacific, but could only make the California-to-Hawaii flight if stripped of all passenger accommodations and fitted with extra fuel tanks. (Kraft Heinz Foods Company)

Some collectors date the Series One trading cards to October 1934. This supposition, based on a group of cryptic lot numbers on the backs of the cards, is not inconsistent with the chronology of events presented here. It is quite plausible that the background drawings for the cards and the booklet were two small jobs billed together, but not printed at the same time.

Correspondence between Col. Roscoe Turner and Heinz Advertising Manager Franklin Bell reveals the unraveling of their relationship during the fall of 1935. Apparently, Turner believed that Howard Heinz had not lived up to his part of the agreement between the company and the aviator. As a result, Series One cards carry information about Turner, while Series Two cards do not. In a letter to Turner in October 1935, Bell stated that his department was working on new aviation inserts, the illustrations for which he had assigned to William Heaslip.[40]

The second series of the Modern Aviation Cards was produced by photolithography from a series of well-developed paintings. Those paintings—with colorful, accurately drawn airplanes rendered three dimensionally in full action mode—are classic Heaslip, but they bear no attribution to the artist. However, a one-page color proof of all the planes discovered in the William Heaslip estate reveals the active participation of the artist in the approval process for the Series Two trading cards. Moreover, the original paintings themselves, auctioned off in September 2017, bear the Heaslip signature, which was apparently eliminated during production of the cards. Until then, the paintings had been in the private collection of Lionel P. "Duke" Cornwall, the Maxon Advertising Agency corporate pilot. Clearly, Heinz had wanted a better-quality card to expand the promotion.

The popularity of the Series Two trading cards generated another Heinz album—this one for Famous Air Pilots. These portraits were based on well-known photographs,[41] but there is no evidence that the portraits were painted by Heaslip. The originals, which were also auctioned off in 2017, display no signature or other markings to designate authorship.

Wanting the overall promotional campaign to have an educational component, the Heinz company also produced a supplemental teacher's guide to accompany the series. The guide, which features a classroom wall map with "correlations and suggested activities for all grades,"[42] illustrates famous flights and air routes throughout the world. It is bordered by the 25 airplanes and 25 pilot cards featured in the Modern Aviation Series Two set. Clearly, the House of Heinz believed that "the useful knowledge of how the air was conquered, the names of those who achieved these triumphs, and the details of the equipment used" would inspire every American boy and girl. This is corporate responsibility at its best.

While Heaslip was working on the Series Two trading cards and collateral material, Clayton Knight continued to illustrate the *Ace Drummond* and *Hall of Fame of the Air* comic strips, which were part of Eddie Rickenbacker's Junior Pilots Club. Early installments of both strips—*Ace Drummond* in 1935 and *Hall of Fame of the Air* in 1936—were reprinted in a Big Little Book format.

Many of the young boys who were exposed to the work of Clayton Knight and William Heaslip during this golden age of aviation would become enthralled by the

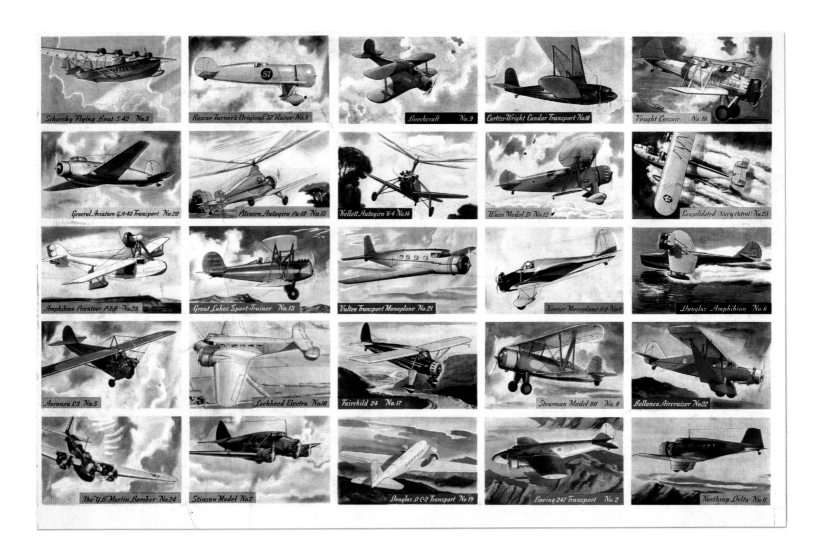

Above: This one-page color proof for trading cards from the Heinz "Modern Aviation" Series Two set is from the estate of William Heaslip. (Kraft Heinz Foods Company; courtesy of Allan M. Heaslip)

Left: Heinz aviation card (Series Two): Bellanca Aircruiser No. 22. (Kraft Heinz Foods Company)

Above: This is the original art work for Roscoe Turner's "57" Racer No. 1, by William Heaslip. (Kraft Heinz Foods Company; courtesy of Mark Finn)

Right: Heinz aviation card (Series Two): Roscoe Turner's "57" Racer No. 1. (Kraft Heinz Foods Company; courtesy of Mark Finn)

Above: This is the original art work for the Waco Model D No. 12, by William Heaslip. (Kraft Heinz Foods Company; courtesy of Mark Finn)

Left: Heinz aviation card (Series Two): Waco Model D No. 12. (Kraft Heinz Food Company; courtesy of Mark Finn)

Right: This is the original artwork for Captain "Eddie" Rickenbacker (No. 3) in the "Famous Air Pilots" series album. Although many have tried to assign these images to William Heaslip, it is the opinion of the authors that the aircraft in the background are not up to Heaslip standards. (Kraft Heinz Foods Company; courtesy of Mark Finn)

Below: This 31" x 42" map was intended to be displayed in classrooms to inspire America's youth to seek a career in aviation. Five pilots from the first printing of "Famous Air Pilots" trading cards—Amelia Earhart, Laura Ingalls, Howard Hughes, Captain Edwin Musick, and Commander Frank Hawks—were not included in the wall map and are thought to have objected to the use of their images. (Kraft Heinz Foods Company; courtesy of Allen McHenry)

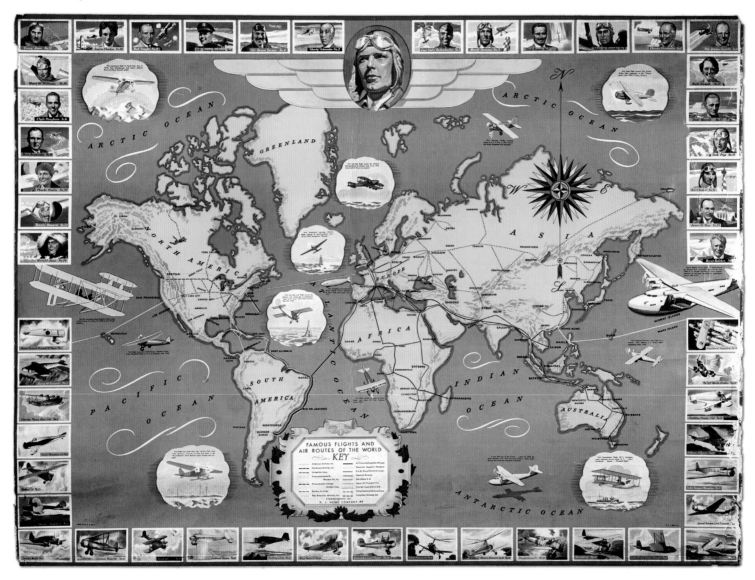

Big Little Books, published by the Whitman Publishing Company of Racine, Wisconsin, started in 1932 with the promise of offering the children of the Great Depression a good read within a compact format of 4 ½″ x 3 ½″ x 1 ½″ for the reasonable price of a dime. The first Big Little Book was *The Adventures of Dick Tracy* to be followed by others with material taken from radio, comic strips and motion pictures. (*Ace Drummond,* ©1935 King Features Syndicate, Inc.; *Hall of Fame of the Air* ©1936 King Features Syndicate, Inc.)

mystique of the airplane itself. They would seek out futures in which dreams of flying would become a reality: some would become pilots; others would become designers, engineers, and mechanics. And some would even provide much needed manpower in the air wars of World War II. It should go without question that today's freedoms are built upon the service, courage, and sacrifice of these men.

CHAPTER SIX

Military and Commercial Aviation 1926–1939

Many Americans believed that aviation fostered such societal virtues as economy, efficiency, and technical innovation. It would help reduce federal spending and enable America to defend itself without becoming mired in another bloody European war. The 1920s and 1930s were the heyday of American technological enthusiasm.[1]

—Charles J. Gross, *American Military Aviation*

Opposite: Clayton Knight produced this image of the USS Lexington with U.S. Navy fighters overhead for the June 1930 issue of *Fortune* magazine. (Clayton Christopher Knight)

In the period between the two world wars, Clayton Knight and William Heaslip built substantial careers, buoyed by the growth of aviation in both the military and commercial sectors. And between them, they captured on paper and canvas many of the innovative aircraft developed during that time.

The Tranquil Skies, 1926–1935

In the 1920s, two able commanders—Major General Mason M. Patrick and Rear Admiral William A. Moffett—helped the government understand what aviation could be to the armed services. Both visionary leaders used their excellent administrative skills to rationalize the production of U.S. military aircraft by directing contracts to companies that knew how to put forth "winning designs."[2]

A graduate of the U.S. Military Academy in 1886, Major General Mason M. Patrick (1863–1942) spent his early military career in the Army Engineers. In 1918, General Pershing tapped him to command the Air Service, American Expeditionary Forces. Patrick succeeded in bringing stability to the chaotic, fledgling organization. After a brief postwar return to the Engineers, Patrick became Chief of the Air Service in 1921, and with the passage of the Air Corps

This photo of Major General Mason M. Patrick, Charles A. Lindbergh, and Rear Admiral William A. Moffett was taken in 1931.

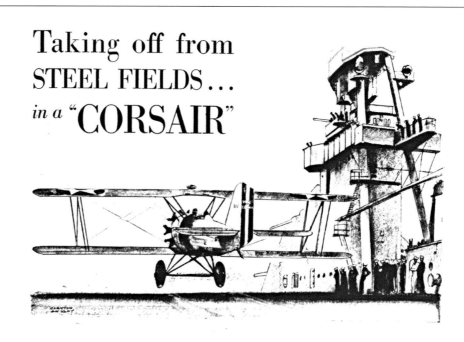

Clayton Knight's ad for aerospace firm Chance Vought portrays Corsair aircraft taking off from the deck of a new carrier. (Clayton Christopher Knight)

Corsair in flight over the newly commissioned carrier USS *Saratoga*. (Clayton Christopher Knight)

Act in 1926, he became the first head of the Air Corps. Patrick was described both as the leader who "ensured the survival of the Air Service" and as a "visionary who saw the full potential of airpower." He also made a wise decision in the early 1920s: in the face of severe funding limitations, he had the foresight to cut back on operations in favor of research and development efforts. This decision helped to bring about more powerful aircraft engines, higher octane fuel, and variable pitch propellers later in the decade. A non-flyer for most of his career, Patrick was to earn his wings at age 59.

Medal of Honor recipient (Vera Cruz, 1914) Rear Admiral William A. Moffett (1869–1933), who became Director of Naval Aviation in 1921, was considered the "architect of U.S. naval aviation." During a period of tight budgets, he used his considerable public relations skills to build support for naval aviation. He also helped to establish the Bureau of Aeronautics and to integrate new technology into the fleet. In effect, he transformed

AUGUST, 1931

81

CORSAIRS

that wear the

GLOBE AND ANCHOR

of the U. S. Marines

Corsairs in service with the Marine Corps are usually in *active* service. It may be in Haiti, whose ragged, mountainous interior affords few landing fields that are even possible. It may be over the inaccessible jungles of Central America. It may be in China in sections where plane failure would write "Finis" to an aerial mission.

Corsairs ask no odds of the men who make their assignments, or the men who do the flying. The stamina to stand rough landings and the performance to get into and out of small fields are traditional with this plane. So, too, are its speed — its climb and its excellent handling qualities.

These distinctly Vought characteristics have carried *Corsairs* through years of strenuous service with the Marine Corps. They have made the *Corsair* a standard observation plane with the Navy. And they make it an ideal ship for fast executive transport and private flying. Chance Vought Corporation. Division of United Aircraft & Transport Corporation, East Hartford, Connecticut. Export representative: United Aircraft Exports, Inc., 230 Park Avenue, New York, N. Y.

CHANCE VOUGHT CORPORATION

The Marine Corps also flew the O2U Corsair with notable success, with Lt. Christian Schilt receiving the Medal of Honor for heroism while on a mission against Sandino rebels in Nicaragua in 1927. (Clayton Christopher Knight)

the naval air service from a "shore-based anti-submarine force of flying boats to a balanced force of aircraft carriers … and shore-based patrol craft, lighter-than-air craft, and floatplanes."[3] Moffett was killed in the crash of the dirigible USS *Akron* in 1933.

The Air Corps Act of 1926 and the Naval Aviation Modernization Act of the same year gave a boost to both services' aviation arms, increasing men and equipment in those services, and creating new offices of Assistant Secretary of War for Air and Assistant Secretary of the Navy for Aeronautics, in the War and Navy departments respectively.

Unfortunately, projected increases in men and material were not realized because of a lack of sufficient funding appropriations. The onset of the Depression forced further reductions in pay and numbers of aircraft. As a result, both air services competed more strenuously for funding from Congress and for the attention of the public in what was described as a competition for "firsts."[4]

The military's ongoing demand for aircraft did help to stabilize and sustain the aviation industry during the calamitous Depression. While the number of aircraft procured by the military was smaller in number than that of the commercial sector, it produced greater revenues. In 1928, the American aviation industry sold 1,219 military and 3,542 commercial aircraft, producing revenues of $19 million and $17 million, respectively; while in 1937, the aviation industry sold 949 military and 2,281 commercial aircraft, producing revenues of $37 million and $19 million respectively. Revenues from the military almost doubled during the Depression, while revenue from commercial sales remained essentially the same.[5]

The Artists as Documentarians

Clayton Knight and William Heaslip's illustrations and articles covered many of the air service's "firsts" as well as their extensive promotional activities during the 1930s. Heaslip had a ringside view of the 1931 Air Corps War Maneuvers, which was described in *Aero Digest* during that same year:

Brigadier General Benjamin Foulois, F. Trubee Davison, Major General James Fechet, and Major Fabian Pratt, MC. (Allan M. Heaslip)

The annual major tactical mission of the Army Air Corps was this year the most ambitious and comprehensive in the history of this branch of the United States air forces. It represented the greatest concentration of military aircraft ever organized in peacetime or wartime [likely only in the USA, and not in a theater of war]. The Air Corps maneuvers of 1931 were organized primarily to test and improve tactical theories regarding aerial defense of the Atlantic Coast against enemy invasion. It was assumed for the purpose of the exercises that a belligerent nation had launched an attack which threatened metropolitan centers on the Atlantic seaboard from New England as far south as Washington, DC. Could the Air Corps summon from stations all over the country every available plane and man, mobilize an efficient air division [to be named the First Air Division] and successfully speed to defense against the invasion? That was the problem to be solved.[6]

F. Trubee Davison, Assistant Secretary of War for Air (1896–1974), seated in the cockpit of a Curtiss B2 Condor bomber. (Allan M. Heaslip)

In preparation for this event, Heaslip mobilized his sketch pad, pencils, and camera, and traveled to Wright Field in Dayton, Ohio, where 672 Air Corps aircraft and 1,484 officers and men were gathering. Among the crowds were many civilian and military luminaries. Heaslip's credentials entitled him to roam freely among the personages and the vast number of assembled aircrew and aircraft. He took full advantage as he sketched many familiar faces. He was well known for his skills as quick sketch artist, and once commented:

> I prefer to sketch a subject when he is unconscious of it, for his mood and expression are more natural. The Assistant Secretary of War [Davison] was at ease in a tilted chair, flanked by Generals Fechet and Foulois, deep in discussion of the probable defeat of the enemy and the inclement weather. The reflected light from the verandah floor playing on the Secretary's face had a tendency to distort his features somewhat. Still and all, I obtained a likeness.[7]
>
> General Foulois was unusually interesting to study. His is a kindly face, but not without the determination of a soldier. His pipe gave an "off moment" touch. But his tobacco—had we been nearer Chicago, I should have blamed the meat packing industry. But if General Foulois found his inspiration for his masterly conduct of the Army Air Corps field exercises in that pipe—may he never exhaust his supply of tobacco, be it ever so rank.[8]

Heaslip also participated in the mass flight over Chicago, recording the view from the rear seat of a Douglas bomber. The resulting drawing reflected the buffeting he encountered in flight:

> We took off into a stormy looking sky. Finally, though, we flew into sunshine. But the going was rough. My sketches from the air bear testimony of that. They are not retouched because I want them to remain

F. Trubee Davison signed this published sketch by William Heaslip. (Allan M. Heaslip)

as they were made under the various conditions. It is exceedingly difficult to get anything that approaches steadiness while putting down impressions in the air.[9]

After the mass flight over Chicago, Heaslip boarded a Fokker F-32 transport, along with Clayton Knight (whom he referred to as his "contemporary"); Eddie Rickenbacker; and Cy Caldwell, editor of *Aero Digest* magazine. Bound for Floyd Bennett Field in New York, they arrived in advance of the First Air Division.

The many military aircraft of the First Division that followed severely taxed the facilities of all of the military and civilian airfields along the route from Chicago to New York … but longer-term benefits would accrue as a result, especially to commercial aviation. According to *Aero Digest*:

> The great influx of military ships created traffic conditions similar to operations five or ten years in the future. The operators have learned how they must prepare for the normal growth of commercial operations.[10]

Moreover, over 75 million people had the opportunity to view some of the maneuvers associated with this massive aeronautical event. As a result, interest in commercial aeronautics increased dramatically.

Mass flight of United States Army Air Corps aircraft over Chicago.

This published sketch, signed by passengers enroute to New York City aboard the Fokker 32 transport, was suggested to Heaslip by Eddie Rickenbacker. (Allan M. Heaslip)

The culmination of the exercise was staged over and near New York City on May 23, 1931. According to *Aero Digest,* the First Air Division engaged in a combat demonstration: they "defended the city from enemy invasion. After taking off from various air fields, they swept down the Hudson River to the Battery in a double-deck column more than ten miles long," ending with the laying of a smoke screen. The Division then joined into one solid formation about 20-miles long and passed in review over Floyd Bennett Field. "What an exciting spectacle for those watching from below!" *Aero Digest* editors observed.[11]

Back in his New York studio the following day, Heaslip noted:

My pencils were worn down to stubs while I was away, but my camera never saw the light of day. It takes quick maneuvers with the pencil to suggest the action of those fleeting moments on land and in the air. Photographs are static after all, and lack that certain spontaneity which is so desirable to portray the very life and throb of living incidents.[12]

The highly successful two-week Air Corps exercise concluded after additional flights were made over New England and the Chesapeake Bay area.

During the early 1930s, when military budgets were tight, some U.S. aviation companies were willing to risk their own capital to innovate and improve the capabilities of military aircraft. A dramatic example of this was the Martin B-10 bomber, a private venture of the Glenn L. Martin Company of Baltimore, Maryland.

Technical innovations during that time brought about major doctrinal changes for both military and naval air services. The Air Corps' Martin B-10 twin-engine bomber, new in 1934, demonstrated speeds superior to fighters then in use. This led the Air Corps to rationalize that well-armed bombardment aircraft flying in close formations could accomplish their missions unescorted by fighters. Thus began a long-running conflict between bomber and fighter proponents, with the bomber forces winning the funding battles for most of the balance of the decade. While the fighter forces were being shortchanged, increased bomber funding led to the development of the B-17 and B-24 long-range bombers, and the incomparable B-29 Superfortress, which would end the coming war by dropping two atomic bombs.

In 1941, the Air Corps was reorganized as the U.S. Army Air Forces (USAAF). And with the adoption of the highly accurate Norden bombsight, the primary mission of the USAAF became precision bombings of strategic targets in daylight. However, unescorted daylight bombing proved a failure in World War II because of prohibitive losses to German fighters. It was only after the development of the P-51 Mustang fighter, capable of sufficient range to get to "Berlin and back," that the USAAF would continue its mission of destroying enemy targets in daylight.

The USS *Langley*, built on the hull of a former collier in the early 1920s, was America's first aircraft carrier. Pioneer carrier pilots learned the rudiments of carrier operations flying from the small deck of this ship. In 1927, the U.S. Navy commissioned two far larger carriers, the USS *Saratoga* and the USS *Lexington*, both of which were capable of carrying close to 80 aircraft (designated as an air group).

Both new carriers joined the fleet exercise in early 1929 to carry out Fleet Exercise Problem (FP) 9 dealing with the defense of the Panama Canal. In prior exercises, the USS

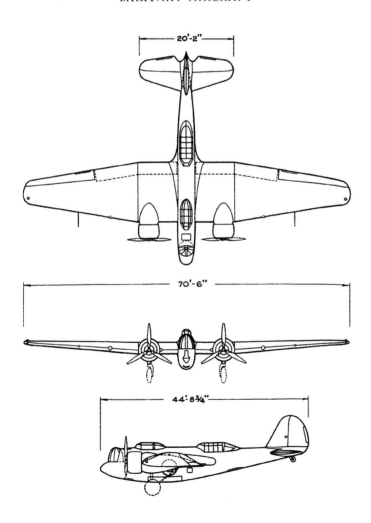

MILITARY AIRCRAFT

20'-2"

70'-6"

44'-8¾"

THE GLENN L. MARTIN COMPANY
Baltimore, Md.
MODEL 139   ARMY BOMBER
ENGINES: 2 WRIGHT CYCLONES

Left: Clayton Knight in cap and goggles in front of a U.S. Navy Boeing F4B fighter aircraft. (Smithsonian Institution Archives, Record Unit 311, National Collection of Fine Arts, Office of the Director of Records, 1892–1960)

Right: Etching of U.S. Navy pilot by William Heaslip, *c.* 1933. (Allan M. Heaslip)

Langley, with its limited complement of 20 aircraft, had been tasked with scouting and maintaining air defense over the fleet. But the new and faster USS *Saratoga* and USS *Lexington*—each carrying an entire air group—were tested as offensive forces independent of the fleet. Many years later, the USS *Saratoga* was given credit for wiping out the enemy on the Pacific side of the Panama Canal.

Clayton Knight was aboard the USS *Pennsylvania* during Fleet Exercise Problem 14 in 1933. He had been sent by air-minded *Cosmopolitan* magazine to illustrate an article written by Floyd Gibbons. In that exercise, the USS *Pennsylvania*, flagship of the "blue fleet," defended two major West Coast cities from the attacking "black fleet," which included the carriers *Saratoga* and *Lexington*. The cities were judged by the fleet's chief umpire as having been wiped out in the attacks by carrier-borne aircraft.[14]

Clayton Knight's original sketch of the USS *Saratoga* landing fighters after a simulated raid. (Clayton Christopher Knight)

NRA
U.S.
CODE

The American
LEGION
MONTHLY

JUNE 1935   25 CENTS

Opposite: Heaslip's image of a Curtiss Hawk (early dive bomber) on the deck of the aircraft carrier USS *Saratoga*. (*American Legion Monthly*)

Left: Heaslip's still life painting of his Curtiss Hawk model alongside pilot's paraphernalia. (Theodore Hamady)

Below: Photograph of Heaslip at his easel painting the same Curtiss Hawk canvas for the cover of *American Legion Monthly*. (Allan M. Heaslip)

In the early 1930s, the U.S. Navy also began experimenting with dive bombing. This method of attack, which delivered a heavy bomb from an aircraft that could dive steeply on its target ship (to maximize the certainly of a hit), rendered enemy surface ships vulnerable to aerial attack. This was borne out on June 4 and 5, 1942, when three squadrons of Douglas SBD Dauntless dive bombers from the USS *Yorktown* and *Enterprise* sank all four Japanese carriers during the battle of Midway.

With lessons learned from experimental innovations and fleet problems, including FP 14, authorization was approved in 1933 for the building of the new Yorktown class of aircraft carriers. Thus began the integration of carrier air power into the fleet. Fleet exercises, including the successful attacks on Hawaii in 1932 (named Grand Joint Exercise 4) and again in 1938, further honed the skills of the military and taught the lessons that foretold the might of the U.S. Navy carrier task forces that ranged throughout the South Pacific in World War II.[15]

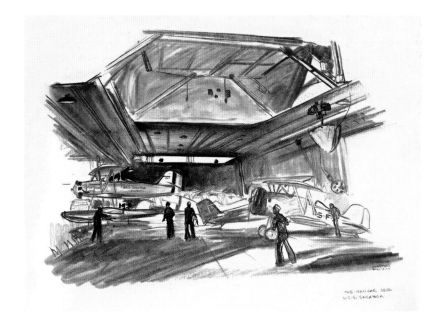

Clockwise from top left:

Clayton Knight's original drawing of an aircraft carrier hangar deck appeared in the May 1933 issue of *Cosmopolitan* magazine. (Clayton Christopher Knight)

Clayton Knight sketched Rear Admiral Harry Yarnell aboard his flagship USS *Pennsylvania*. Admiral Yarnell had directed his new carriers, the USS *Saratoga* and the USS *Lexington*, in a simulated attack on Pearl Harbor in a 1932 fleet problem and won a decisive victory. The Japanese Imperial Navy accomplished the same feat nine years later. (Clayton Christopher Knight)

Clayton Knight sketched this original drawing of a darkened signal bridge aboard the USS *Pennsylvania* battleship before a simulated attack at night. (Clayton Christopher Knight)

This original drawing by Clayton Knight portrays a 14-inch gun crew in simulated action aboard the USS *Pennsylvania*. (Clayton Christopher Knight)

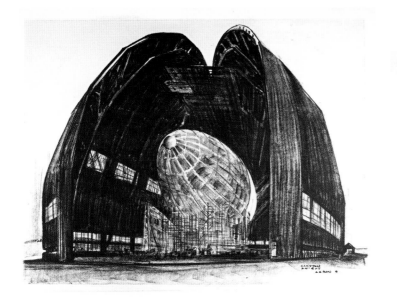

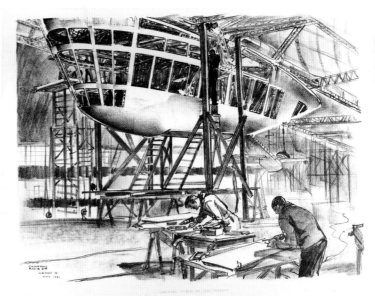

Left: U.S. Navy dirigible *Akron*, under construction. Original drawing by Clayton Knight. (Clayton Christopher Knight)

Right: Working on the dirigible gondola. Original drawing by Clayton Knight. (Clayton Christopher Knight)

The Gathering Storm, 1935–1939

The year 1935 was a pivotal one for military and commercial aviation. When Adolph Hitler proclaimed an end to the limitations imposed by the Versailles Treaty, the threat of another major conflict became a real possibility. Germany began a rapid expansion and modernization of its military services, including a reconstitution of its air force, dubbed the *Luftwaffe*. This renascent air force quickly became a perceived threat to much of Europe.

Italy, supported by its own then-potent air force, sent troops into Ethiopia, daring the British and French to respond. The British Royal Navy steamed into the Mediterranean in a show of force … but to no effect as Mussolini called their bluff. At about the same time, Japan doubled its appropriations to modernize its army and navy air forces in preparation for an aggressive foray into China. And in view of these new threats, Britain and France doubled their aviation appropriations.

In 1935, the United States, with its cash-strapped military budgets, fell to fifth place in the number of combat airplanes in its squadrons, and what had been a three-year technical lead was shortened to 18 months.[16] On a positive note, the U.S. introduced several significant aircraft in 1935. Among them was the Boeing 299, soon to be renamed the "Flying Fortress" by the press.

Consolidated Aircraft Corporation's PBY-1 would gain fame during the coming war as the PBY Catalina. This long-range aircraft served in a variety of roles, including reconnaissance (it spotted the German pocket battleship *Bismarck* in 1941, and the Japanese fleet approaching Midway in 1942), anti-submarine warfare, search and rescue, cargo transport, convoy escort, and even night bombing.

In 1935, civilian aircraft were also introduced, including the much-heralded Martin 130 "China Clipper" that inaugurated Pan American's airmail service to the Philippines in November of that year. The following year, the "Philippine Clipper" began passenger

War Birds are Flying   By W. B. Courtney

May 25, 1935

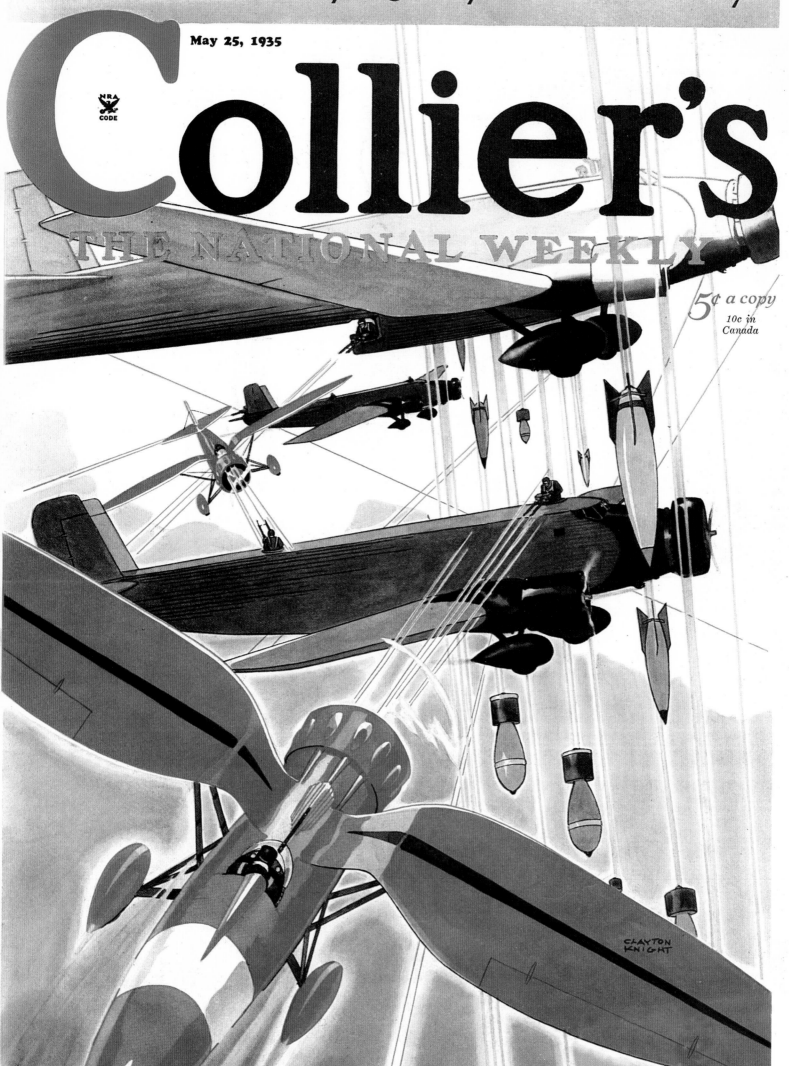

Collier's
THE NATIONAL WEEKLY

NRA CODE

5¢ a copy
10c in Canada

CLAYTON KNIGHT

The illustrious Boeing B-17 Flying Fortress carried the air war over Europe in World War II.

The B-17 variant portrayed in this ad is a prewar B-17B, with larger control surfaces to improve performance at slower speeds.

service from California to Hong Kong. Perhaps the most important aircraft of all was the Douglas DC-3, an aircraft that would equip many of the world's airlines by the end of the decade. Ten thousand C-47s, the military configuration of the DC-3, would be supplied to American and Allied air services during World War II.

Clayton Knight and William Heaslip spent many hours at their drawing boards rendering illustrations of these and other aircraft. In 1937, Knight was commissioned by Pratt & Whitney Aircraft to prepare stone lithographs of aircraft powered by Pratt & Whitney engines: notably, the legendary Twin Wasp R-1830, which produced up to 1,350 horsepower; and the Double Wasp 18-cylinder R2800. This series of lithographs began with the Sikorsky S-42 "Pan American Clipper" in 1937 and ended with the Douglas C-47 in 1944.

The Following portfolio of lithographs was produced by Clayton Knight for the Pratt & Whitney Company. Each aircraft was powered by a Pratt & Whitney radial engine.

Opposite: This prescient 1936 *Collier's* magazine cover by Clayton Knight, dated May 25, 1935, shows a Polish type PZL fighter attacking a German Junkers Ju-52 bomber. (Colliers Magazine)

Capt Harold Gray

"HORNETS" TAKE THE SIKORSKY "PAN AMERICAN CLIPPER"

ACROSS THE ATLANTIC

· 1937 ·

A "DOUBLE WASP"
GIVES THE ARMY'S REPUBLIC P-47 "THUNDERBOLT"
OUTSTANDING PERFORMANCE AT HIGH ALTITUDE
1941

Carl F. Greene

SUPERCHARGED "WASPS"
CARRY THE U.S. ARMY AIR CORPS LOCKHEED INTO THE SUBSTRATOSPHERE TO WIN
THE COLLIER TROPHY
☆ 1938 ☆

Alfred W. Johnson

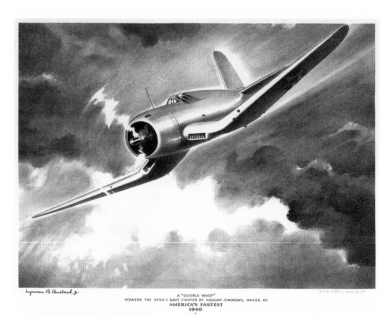

A "DOUBLE WASP"
POWERS THE XF4U-1 NAVY FIGHTER BY VOUGHT-SIKORSKY, HAILED AS
AMERICA'S FASTEST
1940

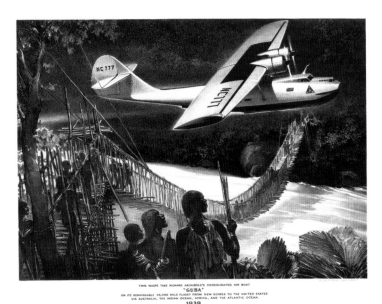

TWIN WASPS TAKE RICHARD ARCHBOLD'S CONSOLIDATED AIR BOAT
"GUBA"
ON ITS REMARKABLE 24,000 MILE FLIGHT FROM NEW GUINEA TO THE UNITED STATES
VIA AUSTRALIA, THE INDIAN OCEAN, AFRICA, AND THE ATLANTIC OCEAN.
1939

THE STEADY DRONE OF TWIN WASPS FILLED THE HEAVENS
AS PARATROOP-CARRYING DOUGLAS C-47'S HERALDED THE OPENING OF
◊ THE INVASION ◊
D-DAY ★ JUNE 6, 1944

Far left

Top: The Sikorsky S-42 met Pan American's 1931 requirement for a long-range Flying Boat, 1937.

Middle: The Lockheed X-35 experimental pressurized aircraft received the Collier Trophy in 1938.

Bottom: "Guba," a PBY twin-engine Flying Boat was used to explore New Guinea in 1937. Built by Consolidated Aircraft, the PBY was widely used by the United States, Great Britain and the Soviet Union as a maritime patrol aircraft during World War II, 1939.

Left

Top: Packing eight .50 machine guns, the Republic P-47 was the largest USAAF fighter in operation during World War II, 1941.

Middle: Vought XF4U-1 was America's fastest fighter plane in 1940.

Bottom: Douglas C-47 dropping paratroopers, 1944.

Right

Top: Grumman F4-F Wildcat naval fighters bore the brunt of the early air combat in the Pacific. The type remained in production throughout the war, 1942.

Bottom: B-24 Liberators on a low-level mission to destroy oil refinery facilities at Ploesti, Romania, on August 1, 1943. Five Medals of Honor were awarded for that mission, three given posthumously.

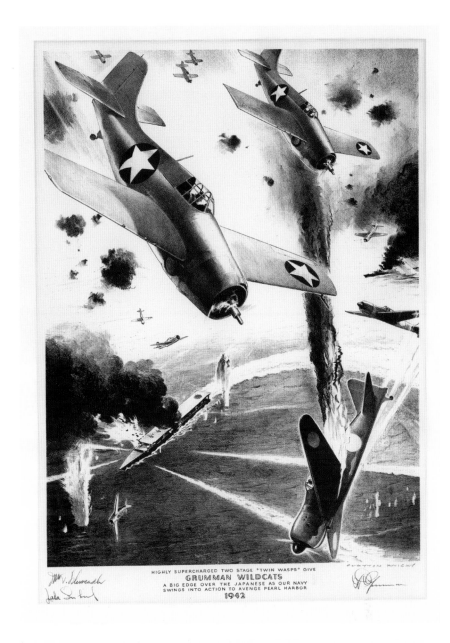

HIGHLY SUPERCHARGED TWO STAGE "TWIN WASPS" GIVE
GRUMMAN WILDCATS
A BIG EDGE OVER THE JAPANESE AS OUR NAVY
SWINGS INTO ACTION TO AVENGE PEARL HARBOR
☆ **1942** ☆

THE NINTH AIR FORCE SWEEPS DOWN
IN CONSOLIDATED B-24 LIBERATORS
POWERED BY TURBO-SUPERCHARGED PRATT & WHITNEY TWIN WASPS
FOR A LOW ALTITUDE RAID
DEVASTATING THE PLOESTI OIL FIELDS
☆ **1943** ☆

Right: This ad for Jacob's airplane engine, produced in 1938, reveals William Heaslip's artistic brilliance. (Allan M. Heaslip)

Below: William Heaslip's etching of Douglas Corrigan's flight to Ireland. Piloting a 1929 Curtiss Robin airplane, Corrigan claimed he had taken off from New York for California, but somehow ended up in Ireland. For this so-called navigational error, he became celebrated as "Wrong-Way Corrigan." (Allan M. Heaslip)

Each season produces at least one perfect combination. This year without question it is the Waco Model A powered by the Jacobs "170". This model was particularly designed for the sportsman pilot. Unmatched performance . . . reasonable first cost . . . remarkably low maintenance. Consult your nearest Waco dealer.

JACOBS AIRCRAFT ENGINE CO.
Central Airport, Camden, New Jersey

JACOBS
AIRCRAFT ENGINES

Heaslip's watercolor draft of an illustration for the cover of Grumman's 10-year history book, published in 1939. The aircraft is the Wildcat F4-F naval fighter. (Allan M. Heaslip)

Heaslip produced this outstanding oil painting of the Grumman Wildcat F4-F naval fighter—the type later sold to many allied countries including Great Britain, where it was known as the Martlet. The ad dates to 1940. (Allan M. Heaslip)

Top left: The luxurious Boeing 314 Flying Boat supplanted Pan American's Martin 130 Flying Boats on trans-ocean routes. (American Aviation Historical Society, A. Hansen photographer)

Top right: The Boeing 307 Stratoliner was the first successful pressurized commercial airliner. Passengers enjoyed a comfortable flight above the weather. (American Aviation Historical Society)

Bottom: Clayton Knight is honored on the cover of Air Services magazine in 1939.

The year 1938 was another banner year for both the U.S. military and commercial aviation. Prototypes of the first production models of the Air Corps' P-38, P-39, and P-40 fighters appeared on the scene, as well as the Navy's Grumman F-4 Wildcat. America's airlines enjoyed another record year as they awaited the arrival of new transport aircraft, such as the Boeing 314 Flying Boat and the Douglas DC-4.

The prestigious Collier Trophy had been awarded to the Air Corps in 1937 for its development of Lockheed's XC-35 pressurized sub-stratosphere plane. This technology was utilized by Boeing for its model 307 Stratoliner, which would become the first pressurized commercial airliner in 1940.

The Munich Crisis, which took place over the summer of 1938, culminated on September 30 in British Prime Minister Chamberlain's "peace for our time" speech and acquiescence to Hitler's demands. In less than a year, most of the Low Countries in Europe would lay prostrate in defeat, with only Britain left to carry on the war against Nazi Germany.

On December 29, 1940, President Franklin D. Roosevelt warned the nation:

> There is danger ahead—danger against which we must prepare. ... We are planning our own defense with the utmost urgency, and in its vast scale we must integrate the war needs of Britain and the other free nations resisting aggression. ... Manufacturers of [peacetime articles] are now making [instruments of war.] But all of our present efforts are not enough. We must have more ships, more guns, more planes—more of everything. ... We must be the great arsenal of democracy.[17]

Clayton Knight illustrated the cover of Lieutenant Colonel Harold Hartney's World War I memoir, which also related his thoughts on the coming war in the air.

Both Clayton Knight and William Heaslip had already begun to mobilize almost exclusively for war work. But their career paths over the next six years would take them in very different directions.

CHAPTER SEVEN

Girding for War

As the threat of war grew throughout the mid-1930s, the United States Congress passed a series of stringent Neutrality Acts designed to limit U.S. involvement in future wars. In September 1939 when war broke out in Europe, President Franklin Delano Roosevelt (FDR)—who was keenly sensitive to public opinion—began to reassure citizens that American boys would not be sent to fight in foreign wars. This mantra would be repeated many times over the next two years.

But as Roosevelt witnessed the defeat of France and the Low Countries in 1940, the Battle of Britain, during which England stood alone in its fight against Nazi Germany and Fascist Italy; and a massive attack against the Soviet Union (unexpected by Stalin) by the German *Wehrmacht* in 1941, he privately chafed under the restrictions of the Neutrality Acts. He believed that greater security for the United States lay in its allies' abilities to defend themselves, especially since the U.S. was still unprepared for war. And like many in his generation who served the nation during the World War I, FDR remembered President Woodrow Wilson's unpropitious charge to the American people to remain neutral in dealing with the then-warring powers. FDR knew that under Wilson's leadership, the United States had failed to mobilize its manpower and industry in time, and consequently was forced to rely on its allies to fully train and equip its military—an added cost that would later appear on casualty lists. This could not be tolerated in 1939 when the dangers were far greater than those of 1917, not just in Europe, but also in the Pacific.

And so, with consummate skill and creativity, plus (his critics claimed) a large measure of deception, President Roosevelt began supplying war weapons to England, and later, to the Soviet Union and China, while at the same time funding massive increases in U.S. military budgets to build production capacity within the military—especially in aviation.

By emphasizing the importance of military preparedness and defense, FDR attempted to influence American public opinion and prepare America for the coming war. But by mid-1941, many Americans were still largely conflicted when it came to voluntarily entering the war. According to historian Marc Wortman:

Opposite: William Heaslip's inspirational illustration "There'll Always Be an England." The scene takes place at London's Cenotaph, a memorial to Britain's war dead from World War I. A ghostlike soldier is seen rising from the dead as *Luftwaffe* bombers range overhead. The king and queen are in the forefront among their people. (Allan M. Heaslip)

Results from Gallup Polls in the spring of 1941 showed that a steadily increasing percentage of Americans wanted to get more aid to Britain even at the risk of war, some 68 percent, and by even larger numbers, 73 percent, they were convinced that an Axis conquest of England could pose a "serious danger," even a military threat to the U.S. By May 1941, 85 percent of those polled thought the U.S. would have to get into the war before it ended. Yet those same polls found that almost the same number of Americans opposed U.S. entry into the war, even at risk of a British defeat.[1]

Artists at War

Clayton Knight and William Heaslip found ample opportunity to chronicle the country's efforts to gird up for war. By September 1939, both were widely sought after by industry, business, and the U.S. government. And in a very short time, their commitments increased to a fevered pitch, remaining so for the duration of the war.

Between 1939 and 1942, Knight traveled extensively across the United States as a special correspondent for the Associated Press, covering the growing activities of the U.S. Army Air Corps and bringing attention to the country's burgeoning aerial defense needs. And from 1943 to 1945, he served as a combat artist for the U.S. Army Air Forces.

In contrast, William Heaslip's war commitment was to the *New York Times*/Wide World syndicate in 1940–1942, followed by an extensive five-year involvement with the Coca-Cola Company. During those years, Heaslip would be confined to his studio in

This assembly line producing P-39 Airacobra fighters clearly reflects prewar production thinking. It would soon change dramatically with every square foot of space utilized along with the increasing presence of skilled women workers. (Theodore Hamady)

William Heaslip's illustration of a Lend-Lease Lockheed Hudson in its anti-submarine warfare role. (Theodore Hamady)

New York City, working 12-hour-plus days in order to meet punishing deadlines before returning home to his family in Rahway, New Jersey, for brief weekend visits.

Apart from illustrating ads for industry and preparing recruiting and production posters for the U.S. Army Air Forces, Knight and Heaslip no longer saw themselves as competing for business as they had done for much of the 1930s. Both shared a strong emotional attachment to England: Heaslip, a former British subject and veteran of the Royal Air Force in World War I, and Knight, a former American Air Service member of an RAF bomber squadron. They both manifested their fervent support for England and the British Empire in the fight against Nazi Germany.

The Clayton Knight Committee

On September 4, 1939, one day after World War II began, Clayton Knight received a telephone call from Air Marshal (Honorary) William A. "Billy" Bishop, recipient of the Victoria Cross, and Canada's Ace of Aces. Bishop had known Knight during World War I and was well aware of his wide circle of influential friends in aviation. He asked Knight if he would be willing to assist the Canadian Honorary Air Advisory Committee in recruiting American pilots who expressed interest in joining the Royal Canadian Air Force. The critical need for trained aircrew to fight the war in Europe was apparent, but the constraints of the strict neutrality laws then in effect in the United States made Bishop's proposal an illegal endeavor. In any case, Knight responded with an enthusiastic yes, and he was quickly brought on board.[2]

The immediate concern of Americans entering the military service of another country was quickly dealt with by FDR, who assured the British and Canadian ambassadors that recruitment of American pilots could be done ... *but only if it were done discreetly.* The goal was achieved through the creation of front organizations that successfully masked the activities of what came to be known as the Clayton Knight Committee, later renamed the Canadian Aviation Committee. A similar process was undertaken two years later to mask the creation of the American volunteer group Flying Tigers before the U.S. entered the war.

30 American Youths Here To Join Canada's Air Force

Prospective Recruits Are Sent to Ottawa Under Auspices of Clayton Knight Committee

Scattered about in Ottawa hotels today, many of them quartered at the Chateau, were some 30 American youths recruited by the Clayton Knight Committee associated with Bundles for Britain, and sent to Canada's Capital for enlistment with the Royal Canadian Air Force.

In the group were truck drivers, salesmen, college students, chemists; but there was also a flying potato-bug exterminator, and a lad who had devoted his post high school years to thumbing his way through 46 states and Mexico.

Sent by Committee.

Each young man had been approached by an agent of the Clayton Knight Committee, formed by a group of patriotic U. S. citizens, convinced that full-out aid for Britain is America's best defence.

The Clayton Knight Committee, working in association with Bundles for Britain, "recruited" these young Americans, providing each youth with transportation and hotel expenses for the trip north to Ottawa.

"Agents of the committee are active in every state of the Union", explained 25-year-old George Corneal, an Alabama "crop-duster".

His statement was borne out by the other American youths who hailed from California, Louisiana, New York, Pennsylvania and other states.

Corneal the "crop-duster" was busy spraying insecticide from a 'plane over Alabama potato fields when approached on the idea of joining the R. C. A. F. by one of the many Clayton Knight Committee agents.

"Sold" on Idea.

The flying potato-bug exterminator, like the other American youths, quickly was "sold" on the adventure offered by the R.C.A.F. in "shooting up the Nazis".

"It seems like I just can't stay put", explained 20-year-old Leonard L. Slego, who "just by accident" happened to be pausing between trips when a committee agent called around at his Donmore, Pennsylvania, home.

Slego had hitch-hiked his way around 46 states, covered Mexico, but had never been to Canada.

Because he "never could stay home", he headed north to Ottawa to be fitted with the Air Force Blue.

John Mathews, 20 - year - old

Order of the British Empire citation awarded to Clayton Knight. This officer-rank citation, given for service to the British Empire by a civilian, was "honorary," since Clayton Knight was an American citizen. (Clayton Christopher Knight)

Armed with a list of 300 prospective pilot recruits, Knight embarked on a tour of American flying schools and college campuses. He set up interview offices in luxury hotels in nine major U.S. cities in anticipation of a groundswell of interest.

The author (Hamady) recalls a former business associate who responded to Clayton Knight's proposal while a student at Texas A&M in 1940. The young man traveled to Canada, and after receiving his wings, was posted to North Africa as a fighter pilot. Downed over the desert after an encounter with enemy fighters, he was taken prisoner by hostile Bedouins, but ultimately rescued by elements of the Long Range Desert Group, a legendary British unit that wreaked havoc behind German and Italian lines. By this time, the United States was at war, and by prior arrangement, all Americans who wished to join U.S. military service could do so. The former Texas Aggie returned to the United States for additional training, joined a B-24 unit in the 445th Bomb Group of the vaunted Eighth Air Force, and was deployed to England. (Actor Jimmy Stewart was the 445th Bomb Group's operations officer at the time.) This former Royal Canadian Air Force/U.S. Army Air Forces pilot ultimately made a career in the postwar United States Air Force.

Over two and a half years, the Clayton Knight committee recruited 2,650 American trained pilots and trainee aircrew for the Royal Canadian Air Force (RCAF). The Committee also provided over 90 percent of the men who made up the Eagle Squadrons (Americans who flew for the British Royal Air Force). The Clayton Knight Committee officially ceased operation in May 1942.[3]

On July 10, 1946, Knight received the Order of the British Empire (OBE) in recognition of his services to the British Empire. He accepted the honor from the British ambassador aboard the RMS *Queen Mary* in New York harbor, as custom dictated that it be presented on British land.

William Heaslip and the Sunday Photogravure

In 1939, the *New York Times/Wide World Photos* decided to illustrate the new war's unfolding events. The editors got the idea from the popular *Illustrated London News*, which had featured illustrations of the Great War years earlier by noted artist Fortunino Matania. William Heaslip, who considered Matania a mentor, was hired to undertake the job.[4] According to one publication commenting on the arrangement:

> [Heaslip] is the illustrator or artist whose job it is to present as realistically as possible an interpretation of these tremendous events [the early battles of World War II]. Because of the nature of his work, his job also is to dramatize these events. Guided by a realistic news interpretation of the scenes, his task is to inject an eye-witness account of the inferno of crashing tanks, screaming dive bombers, heavy artillery barrages, screens of machine-gun fire, flame throwers, etc.[5]

Heaslip was an inspired choice for this task. His renderings of aircraft were unsurpassed, and he was equally facile in accurately capturing the details of tanks, ships, troops and uniforms, and weapons large and small. His quest for accuracy took him on occasion to the German consulate in New York City whose officials were happy to provide him with detailed photographs of German weapons (at least until Germany's declaration of war on the United States on December 11, 1941). In addition, he frequently consulted his own enormous collection of photographs and information gathered from a multitude of sources.

Heaslip's careful research work paid off, although he gave little indication of the enormous and exhausting effort involved. An article in *Flying* magazine offered an idea of the price he paid:

William Heaslip at easel with completed canvas of Royal Air Force fighting planes. (Allan M. Heaslip)

A flying veteran of first World War, Mr. Heaslip is one of few artists whose work is recognized in the aeronautical field for meticulous accuracy and fine details.

On a double-page illustration of fighting planes for the *New York Times Sunday Magazine*, [Heaslip] worked for 67 hours without rest. He tied a pillow around the seat of his pants to alleviate the soreness of sitting steadily so many hours; he sent out for food; he worked unceasingly to make the deadline—and did … but he was sore for weeks.[6]

Heaslip's first weekly submissions for *Wide World Photos* began appearing in Sunday newspaper supplements shortly after the war began in September 1939. The German *Wehrmacht*'s *blitzkrieg* had just overrun Poland, and the Low Countries of Europe would soon follow.[7]

Heaslip's original painting of RAF fighters, c. 1941. (Allan M. Heaslip)

Heaslip's original painting of RAF bombers in operational use in 1941. (Allan M. Heaslip)

Heaslip's dramatic illustration of Heinkel He 111 nose gunner taking aim at a Royal Navy ship in the Channel. (Allan M. Heaslip)

In this Heaslip rendering, Londoners under aerial attack flock to shelters, many of which are located in Underground stations. After the bomb explosions ceased and the all-clear siren sounded, crowds would emerge from those shelters smelling smoke and surveying the widespread damage. (Allan M. Heaslip)

Clusters of incendiary bombs raining down on London, original painting by William Heaslip. (Allan M. Heaslip)

Civilians calmly smothering incendiary bombs with sand stored on the roofs of buildings, original painting by William Heaslip. (Allan M. Heaslip)

A Vickers Wellington bomber hits German dock facilities during a night attack, original painting by William Heaslip. (Allan M. Heaslip)

Heaslip's RAF bombers over Berlin's Brandenburg Gate in 1940. *Luftwaffe* Chief Reichsmarschall Herman Goering had claimed in 1939, "No enemy bomber can reach the Ruhr. If one reaches the Ruhr, my name is not Goering. You may call me Meyer." The Royal Air Force, and later the U.S. Army Air Forces, would prove him wrong. (Allan M. Heaslip)

The loss of the venerable battle cruiser HMS *Hood* enraged the Royal Navy, which rushed to locate the German battleship *Bismarck* and destroy her. Here Heaslip depicts the *Bismarck* under attack by Fairey Swordfish torpedo bombers from the carrier HMS *Ark Royal*. Damaged by aerial attack and set afire by Royal Navy surface ships, the *Bismarck* sank (with help from her crew who scuttled her) on May 27, 1941. Of the *Bismarck*'s crew of 2,310 men, 110 survived. (Allan M. Heaslip)

The Case for Military Ramp-Up

As America's entry into the war became imminent, military production, heralded for the defense of the country, became a primary focus for the nation—and for the two artists. In spite of their commitments elsewhere, Heaslip and Knight both became deeply involved in advocating for and showcasing U.S. military preparedness.

Americans were heartened as the 1941 Christmas season approached. The Depression had ended, they had money in their pockets, and stores were filled with clothes, toys, and all manner of gifts, most with military motifs. Few Americans realized, however, that they would not enjoy this bountiful experience again for four years as vastly increased military

Heaslip's automobile and B-26 Martin Marauder medium bomber being refueled with Shell gasoline.

Your car's a plane— to your Shell Dealer's

"Ground Crew"

This Army Air Corps Ground Crew member is checking the air pressure in the landing wheels of a giant bomber. Exacting Ground Crew Service is a "must"—human life and precious ships depend upon it.

"Tires are okay now, Sir!"
Shell Dealers wearing the Shell "Ground Crew" service wings know how to give your car complete "Ground Crew" Service... the kind of service you need now that automobile production has been stopped and tires are being rationed.

FREE Official U.S. ARMY AIR CORPS Squadron Insignia (27TH PURSUIT SQUADRON)—
Made on cloth in full color, these insignia are fine for sewing on sweaters, jackets or shirts. Thrill your youngsters. Start a collection of regulation Air Corps Squadron Insignia—the kind actually on fighters and bombers. A new one FREE each week at Shell Dealers displaying Shell's "Ground Crew" Service Wings.

DRIVING and flying are a lot alike. Your car has to be *right* when you pilot it in modern traffic.

That's why Shell Dealers displaying Shell's "Ground Crew" Service Wings now offer your car "Ground Crew" Service patterned after that of the Army Air Corps. They *"thoro-check"*:

1. Oil condition
2. Tires
3. Lights
4. Radiator
5. Battery
6. Windshield & rear window (cleaned)
7. Sparkplugs
8. Windshield wiper

They help you get extra mileage from your tires by switching wheels periodically and by checking tires regularly for proper pressure.

They provide expert lubrication—*the right amount of the right Shell lubricant in the right place!*

Ask your Shell dealer about the Ground Crew Log Book he has for you. It will show you how "Ground Crew" Service *lengthens car service*. It's a patriotic duty to—*Care for your Car...for your Country.*

SHELL
GROUND CREW SERVICE

4077-A Revised

American Engines Prove Their Mettle

Direct From the Airdromes of England Comes New Recognition of RELIABILITY as a Vital Military Asset

DAY after day, under the relentless pressure of continuous combat, thousands of Pratt & Whitney engines are answering the call of the Royal Air Force with eager power. Report after report reaffirms the ability of these air-cooled engines to take terrific punishment and still continue to pour out dependable power.

This reliability is the natural result of a great American characteristic— the genius for quantity production to high standards of precision. It was

the dependability of American air-cooled engines which in peacetime led to their sweeping success on airlines all over the world. Now this same quality becomes vital to the defense of a nation.

Americans can congratulate themselves that this dependability of engine performance is a traditional American quality. It is bred into every Pratt & Whitney engine that goes out to the flying forces of the United States Army and Navy.

UNITED AIRCRAFT CORPORATION

EAST HARTFORD · CONNECTICUT

PRATT & WHITNEY ENGINES · VOUGHT-SIKORSKY AIRPLANES · HAMILTON STANDARD PROPELLERS

89

Heaslip's ad for Grumman's Martlet, which was provided to the Royal Navy under Lend-Lease legislation. The U.S. Navy designation for the fighter was Grumman F4F Wildcat. (Allan M. Heaslip)

production resulted in rationing that soon curtailed the availability of consumer goods.

The Japanese surprise attack on December 7, 1941—the "Day of Infamy" that thrust the United States into war—brought together Americans in a total commitment to winning. Anti-war sentiment and protest stilled overnight as the country unified. But industrial mobilization would take time. President Roosevelt, decrying the major losses to U.S. military and naval forces at Pearl Harbor, prophesied that "we will have to take a good many defeats before we have a victory.[8] And in fact, the United States would not reach full wartime production until 1943.[9]

These sentiments, and the sacrifices required of all Americans, would be unambiguously reflected in the works of artists Clayton Knight and William Heaslip as America's war progressed into 1942.

Heaslip's ad for the Consolidated B-24 Liberator bomber, which saw service with the Royal Air Force as an effective maritime surveillance aircraft. (Allan M. Heaslip)

Heaslip's ad for the Chance Vought F4U Corsair Navy fighter, which was provided to U.S. allies under Lend-Lease. (Allan M. Heaslip)

Clayton Knight's package design for a Mennen's gift set, reflecting the pervasive, defense-oriented marketplace theme for the 1941 Christmas season. (Theodore Hamady)

筆二堅岡吉　　　襲強灣珠眞イワハ

This Imperial Japanese Navy propaganda postcard shows Japanese Nakajima BSN2 bombers on their way to attack the U.S. Fleet at Pearl Harbor—an attack that galvanized the American people. Soon almost all U.S. industry was converted to wartime production, with military and naval aviation taking center stage.

THE GREATEST TEAM **AAF** IN THE WORLD!

IF YOU ARE 17 AND LESS THAN 18 CALL FOR INFORMATION AT ANY

AAF EXAMINING BOARD OR U. S. ARMY RECRUITING STATION

CHAPTER EIGHT

All-Out Support for the War Effort

When Pearl Harbor was bombed on December 7, 1941, and America's neutrality constraints disappeared, mobilization of U.S. industry and manpower was still in its nascent stages. President Roosevelt had predicted that the nation would suffer defeat until it was ready to fight a sustained world war—and full mobilization would not be realized until 1943. As a result, Roosevelt faced a multitude of war-related emergencies in early 1942—including the need to steady the American populace.[1]

During this time, William Heaslip and Clayton Knight, together with other artists and illustrators, took on the task of helping to inform Americans of what to expect and how to prepare for war.

Heaslip's Work Informs the Public: There's a War On!

Heaslip's love of country and sacrifice became evident early in the war through his moving and highly patriotic illustration surrounding the poem *Our Country*. It is a good example of his efforts to mobilize the country for its struggles ahead.

Heaslip provided similarly powerful illustrations to accompany "The Inside Story of Kelly's Exploit," an article that appeared in the February 10, 1942, issue of *Look* magazine. The article features the exploits of Captain Colin P. Kelly, a B-17 pilot who lost his life while on a bombing run against a Japanese warship during the initial assault against the Philippine Islands.

In the article, Kelly was credited with being the first American pilot to sink an Imperial Japanese Navy (IJN) ship—the *Haruna*—on December 11, 1941. Kelly died on that run after sticking at the controls of his burning aircraft and allowing his crew to bail out before the aircraft exploded. He was deemed an early hero for his efforts and was posthumously awarded the Distinguished Service Cross, the country's second highest award for valor.

Heaslip's illustrations present Kelly's actions as great heroism—but some of the story was, in fact, an exaggeration. The *Haruna* survived until July 25, 1945, when it was sunk at its moorings in Kure, Japan.[2]

Just hours after the attack on Pearl Harbor, the understrength First Marine Defense

Opposite: U.S. Army Air Forces recruiting poster featuring B-26 Martin Marauders attacking a Luftwaffe airbase.

William Heaslip illustrated the patriotic poem "Our Country" by Merrick Fifield McCarthy to benefit Bundles for America, an organization set up to support U.S. troops and families disrupted during wartime. The illustrated poem was printed on postcards and in sheet music—both of which were sold to raise funds for the organization. Bundles for America emulated the popular program Bundles for Britain, which had been established earlier in the war. (Allan M. Heaslip)

Original painting *Battle for Wake Island* by William Heaslip. (Gift of Allan M. Heaslip, Art Collection, National Museum of the Marine Corps, Triangle, Virginia)

"The Inside Story of Kelly's Exploit," *Look* magazine, February 10, 1942. Illustrations by William Heaslip.

Battalion—comprised of U.S. Marine artillery, fighter, and infantry personnel, plus volunteer civilian contractors—was attacked on Wake Island. While the battalion fought heroically, inflicting heavy losses, the Japanese responded by deploying over 1,500 crack marines plus aircraft from two carriers, causing the depleted U.S. forces to lay down their arms on December 23, 1941.

Despite the defeat, America was electrified by the heroism and sacrifice made by this small contingent of U.S. Marines. Within five days of the defeat, William Heaslip released a dramatic illustration of the battle for Wake Island. Paramount Pictures began planning a film about the event, *Wake,* which starred William Bendix and Brian Donlevy and was released on August 11, 1942.

The U.S. Marine Corps' public relations department became keenly interested in obtaining Heaslip's illustration. The request was honored by his son, Allan, after the war, and the illustration now resides in the National Museum of the Marine Corps near Quantico, Virginia.

Heaslip continued to portray the heroism of the American troops and their military leaders during the dark days of 1942.

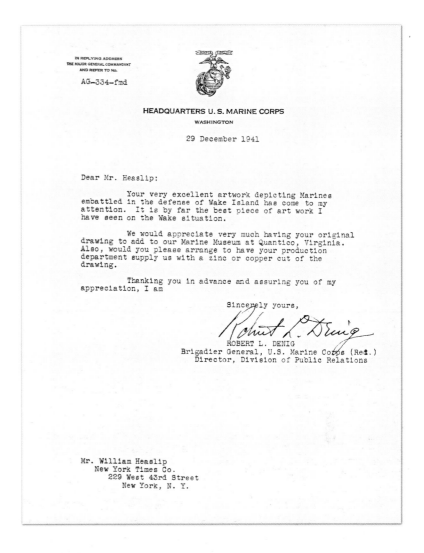

Letter from U.S. Marine Corps requesting William Heaslip's illustration of Wake Island battle. (Allan M. Heaslip)

Under the command of General Douglas MacArthur (1880–1964), American and Filipino forces held the Japanese at bay on the Philippine Bataan Peninsula during the early months of 1942. But the Allied forces were compelled to surrender on May 7, 1942, after MacArthur turned his attention to and concentrated the bulk of his forces on the island of Corregidor at the mouth of Manila Bay. Despite the defeat, MacArthur would become Commander of Forces in the Southwest Pacific, achieving five-star rank before the end of the war.[3]

During this period, American Patrol Torpedo Boats—"PT Boats"—were active in Manila Bay and the surrounding area. Motor Patrol Squadron Three, under the command of Lt. John D. Bulkeley, U.S. Navy, participated in the defense of Bataan and later took General MacArthur and his family away from Corregidor to Cagayan Island where he and others would be flown by B-17 to Australia. Bulkeley's heroism in combat earned him the Silver Star, the Distinguished Service Cross (a U.S. Army decoration), the Navy Cross, and the Medal of Honor, which he received directly from President Roosevelt at the White House after his return to the United States.

The United States had supplied Nationalist China with war materiel since before Pearl Harbor and had utilized the Burma Road to truck munitions from Lashio, Burma (Myanmar), to Kunming, China. In December 1941, Japanese forces began a ground and air offensive against British and Chinese troops (including members of the American

volunteer group Flying Tigers). The Japanese succeeded in taking Lashio in April 1942, effectively cutting off the Burma Road—the only lifeline into China. Heaslip illustrated this dramatic event.

In 1941 President Roosevelt organized the Office of Civilian Defense (OCD) to coordinate state and federal measures for the protection of civilians in the event of war. In the absence of an immediate threat, the civilian population took little notice until Pearl Harbor was bombed. Then, motivated by intense anger at the nature of the attack and wanting to do their bit for the war effort, civilians flocked to join the many OCD organizations forming throughout the United States.

Heaslip was tapped to produce a cover for both the U.S. and British version of the booklet *If Bombs Fall,* which was used to educate civilians and OCD volunteers should the war reach U.S. shores. Air raid wardens and fire fighters are probably the best-remembered volunteers of the OCD, whose numbers ultimately exceeded over 10 million Americans. Fortunately, the Axis powers lacked long-range strategic bombing capabilities, which could have wreaked havoc on the American war industry from East to West Coast.

Civil Defense poster designed by William Heaslip. (Allan M. Heaslip)

Heaslip produced numerous illustrations during this period. He even produced a version of the Civil Defense logo, which appeared across the United States throughout the war.

The United States achieved several victories during the dark days of 1942: successful carrier attacks against Japanese-held islands, Jimmy Doolittle's dramatic attack on Japan, and the U.S. Navy's strategic victory at the battle of Coral Sea. The battle of Midway in June 1942 put the Japanese Empire on the defensive and became the turning point of the Pacific War. That battle took place exactly six months after the attack on Pearl Harbor. Admiral Yamamoto, the Japanese naval commander-in-chief, had predicted to his superiors that Japan would prevail for only six months to a year against the United States. He had been correct.

The battle of Coral Sea (May 4–8, 1942) was a tactical victory for the Imperial Japanese Navy (IJN), but a strategic victory for the U.S. Navy. In this air

Heaslip's cover for the U.S. version of *If Bombs Fall,* 1942. (Allan M. Heaslip)

Clayton Knight illustrated the cover of this early wartime aircraft identification book. These reference books proved of interest to civilians as well as airmen. (Clayton Christopher Knight)

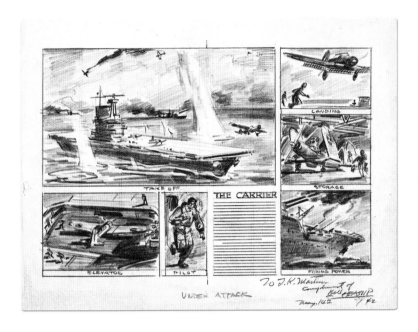
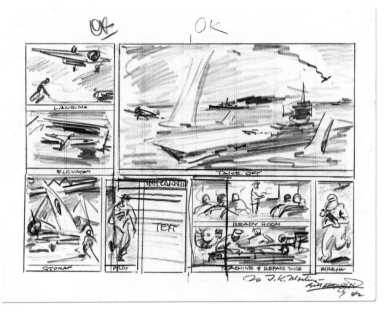

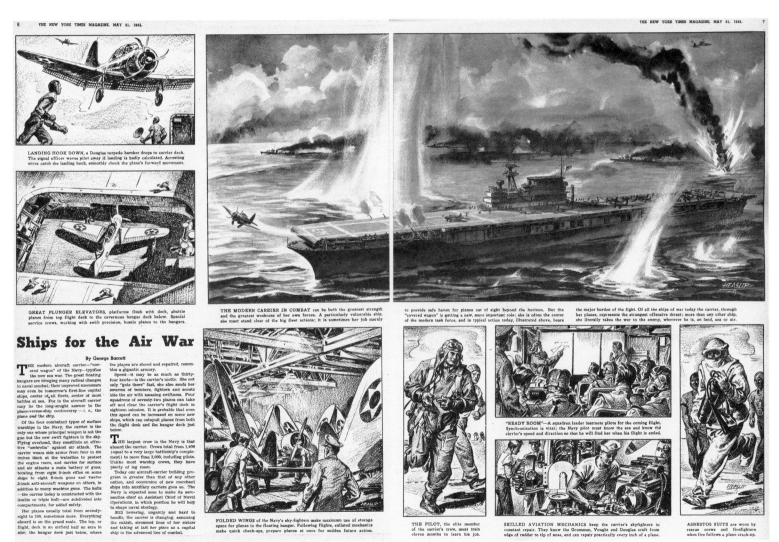

Top: William Heaslip prepared work studies for carrier battle illustration, one of which is marked OK for approval.. (Allan M. Heaslip)

Bottom: Finished art for a *New York Times Sunday Magazine* article, May 31, 1942. The date of publication was propitious, for it appeared shortly after the carrier battle of the Coral Sea with the carrier battle of Midway only four days later. Midway turned the tide of battle in the Pacific. (© *New York Times*. All rights reserved.)

ALL-OUT SUPPORT FOR THE WAR EFFORT   **219**

battle, where neither fleet saw the other, the IJN assault force was repelled and Allied sea lanes to Australia were protected. The battle of Midway, one month later, would turn the tide against the Japanese Empire. Heaslip took great pains to illustrate the drama of carrier battles.

This humorous greeting card by William Heaslip reflects the prevailing sentiments against the Axis leaders—Adolf Hitler, Benito Mussolini, and Hideki Tojo—during wartime. (Allan M. Heaslip)

Heaslip and Knight at the Turning Point: Mobilizing U.S. Manpower and Industry

The growth in the effectiveness of U.S. military air power was the result of the recruitment and thorough training of air crew and ground personnel, as well as a dramatic increase in aircraft production. William Heaslip, Clayton Knight and hundreds of other artists and illustrators made small, but important contributions to achieving massive increases in such production through their work on magazine covers, ads and the like.

Collectively, their efforts and patriotic fervor, combined with government and industry support, brought about a miracle of production that delivered over 300,000 military aircraft to the United States and Allied air services during World War II. (In contrast, during World War I the United States government failed to deliver a single combat aircraft to the U.S. Air Service's American Expeditionary Force.)

Next are examples of the illustrations produced by both Heaslip and Knight in support of this effort.

Hell-bent Son of Heaven

North American P-51 Mustang Fighter

North American Aviation *Sets the Pace*

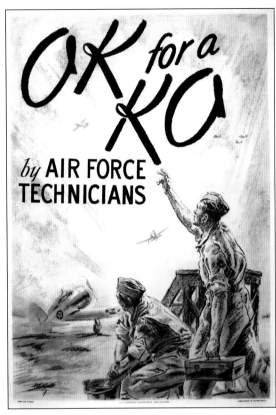

Left: Heaslip was one of several artists who helped North American Aviation promote its high-performance P-51 Mustang Fighter. (Allan M. Heaslip)

Right: Poster for recruitment of aviation technicians, by William Heaslip. (Allan M. Heaslip)

Below: Heaslip produced a series of "Give Us More…" posters for every major military aircraft in the U.S. Army Air Forces inventory. The Boeing B-29 Superfortress, the Very Heavy Bomber type that dropped the atomic bombs on Hiroshima and Nagasaki, is shown here. (Allan M. Heaslip)

U.S. ARMY OFFICIAL POSTER

Biggest Fastest Deadliest… SUPERFORTRESS

SILVER GNATS IN THE SKY. Soaring higher than any other bomber, majestic B-29's are the tiniest of targets, mere silver specks, to enemy gunners far below. Fast as fighter planes, they need no escort.

B-29 SUPER STREAMLINES show up vividly in comparison with the smaller B-17. Note the slender, 141-foot wings, brand-new in design. They lift a heavier weight than any other plane's wing.

8800 POUNDING HORSES—nearly twice the B-17's horse-power—in the Superfort's four Wright Cyclone engines. Four-bladed, 16½-foot Hamilton propellers dwarf those of every other plane.

TEAMWORK DOES IT!

In the bright sun of mid-morning, a Jap convoy crawls over the Burma Road. Suddenly the look-outs yell... point to a flash of silver wings in the sky... jump and run as the road under their wheels explodes in a splash of bomb-bursts that hurl men and trucks and Jap supplies into the gorge below. Then, with her bombs away, the "Old 59" streaks down, fighting off Zeros as she comes... rakes the wrecked convoy with flaming tracer streams... and disappears over the peaks into India.

Here is the crew of the "Old 59"... and here's how they do their jobs:

★ "Teamwork does it," says Capt. Robert Ebey, pilot, of Stillwater, Okla. "Every man on our crew is a specialist, but we don't have any 'individual stars'. In the air we fight together, as a team. And that's the way to win." Co-pilot is 1st Lt. Paul Sjoberg, of Grand Marais, Minn. "Salami", a dachshund mascot, rides behind the pilot's seat.

★ The plane, the crew, the mission's success, depend upon split-second timing, pinpoint accuracy. 1st Lt. Hilliard Peavy, navigator, of Montgomery, Ala., checks course by "shooting the sun"... while in the waist behind him, Sgt. Francis Donnelly, radio-gunner, of Philadelphia, mans the world's most modern radio equipment.

★ Sgt. Donnelly shares his "office" with S/Sgt. Lyle Wilson, mechanic-gunner, of Conneaut Lake Park, Pa. Besides firing the top-turret guns, Sgt. Wilson is the "Old 59's" engineering specialist... takes care of engines, bomb-release mechanism, electric, hydraulic and oxygen systems—and in emergencies has repaired them in the air.

★ 1st Lt. George Jernigan, bombardier, of Charleston, W. Va., lets his bombs go, and then gives the gunners a hand. The "Old 59's" bombs have blown Jap shipping out of the Tongking Gulf, plastered Jap airfields from Helo to Mandalay, blasted railroad yards, bridges and ammo dumps all over the China-Burma-India theater.

★ All AAF gunners are aerial sharpshooters... and S/Sgt. Rudolf Madsen, of Eugene, Ore., tail-gunner, is a dead-shot with twin 50-calibers. Flying, fighting, working *together*, the air combat crew of the "Old 59" is typical of the thousands of such crews that have made the AAF the "greatest team in the world."

MEN OF 17...

U.S. Army Air Forces recruiting advertisement featuring a B-25 Mitchell medium bomber attacking ground targets, illustrated by Clayton Knight.

U.S. Army Air Forces recruiting poster depicts a B-24 Liberator heavy bomber bombing Pacific Island targets by Clayton Knight in 1944. (Swann Auction Galleries)

BLASTERS!

● Bombs to blast the Axis—that's the pay-load of the Brewster *Buccaneer* and *Bermuda*. Packed with destruction for dictators, these newest American dive-bombers are built to hit the enemy, hit him hard, and then to hit him again.

BREWSTER *Blasters*

B U C C A N E E R   A N D   B E R M U D A   D I V E   B O M B E R S

Above: William Heaslip produced numerous ads for Aerol. He continued to work with the company after the war as it reverted to manufacturing civilian products. (Allan M. Heaslip)

Right: Cover illustration featuring Republic Aircraft's P-47 Thunderbolt, by Clayton Knight;

Left: William Heaslip produced this powerful action ad for the Brewster Blaster, more commonly known as the Brewster Buccaneer. This aircraft did not prove successful in service and many were then relegated to the role of towing targets. (Allan M. Heaslip)

THEY FLY WITH THEIR BOOTS ON—SAFER

Normal vibration can severely tax a plane. But imagine the strain vibration puts on the fastenings of big bombers which have been ripped and torn by enemy fire. That these huge craft, so punished, don't "shake apart" in mid-air is due in important measure to the stout, vibration-proof Boots Self-Locking Nuts they wear.

Boots Nuts, used on every type of U.S. aircraft, can't come loose no matter how severe the plane vibration. Lighter than any other nuts, Boots have greater re-usability too. In addition, they withstand the corrosive action of oil, water or chemicals—literally "outlast the plane." They simplify repairs and maintenance. And they meet the exacting specifications of all government aviation agencies.

VIBRATION a Peace-Time Problem Too

Very often costly repairs result from vibration-loosed connections in your vacuum cleaner, radio, electric refrigerator and other household appliances. Boots Self-Locking Nuts, used on these appliances, will eliminate repair bills caused by this type of mechanical failure. Boots Nuts can't come loose, even under the severest vibration. After victory insist on products protected with vibration-proof Boots Nuts. They will be your assurance of more economical and efficient service from the household appliances you purchase.

BOOTS
Self-Locking Nuts For Application In All Industries

BOOTS AIRCRAFT NUT CORPORATION ★ GENERAL OFFICES, NEW CANAAN, CONNECTICUT

Left: BOOTS (sub-contractor to Boeing) ad for Boeing B-17 bomber, illustrated by Clayton Knight.

Right: *Air Transport* magazine cover, illustrated by William Heaslip. (Allan M. Heaslip)

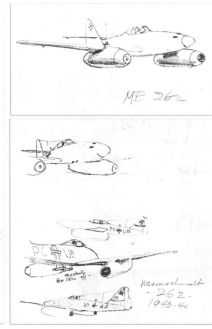

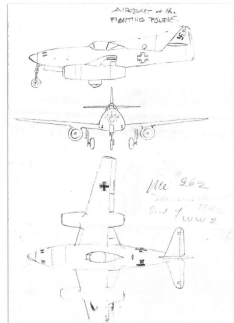

Clockwise from top right:

Work studies of a German ME 262 jet fighter done by William Heaslip, to familiarize himself with the features of the jet aircraft. (Allan M. Heaslip)

A finished illustration of the German ME 262 jet fighter/bomber appeared in a 1958 issue of *Boy's Life*. (Allan M. Heaslip)

Work studies of ME 109 attacking B-24, by William Heaslip. The illustration at the bottom was approved and finished by the artist for publication. (Allan M. Heaslip)

First in a series of true adventure tales, here's a story of the unexpected.

WE SAW THE FIRST JET

By WM. F. HALLSTEAD

SHORTLY BEFORE noon on April 25, 1945, a pilot we will call Captain Ernst Kretschmer—a fighter pilot in the Nazi Luftwaffe—leaped from a moving truck and vaulted into the cockpit of his Messerschmitt 262. The klaxon alarm had sounded just minutes ago. Allied bombers were on the way, thundering northward from their bases in Italy.

It was hopeless, the captain knew. Nothing could stop the Americans and the British now. Not even this super fighter in which he crouched made a particle of difference. He knew that, despite what he was told by the colonel who had to say what he was made to say. Kretschmer wasn't one of the new young pilots who still insisted there was hope for victory because they had never been allowed to think anything else.

Captain Kretschmer, tall, fair, eyes squinting in the sunlight, knew his flight today couldn't affect the obvious outcome of the war. But men were ordered to fight and so they fought. Captain Kretschmer pulled on his black leather helmet, adjusted his earphones and mike, and nodded to his mechanic. The corporal scurried off the wing and signalled to the battery crew. The battery cart was plugged into the fighter's electrical system and the captain pushed the starter button.

The left engine whined, a high-pitched screech that shivered through the trees along the edge of the fighter strip. This was no wheezing pop of the propeller-driven aircraft. This was more power than anyone had dreamed would be crammed into a single plane. This was the most deadly weapon that Willy Messerschmitt, the genius fighter plane designer, had ever turned out. It was the world's first operational jet fighter.

The Americans and their allies had nothing in the air like it, the captain knew. And that was a bitter joke on them because the first jet engine actually had been developed by an Englishman, and the Americans had tested an experimental jet at Dayton two years before.

But Germany now had squadrons of them, and they were deadly. Too fast for the bomber gunners to aim at, the Me 262 could snap in and out of a formation like a striking cobra. This plane at least was real, Captain Kretschmer reflected, even if the war was now like a terrible nightmare.

His number two engine screeched into noisy, burbling life, and the ground crew stood clear.

"You are cleared to taxi," the controller said in his earphones, and the captain guided his sleek green fighter to the head of the (*To page 64*)

ILLUSTRATED BY WILLIAM HEASLIP

WE BOMBED TOKIO! 46 ACTUAL PHOTOS OF JIMMY DOOLITTLE'S MEN WHO DID IT

A special feature of this book is the first, most complete collection of pictures of the heroes of the initial attack on Japan, in life-like rotogravure.

THE ROMANCE OF FLYING

BY CLAYTON KNIGHT

10¢

THE THRILLING STORIES OF
PILOTS AND THEIR FLYING FEATS
FROM THE DAWN OF AVIATION
—THROUGH PEACE AND WAR
ACES OF THE LAST WAR
AIR RECORD HOLDERS
HEROES OF THIS WAR

During the early dark days of the war, Knight also wrote and illustrated *The Romance of Flying*, a publication in comic book format that chronicled the early aviation experimentation of Otto Lilienthal and Octave Chanute; the flying successes of the Wright Brothers, Louis Bleriot and Glenn H. Curtiss; and the bravery of World War I heroes Georges Guynemer, Raoul Lufbery, William Avery Bishop and Eddie Rickenbacker. He wrote of the achievements of Charles Lindbergh, Richard Byrd, Amelia Earhart, Frank Hawks, Claire Chennault and Jimmie Doolittle. In all, *The Romance of Flying* covered the contributions of 47 pioneers who flew all manner of airplanes—from those made of wood, wire, and stretched fabric to all-metal heavy bombers.

In the conclusion to that publication, Knight addressed with great eloquence, the young men of the United States of America:

> You, who are now reaching the age when you, too, can fight in the air against the sinister forces who threaten our precious American freedom, should know about those young and resourceful men who founded the traditions of aviation. … Pilots, navigators, bombardiers and gunners all have their own particular tasks to perform toward a successful mission. That mission is to destroy the enemy who have challenged our right to live in the manner we believe best, and I have the greatest confidence in the young men of America who are daily coming forward to master the complex details of flying and fighting. You will not fail us. Of that I am certain.[4]

Knight Reports on the Fledgling VIII Bomber Command, USAAF, in England

During the early days of the war, Knight also served as a Special Correspondent for the Associated Press (AP). In mid-1942, he was sent by AP to Europe to report on the VIII Bomber Command, a UK-based bomber arm of the U.S. Army Air Forces (USAAF). His assigned task was to talk to everyone involved with what was to become a massive strategic bombing assault on Nazi Germany and its many assets throughout Europe.

Knight was an ideal war correspondent for this assignment. As a bomber pilot in World War I, he had experienced close combat. Moreover, he knew many of the USAAF commanders in Europe, military leaders from the Royal Canadian Air Force (RCAF) and Royal Air Force (RAF), and commanders of the American-manned Eagle Squadrons, some of which he had recruited for the RCAF through the Clayton Knight Committee before the U.S. entered the war. And of course, he was recognized as one of the outstanding combat artists in the world.

His trip was intended as a morale booster for the American public and as a fact-finding mission to answer some concerns about the poor performance of American aircraft (e.g., the P-39, the P-40, and early variants of the B-17). He was also interested in the morale and performance of combat crews, and in how the USAAF was cooperating with the blooded RAF and RCAF who had already experienced three years of war.

Throughout his trip, Knight made sheaves of sketches. His illustrations later appeared in various newspapers in the Associated Press network.

Opposite: *The Romance of Flying*, written and illustrated by Clayton Knight in 1941. (©1941–1942 King Features Syndicate, Inc)

Clayton Knight would not have known at the time, but several of the military leaders he interviewed and sketched on his trip provided the inspiration for *Twelve O'Clock High*, one of the finest movies ever made about American strategic air power over Germany during World War II. Military leaders portrayed in this film included Colonel Frank A. Armstrong, portrayed by actor Gregory Peck (as Colonel Frank Savage); and William Howard Stovall, played by Oscar-winning actor Dean Jagger (as Major Harvey Stovall). Many others of the VIII Bomber Command, including Major General Ira Eaker, were portrayed in this highly regarded film.

Officers' Lounge at Headquarters, U.S. Army Air Force Fighter Command at Bushey, England. Illustration by Clayton Knight. (Clayton Christopher Knight)

Illustration by Clayton Knight. Carl Andrew "Tooey" Spaatz (1891–1974), a 1914 graduate of the U.S. Military Academy, transferred from the Infantry to the Aviation Section of the Signal Corps in time to see service with Brigadier General Pershing in Mexico in 1916. After serving in Europe with the American Expeditionary Forces during World War I, he continued in the U.S. Air Service during the interwar years, commanding the Seventh Bombardment Group in the early 1930s.

By 1943, Spaatz had assumed command of the 12th and 15th Air Forces in North Africa. He returned to the United Kingdom in early 1944 to prepare for the assault on Normandy and the destruction of the *Luftwaffe* and the German oil industry. In 1945, he became Strategic Air Force Commander with headquarters on Guam, during which time he supervised B-29 operations against Japan.

Spaatz became the first chief of staff of the new United States Air Force in 1948. He retired shortly thereafter with the rank of general. (Clayton Christopher Knight)

BRG·GEN, IRA EAKER
HEAD OF U.S. AIR FORCE BOMBER COMMAND

Left: Illustration by Clayton Knight. Ira Eaker (1896–1987), a Texas native, transferred from the U.S. Infantry to the U.S. Air Service in 1918. He remained in service as a pilot after World War I and flew fighters and bombers in the 1920s and 1930s.

Early in 1942, then Brigadier General Eaker assumed command of the VIII Bomber Command. Initial elements of personnel and aircraft were transferred to England along with Brigadier General Frank O'Donnell Hunter's VIII Fighter Command. The commands were equipped with Eaker's B-17 and B-24 bombers, and Hunter's P-38 and Spitfire fighters.

Brigadier General Eaker was credited with organizing what later became the VIII Air Force, but his command was depleted as newly organized groups were transferred to North Africa. As a result, he lacked escort fighters with sufficient range to cover his bomber formations. At the same time, the *Luftwaffe* was deploying more fighters, flak, and effective defensive tactics along the routes to and from targets in Europe. In the end, his command experienced heavy combat losses.

Relieved by Lieutenant General Doolittle in early 1944, Eaker took Command of U.S. Army Air Forces in the Mediterranean Theater. He retired as a Lieutenant General in 1948. In 1985, he received his fourth star by act of Congress. He died in 1987. (Clayton Christopher Knight)

Right: Illustration by Clayton Knight. Harold A. Edwards (1892-1952), a Canadian Air Force officer, worked with the Clayton Knight Committee before the U.S. entered the war to build the strength of the RCAF with an infusion of American volunteers.

In January 1942 he was sent to the United Kingdom as Air Officer, Commander-in-Chief, in charge of all Royal Canadian Air Force (RCAF) personnel overseas. Upon his arrival, he found that RCAF personnel were widely dispersed throughout the UK. Edwards gathered them up and formed what became the fourth largest Allied air force in Europe by war's end. In the process, he improved the performance of the RCAF and clearly established it as a Canadian fighting force. (Clayton Christopher Knight)

AIR MARSHAL H. A. "GUS" EDWARDS
COMMANDING THE ROYAL CANADIAN AIR FORCE
IN ENGLAND.

Left: Arthur Travers "Bomber" Harris (1892–1984) was an air marshal (general) in the Royal Air Force. A bomber commander in World War I and between the wars, Harris became a strong proponent of strategic area bombing at night—rather than costly daytime raids—because he believed that these kinds of devastating area bombings would better demoralize and defeat the enemy.

He demonstrated his premise in May 1942 when he launched a 1,000-plane raid against Cologne, a tactic that produced widespread destruction of civilian lives and targets.

But Harris' tactic contrasted with America's precise daylight bombing of carefully selected German military targets—a tactic heavily dependent on the precision of the Norden Bombsight. Toward the end of the war, British and American bomber commands better coordinated around-the-clock bombing attacks on German cities and military targets. (Clayton Christopher Knight)

Right: Illustration by Clayton Knight. Frank A. Armstrong (1902–69), colonel in the USAAF, was among the most successful bomb group commanders to emerge from the European Theater during World War II.

Armstrong was born in Hamilton, North Carolina, and educated at Wake Forest College. He entered the U.S. Army Air Corps as an air cadet and received his wings in 1929. Lieutenant Armstrong received extensive training in flight instruction, navigation, and instrument training in the 1930s, as well as flying and command experience with several bombardment units.

Posted to England after America's entry into the war, Colonel Armstrong led USAAF's first daylight raid over Axis territory in August 1942. He was decorated for this mission with the Silver Star by the USAAF, and with the Distinguished Service Cross by the RAF. He inspired the officers and men of the VIII Bombardment Command with his courage and leadership.

As related in the post-war novel *Twelve O'Clock High*, Armstrong taught his men well during the time he led them. It should be noted that unlike his movie character portrayed by Gregory Peck, Armstrong did not suffer a breakdown after a particularly stressful mission; rather, that incident happened to another B-17 group commander whom Armstrong replaced. (Clayton Christopher Knight)

Left: Illustration by Clayton Knight. William Howard Stovall (1895-1970), colonel in the USAAF, was born in Stovall, Mississippi. After attending Yale in 1916, he enlisted in the Air Section of the Signal Corps and became a member of the Thirteenth Pursuit Group in France. Lieutenant Stovall was credited with six aerial victories before World War I ended.

Like many "retreads" from World War I, Stovall rejoined the U.S. Army Air Forces in 1941 and became deputy chief of staff for personnel under Brigadier General Frank Hunter. This gave him an opportunity to closely observe the enormous stresses experienced by leaders and aircrew during the formative years of the VIII Air Force. His own son, a fighter pilot, was killed in action during his service in England.

Stovall returned home after the war and continued his peacetime career as a highly regarded agronomist. Among his closest wartime friends were Sy Bartlett and Beirne Lay, authors of the book *Twelve O'Clock High*. (Michael G.C. Webster, grandson of Colonel William Stovall)

Right: Illustration by Clayton Knight. Jimmy Nelson is dressed in a blue RAF uniform distinguished by an Eagle Squadron patch worn on the left sleeve. Nelson was among 250 Americans recruited prior to December 1941 by the Clayton Knight Committee to join three RAF fighter squadrons known as the Eagle Squadrons. (Clayton Christopher Knight)

Eagle Squadron patch, from Royal Air Force Museum.

Left: A Douglas A-20 attack aircraft, popular with aircrews in Europe, the Mediterranean, and the Pacific. It was fast (maximum speed 330 mph), had a range of 1,200 miles, a ceiling of 30,000 feet, bomb capacity of 2,000 pounds, and was armed with two to four fixed machine guns and two flexible machine guns. It was easy to fly and could be flown with an engine out.

Below: In this illustration, Clayton Knight depicts an American A-20 attack aircraft, one of six borrowed from the RAF, in a low-level attack against a German flak tower at an airfield in Holland. In the first mission mounted by the USAAF VIII Bomber Command on July 4, 1942, the A-20, flown by Captain Charles Kegelman, was heavily damaged, but Kegelman, managed to fly it safely back to base. He was awarded the Distinguished Service Cross for this feat of valor.[5] The A-20 was known as a *Boston* in the RAF service, and a *Havoc* in the USAAF. (Clayton Christopher Knight)

Flying Fortresses Finally Prove Worth Against Germans

(Editor's note: Clayton Knight, whose stories about our flying forces in England and Iceland are appearing in the New Era daily this week, is no stranger to air war. He flew for us in the last world war, won many air battles until shot down by the Germans a short time before peace came. Next, Mr. Knight tells you about the fighting qualities of our men.)

By CLAYTON KNIGHT
For the Associated Press

London — When the first batch of Flying Fortresses arrived in England from America, the British airmen took one look at them and said:

"They look very pretty, but they'll never get back from bombing runs."

American airmen disagreed and it wasn't until some of the "forts" participated in the raid on the German battleships Gneisenau and Scharnorst at Brest — and were virtually shot to pieces—that they decided the British were right, at least in part, about these huge four - motored battleships of the air.

The Americans didn't give up. They believed in the Flying Fortresses and set out to prove their worth. They added guns, plenty of guns, until the new "Forts" boasted death - dealing snouts sticking out in every direction.

And then the Flying Fortresses went out again to do battle. I was interested in how they were performing after the new guns had been added, and on my tour of British, Canadian and American air stations in the British isles, found that they are now doing right well for themselves.

Perhaps, the best illustration of just how good the "Forts" are, however, was brought home to me after I arrived back in London. It was in the form of a letter from a friend of mine, Col. Frank Armstrong, a native of North Carolina and formerly of Richmond, Va., commanding an American bomber group that has seen plenty of action over Nazi - held territory. I had spent several days at his headquarters. The letter brought this good news:

"No doubt you have read of our attack last Sunday — it certainly was a 'doozie.' We fought approximately 40 enemy aircraft all the way in and to the target. Their attacks were head-on — nose-to-nose —when the bombing run was being made. Once I was forced to pull straight up to prevent a head - on collision with a Messerschmitt 109. I am delighted to say that one of my boys was denied. My number three man was hit in three motors, but he managed to stay in long enough to unload — and only then went down. It is estimated that we accounted for 15 Huns. One of my nose - gunners set a Hun on fire and he fell just beyond the leading element as it moved over to give him room. He was a beautiful sight."

Now the significance of the colonel's letter as regards the performance of the new Flying Fortresses was this:

That raid was one of the early ones which the American "Forts" made along — protected by fighters, of course, but aided by, no other bombers. Where the colonel said one of the "Forts" carried out its mission on only one motor before crashing, he gave a good indication of the way these big bombers can account for themselves.

And where the airman emphasized tht the Germans were attacking the "Forts" head-on—one Messerschmitt trying to crash into the Colonel's plane — that meant hte German fliers had bee ordered to bring one of these winged battleships down at any cost so they could see what made it tick.

The Hun did bring two "Forts" down in this particular raid, but, although he probably got a good look at the gun set-up, the chances are he found out nothing about the secret bomb sight which has made the "Forts" the champion precision bombers. There are gadgets to take care of their destruction.

Let's take another raid — an earlier one than Armstrong described in his letter, but made by the same "Forts" under his command.

This was one that proved the "Forts" were revolutionizing day bombardment.

Without the cover of darkness, without even friendly pursuit protection, armstrong's big bombers set out for a daylight raid on occupied France.

How did the "forts" perform?

"The Hun paid for that attack," Armstrong told me later, "with three enemy aircraft confirmed and a total of 12 probable aircraft shot down. That makes a total of one entire enemy fighter squadron. And they never had the satisfaction of seeing even one of our aircraft shot down."

Of course, even the Flying Fortresses wouldn't be much good without a highly trained crew. I stood around a bomber station one day while the men were getting ready to go on a raid, and to look at some of the crewmen you'd never suspect what deadly fighters they are.

The prospect of facing death doesn't mean anything to a Fortress crewman, either. They never believe it can happen to them, and when someone is wounded during a battle, he usually manages to joke about it.

One day a squadron returned from a raid and the lead plane had asked for the ambulance to meet him at his dispersal station.

As the crew tumbled out, the ambulance said, "which one is hurt?"

"Me," grinned the co - pilot holding up his left hand. About an inch of the index finger was missing. A shot from a Focke-Wulf cannon had passed right through the cabin and taken off the tip of the co - pilot's finger as it gripped the wheel.

"Just my luck," the wounded airman smiled. "If I'd have been scratching my ear at the time this wouldn't have happened."

The job the crews and their new "forts" are doing has justified American belief in the bombers and has won the whole - hearted admiration of the British.

The only ones not satisfied with their performance are the Germans — and that's because they're on the receiving end of it.

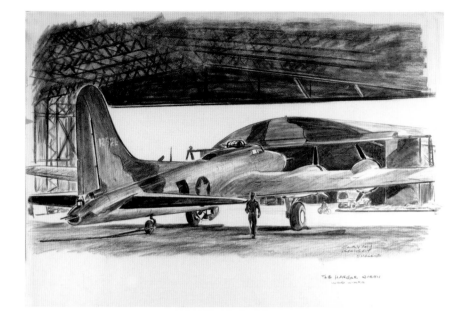

Left: *Hope Star*, Arkansas, Clayton Knight's newspaper article, "Flying Fortresses Finally Prove Worth," published during the fall of 1942.

Top right: Hangar Queen *Wild Wimpie*—a heavily damaged B-17 whose parts were scavenged to repair other B-17s. Illustration by Clayton Knight. (Clayton Christopher Knight)

Bottom right: B-17 on the flight line being fueled before a mission. Illustration by Clayton Knight. (Clayton Christopher Knight)

The Boeing 307 Stratoliner, America's first pressurized airliner, entered service in 1940. Soon after the start of World War II, five of them—built for TWA—were appropriated by the USAAF, stripped of their pressurized system, and reconfigured for military transport use. These aircraft, redesignated C-75s, were flown for the duration of the war by TWA flight crews. Clayton Knight drew this illustration of the cockpit of one of these aircraft—the *Zuni*—while on a flight from the UK to Iceland. He and others aboard the flight signed the illustration.[6] (Clayton Christopher Knight)

On his way home from his assignment in England, Knight spent four days in Iceland. He interviewed members of the Ferrying Command and wrote a thoughtful and revealing article about the crushing boredom experienced by the military personnel who were living their lives on this cold island nation. These men freely confessed that they would rather be serving elsewhere—where they could enjoy some of the comforts of home, such as entertainment, good food, and the chance to meet attractive girls, instead of seeing nothing but soldiers and war materiel headed for the aerial battles over Europe. Knight did not paper over those widely-voiced complaints; rather, he pointed out the sacrifice the men made in carrying out their important jobs.

After Knight returned from his whirlwind three-month tour, his sketches and articles were published in the Associated Press's American and Canadian newspapers during October, November, and December of 1942.[7] He dutifully reported on the early efforts of the VIII Bomber Command and relayed the observations of its key leaders and those of our allies in the RAF and RCAF, and of members of combat aircrew, including those working on the flight line.

Knight reported that service cooperation was excellent between the Allies, with Brigadier General Ira Eaker adopting the most effective measures learned from the RAF's three years of combat. He also reported that the RAF were not impressed with the early B-17s: "They are pretty airplanes," said a British aircrew member somewhat derisively.

What he observed but could *not* report were some of the serious operational problems

Hut on Iceland where Clayton Knight interviewed his subjects. Illustration by Clayton Knight. (Clayton Christopher Knight)

that were brewing at the time. The *Luftwaffe,* aware of the growing might of the VIII Bomber Command, had shifted many of its fighter squadrons and flak units from the Eastern Front and arrayed them along the routes between the UK and German military targets. As a result, losses of USAAF bombers increased to an unacceptable level during the summer and fall of 1942, and the VIII Bomber Command was forced to stand down.

The missing element in the arsenal of the USAAF turned out to be a fighter that could escort the bombers throughout their missions. The long-range Mustang P-51 fighter (powered by the Rolls Royce Merlin engine, built under license in the U.S. by the Packard Motor Car Company) became operational in the spring of 1944. And once it was deployed, Lieutenant General Jimmy Doolittle freed the fighters from bomber escort duty to attack *Luftwaffe* wherever they could be found. The P-51 Mustang fighter, and its newly adopted tactics, then proceeded to destroy the the *Luftwaffe* over western Europe.

Heaslip Signs on with Coca-Cola for the Duration

Not long after the United States entered the war in 1941, William Heaslip began a close association with the Coca-Cola company, a relationship that lasted until 1946. In many ways, his involvement with Coca-Cola became the capstone of his career as an artist and illustrator.

The outbreak of World War II in Europe in 1939 had made Coca-Cola's fledgling operations "increasingly difficult and even dangerous,"[8] especially in Germany where Coca-Cola had enjoyed considerable prewar success. At home, the company confronted aggressive competitive pressures, as well as the prospect of strict rationing should the United States enter the war.

Once the U.S. entered the war, the government imposed tight quotas on sugar; the price of caffeine jumped 500 percent as stocks were depleted; and the source of one of Coke's secret ingredients was now behind enemy lines in China. "Everything seemed to be in short supply: gas, glass, cardboard for cartons, tinplate for bottle caps. Eventually the company even ran out of rubber bands and other office supplies."[9]

Coca-Cola's management responded quickly and adroitly to this wartime crisis: company chemists modified the secret recipe, being careful not to alter the taste; and management used its political clout to acquire an exemption from the sugar quota for soft drinks supplied to the military, a burgeoning market. Company executives decreed that bottles of Coca-Cola would be available for a nickel each to American troops in combat areas around the world, regardless of the cost to the company.

This plan was approved by the War Department so long as area military commanders in each theater requested the Coca-Cola brand by name. In 1943, General Dwight Eisenhower was the first to make such a request. He asked for "ten bottling plants and enough syrup to provide his men [in North Africa] with six million bottles of Coca-Cola a month."[10] Coca-Cola soon became the preferred brand of soft drink among American troops as they advanced in all combat theaters, the familiar six-ounce bottles a tangible reminder of home.

However, the U.S. domestic market was a different matter. In 1941, the company decided to launch a wartime-long advertising campaign to keep the Coca-Cola brand in the public eye, and to let citizens know what was being done to support GIs both at home and overseas.[11] Coca-Cola's advertising department and D'Arcy, its advertising agency, joined with Snyder & Black, an advertising agency that specialized in the creation of point-of-sale display material, to create a campaign of magazine ads and point-of-sale posters, many of which featured servicemen and servicewomen enjoying a Coke.

For that campaign, Snyder & Black became responsible for producing a series of cardboard airplane cards (metal being no longer available) with string hangers, featuring America's arsenal of military and naval aircraft. These cards were design for Coca-Cola bottlers to use as promotional items. Snyder & Black oversaw the production process: hiring an aviation artist, setting deadlines and daily work schedules, and vetting rough or "comp" (composition) art before a finished work was accepted for publication. The result became the first series, or Set No. 1, of Coca-Cola aircraft hanger cards.[12]

This illustration of a Fourteenth Air Force American fighter pilot—a Flying Tiger—sharing a friendly bottle of Coca-Cola with a Chinese officer was created by New York City native Saul Tepper (1899-1987). It appeared in the ID booklet *Know Your Warplanes,* and a full-size version was published in the November 6, 1943, issue of *Collier's* magazine. (Coca-Cola Company)

Around the world, Coca-Cola brings refreshment to Americans, helps make them new friends.

Right: In this original watercolor by Heaslip, a Grumman TBF Avenger is shown dropping a torpedo that will destroy an oncoming enemy warship. This example of original artwork was included in Coca-Cola's Hanger Card Set No. 3. (Theodore Hamady)

Below: Here is the published hanger card featuring the Grumman TBF Avenger (Set No. 3) with simulated frame, Coca-Cola logo and bottle, and aircraft identification. (Coca-Cola Company)

Grumman "Avenger" TBF Torpedo Bomber • U. S. Navy
Releases torpedo in path of enemy warship

Despite the fact that William Heaslip had a vital, longstanding relationship with Snyder & Black, Set No. 1 was not Heaslip's work.[13] That set is comprised of 12 pictures of U.S. aircraft, each in simulated frames measuring 21″×22″. Designed in 1941 and distributed in 1942, the set featured military and naval combat aircraft plus one trainer, all decked out in prewar colors. The aircraft were portrayed in flight, but not in combat mode as America had not yet entered the war. The Coca-Cola logo was prominently displayed in the bottom left corner of the framed illustration.

Set No. 2 appeared in 1943, with 20 all-new illustrations, each measuring 13″×15″. For this set, Snyder & Black turned to Heaslip to produce the artwork—and Heaslip portrayed individual aircraft against a dramatic sky. This set also came complete with string hangers, and a Coca-Cola bottle was added next to each logo. The illustrations were also offered in presentation sets without the logo.

Set No. 3—again with all-new, 13″×15″ illustrations—appeared in 1944. It is arguably the most popular set of the series, for Heaslip had now dramatically portrayed many of the aircraft in close combat with the enemy. The set was also offered in miniature trading cards, each 3″×3″, which proved very popular with kids.

Around the same time, an aircraft identification booklet titled *Know Your Warplanes* was produced for the Ground Observer Corps. It included numerous black-and-white illustrations of American, Allied, and enemy aircraft shown together, in addition to color illustrations of American aircraft alone. It incorporated all 20 illustrations from Set No. 3 plus an additional five. The booklet was available from the Coca-Cola Company for "10 cents each (stamps or coin)."

The entire run of Set No. 3 Coca-Cola hanger card illustrations appears on the following pages.

Know Your War Planes incorporated all the illustrations from Set No. 3 in addition to silhouettes of aircraft useful to the Ground Observer Corps. In addition to this booklet and the hanger cards themselves, larger prints were offered to bottlers and friends. (Coca-Cola Company)

Top row, left to right:
North American A-36 Invader
Lockheed P-38 Lightning
Republic P-47 Thunderbolt
Bell P-39 Airacobra

Middle row, left to right:
Curtiss P-40 Warhawk
Douglas P-70 Havoc
Boeing B-17 Fortress
Consolidated B-24 Liberator

Bottom row, left to right:
American B-25 Mitchell
Martin B-26 Marauder
Grumman F4F Wildcat

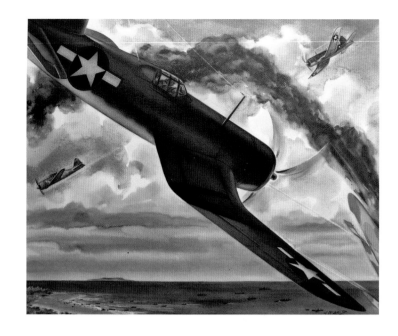

Top row, left to right:
Grumman F6F Hellcat
Vought-Sikorsky F4U Corsair
Curtiss SB2C Helldiver
Consolidated PBY Catalina

Midddle row, left to right:
Grumman TBF Avenger
Martin PBM Mariner
Lockheed C-69 Constellation

Bottom row, left to right:
Vought-Sikorsky OS2U Kingfisher
Vought-Sikorsky YR4 Helicopter

Coca-Cola Hanger Card Set No. 4—the final series—was introduced in 1945 as "Planes That are Smashing through to Victory." Twenty 13″×15″ hanger cards featuring Heaslip's illustrations were distributed to military bases; to retail establishments, such as restaurants, drug stores, and banks; and even to homes and hospitals all over the country.

The following excerpt from an article published two years after the war confirms the success of Coca-Cola's brilliant wartime promotion—and William Heaslip's part in it:

> The Coca-Cola Company did mighty well for themselves and the Allied nations with their full-color aircraft recognition series. It was supplied to the armed services in every theater of war around the globe. These keenly accurate illustrations were painted by William Heaslip, the world's outstanding commercial illustrator of aircraft. The expense for artwork was terrific … but so was the job

Set No. 1: B-17 D, Flying Fortress, circa 1941–42

Set No. 2: B-17 E, Flying Fortress, circa 1943

Set No. 3: B-17 F, Flying Fortress, circa 1944

Set No. 4: B-17 G, Flying Fortress, circa 1945

These four images of a B-17 aircraft are from the Coca-Cola Hanger Card Sets Nos. 1–4. Sets No. 2, 3, and 4, which were signed by William Heaslip, differ markedly in artistic quality and accuracy from Set No. 1, which was produced by an unnamed illustrator. In his series, Heaslip paid careful attention to accuracy of detail as both the U.S. Army Air Forces and Navy fielded new or modified aircraft with new colors and revised national insignia—a difficult task during wartime because of tight security. Sets No. 2, 3, and 4 clearly illustrate Heaslip's mastery of detail as well as his increasingly dramatic and accurate presentation as the war progressed toward victory. (Coca-Cola Company)

this series did. It helped our fliers and ground forces to better recognize friend from foe in the air … and helped millions in the armed services to recognize Coca-Cola as a real benefactor. And did that help Coca-Cola sell their beverage? It did and still does … for the memory of that service lingers warmly in the hearts and minds of returning veterans.[14]

Heaslip contributed a significant amount of time and energy, as well as immense creative talent, to the success of the Coca-Cola airplane hanger card promotion. As a small measure of his work, a complete set of No. 3 Coca-Cola airplane hanger cards currently commands a high price in Coca-Cola's very active collectors' market.[15]

Knight Chronicles the Japanese Surrender: The War Is Won

In 1944 Clayton Knight officially became a U.S. Army Air Forces combat war artist assigned to Alaska, the Aleutian Islands, and the Central Pacific area. The vulnerability of the United States and Canada in the northern Pacific had been recognized since before the war, and major efforts were near completion to build a roadway through Canada to transport troops, laborers, and materiel to Alaska and the Aleutian Islands.

Six months after the attack on Pearl Harbor, Japanese carrier aircraft bombed Dutch Harbor in the Aleutians, and assault troops took control of the islands of Kiska and Attu. The United States responded with a rapid buildup of troops, aircraft and airfields, and succeeded in re-taking the islands—but only after a very bloody campaign to recover Kiska in May 1943. Attu was assaulted shortly thereafter, but U.S. troops found that the Japanese had already evacuated by sea.

With the recovery of Kiska and Attu and the building of a new base on Shemya Island at the tip of the Aleutian chain, U.S. forces were now within 750 miles of the Japanese Kurile Islands, which extend north from the main islands of Japan. Clayton Knight arrived in that area in the spring of 1945 and proceeded to report on many military activities underway along his route to Shemya.

U.S. military sites in Alaska, 1945.

Airfields such as Ladd Field, built near Fairbanks, Alaska, became the training grounds for Soviet pilots and aircrew sent to the United States to pick up the thousands of Lend-Lease fighters and bombers delivered to them during the war. The aircraft, newly emblazoned with red-star insignias and crewed by Russians, were then flown to Nome for refueling before continuing into Siberia and ultimately to Moscow. Ladd Field also housed the principal site for cold-weather testing of aircraft and equipment.

Clayton Knight's illustrations from this period offer only a slight hint of the extreme conditions endured by ground troops and

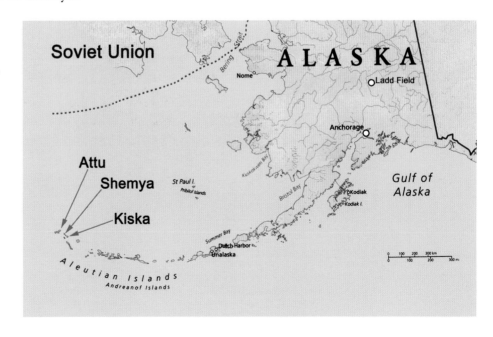

aircrew operating in this forbidding area: conditions that included savage weather with intense fog, rain, high and rapidly changing winds (more aircraft were lost to accidents in this environment than to combat); and crushing boredom.

Knight went directly from the Aleutian Islands to warmer climes in the central Pacific. On Guam he reported on the buildup of B-29 forces. The sketches below are from that part of his assignment.

On August 14, 1945, 143 bombers of the 315th Bomb Wing unleashed the longest continuous mission attempted by the Twentieth Air Force—17 hours and 3,760 miles-—against major refinery facilities at Akita, Japan. Japan announced its surrender as the 315th Bombardment Wing was on its return flight to Guam.

Brigadier General Frank Armstrong, who had led the first daylight VIII Bomber Command over German territory in August 1942, flew his last B-29 combat mission with the 315th Bomb Wing against Japan in 1945.

Pilots viewing ship formation. Drawing by Clayton Knight. (USAF Art Collection)

Eighteenth Fighter Squadron on alert at Attu. Drawing by Clayton Knight. (USAF Art Collection)

Clockwise from top right:

Under the command of Brigadier General Frank Armstrong (a strategic bomber leader well-known to Clayton Knight), the 315th Bomb Wing deployed to Northwest Field on Guam in April, 1945.[16] Equipped with Bell Aviation-built B-29 B-model bombers that had been stripped of their General Electric gun systems to save weight and carry more ordnance, the wing's crews were trained for low-altitude, pathfinder missions. (315th Bomb Wing Association)

Bomb Group HQ, a component of the 315th Bomb Wing, proudly displays a Texas state flag. (Clayton Christopher Knight)

The 315th also possessed several B-29A aircraft equipped with the APQ 7 Eagle radar system used for navigation and bombing purposes. In this illustration, a B-29 air gunner sits at his station in a pressurized fuselage. The wing began combat on August 1, 1945, focusing its operations on Japan's oil production facilities. Drawing by Clayton Knight. (Clayton Christopher Knight)

Working on the underside of a B-29. Drawing by Clayton Knight. (Clayton Christopher Knight)

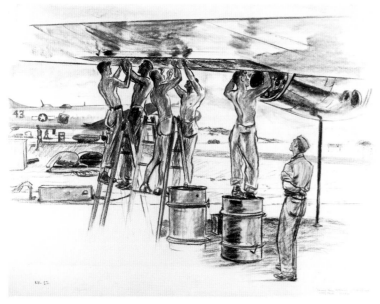

Top to bottom:

Tower at Northwest Field, Guam. Drawing by Clayton Knight. (Clayton Christopher Knight)

Japan: target for tonight. Illustration by Clayton Knight. (Clayton Christopher Knight)

Brigadier General Armstrong, at the controls of *Fluffy Fuzz*, prepares for takeoff on first mission against the Japanese Empire on July 26, 1945. (315th Bomb Wing Association)

Left: Photo of overflight of U.S. Army Air Forces and Navy aircraft. *Right*: Original lithograph by Clayton Knight depicting the massive overflight of American Airpower during the surrender ceremony. (Clayton Christopher Knight)

The war-wounded Dove of Peace wears a Purple Heart medal. (Theodore Hamady)

On September 2, 1945, Clayton Knight joined hundreds of U.S. Navy officers and men, as well as representatives from the media and delegations of victorious Allied officers, at the surrender of the Japanese Empire aboard the battleship USS *Missouri*. Knight positioned himself high on the masthead where he could sketch the overflight of 450 U.S. Navy carrier fighters, plus formations of U.S. Army Air Force B-29s. The flight impressed the Allied fighting men, and, no doubt, sobered the Japanese surrender delegation.

Left: Photograph taken looking down at the surrender ceremony on the deck of the USS *Missouri*, September 2, 1945. *Right*: Once at peace with the Allies, the Japanese delegation was rendered full military honors by U.S. Naval officers and sailors as they departed the USS *Missouri*.

This beautiful poster, produced by William Heaslip for the Coca-Cola Company, celebrates the promise of peacetime travel via aircraft that had only recently served the United States in wartime. The large transport aircraft depicted in flight is the Douglas DC-4 (designated C-54 and R5D by the USAAF and USN respectively) and the tri-tailed aircraft depicted on the modern airport tarmac below are Lockheed Constellations (designated C-69 and R7O-1 by the USAAF and USN respectively). (Coca-Cola Company)

The HOW AND WHY Wonder Book of

5005   50¢

ROCKETS AND MISSILES

How and Why Wonder Books

CHAPTER NINE

For God and Country

Throughout the "Golden Age of Aviation"—by our definition, the period from Charles Lindbergh's epochal transatlantic flight in 1927 to the beginning of World War II—Clayton Knight and William Heaslip inspired Americans to see the promise inherent in the emerging field of flight. Their illustrations, which appeared early in slick magazines such as *Sportsman Pilot* and later in newspapers covering the lead-up to World War II, educated Americans about aviation technologies. Their commercial promotions—featured on everything from Heinz cereal-box trading cards, Coca-Cola point of sale materials, patriotic sheet music, and Christmas cards to jigsaw puzzles,[1] aviation movie serials, and Sunday comics—made heroes of air racers, military and naval pilots, aircraft designers, and sometimes the airplanes themselves. Together Knight and Heaslip helped to turn aviation pioneers such as Amelia Earhart, Roscoe Turner, "Wrong Way" Corrigan, Howard Hughes, and many wartime American and Allied Air leaders into hero-celebrities.

The Roots of the Celebrity Culture

Clayton Knight and William Heaslip were not the first to create celebrity around the aviator through their art. Such celebration can be traced back as far as 1784, when aeronaut Vincenzo Lunardi became the first man to successfully pilot a hot air balloon across France, Scotland, and England. Lunardi's achievement was memorialized in the artwork by John Francis Rigaud.

After that brief fascination with balloon flights, popular interest waned until the Wright brothers demonstrated the first successful controlled flight of an aircraft under its own power in 1903. Artists' impressions of these early powered flights, at first whimsical, quickly turned serious as the public recognized the staggering potential of the airplane as a war weapon.

Henri Farré, (1871–1934) may have been the first artist to celebrate modern aviators in war. He was appointed by the French government during World War I to record aerial warfare as an observer-bombardier, and he flew many combat missions as air crew. As a result of first-hand experience, he created illustrations that were both beautifully executed and realistic.

Opposite: *Rockets and Missiles*, written and illustrated by Clayton Knight, Wonder Books, 1960.

Clockwise from top left:

Captain Vincenzo Lunardi with his assistant George Biggin and Mrs. Letitia Anne Sage, in a balloon, by John Francis Rigaud.

Britisher John Bull, standing astride England with tethered Royal Navy ships at his feet, gazes up at a new, potentially devastating threat from above as depicted in a 1909 issue of PUCK Magazine. (Theodore Hamady)

Henri Farre's oil painting of a French ground crew doing maintenance on a Voisin two-place bomber. Aerial bombs lie in the foreground while other bombers have already taken off on a daylight mission. (Charles Walthall)

But America's aviation craze after World War I transcended all other eras by many orders of magnitude: the audience was far larger, major milestones in aviation were taking place almost continuously, and the duration of the craze was far longer. Moreover, the media through which aviation art spread reached far more people. It was during this time that Knight and Heaslip did their best work.

The Changing Landscape Post World War II

When the atomic bombs dropped on Hiroshima and Nagasaki from B-29 Superfortresses brought World War II to an end, the fervor for flying faded once again. By August 1945, Knight and Heaslip found themselves facing a very different world. Hundreds of young war-trained artists, illustrators and draftsmen, unleashed into civilian life, became aggressive competitors in the marketplace of graphic art.

Much of the illustration work of that period shifted from war planes to commercial aircraft. The War Production Board removed wartime restrictions on the production of general aviation aircraft, and that segment of the market began to expand rapidly. Planes that had been conscripted for the war effort were repurposed and returned to the civil airlines, and surplus military aircraft were sold or scrapped.

Moreover, upon returning home from war, thousands of war-trained pilots moved to the suburbs. This caused market analysts to project that unit sales of private planes would grow as people forsook their automobiles for commute by plane. Sales projections made in May 1945 for personal aircraft were extremely optimistic,[2] and indeed actual unit sales in 1946 exceeded 33,000 aircraft, an astounding increase over prior years. But with the much-improved national highway system introduced in the 1950s,[3] automobiles remained the preferred mode of transportation, and sales of private aircraft would never again come close to 1946 levels.

It was also a time of changing trends in illustration. According to respected illustrator Al Parker, burgeoning advertising budgets and an abundance of magazine fiction offered illustrators much opportunity. But art directors began to eschew the realism and practiced craftsmanship of traditional illustrators for a more modern approach—one that featured unfinished looks to finished art. "The ferment of ... drastic concepts and techniques," Parker wrote, "developed as the major influence of [the post-war] illustrator."[4]

By the 1950s, the rebellion against realism was full-blown. Illustrator Austin Briggs explains the "revolution" as

> ... accelerated by the demise of several national periodicals in a losing competition with television for presentation of fictional escapism. Other floundering publications sought salvation in acquiring a new image—anything different and strident enough to retain the attention of a wavering public.[5]

Many skilled illustrators adapted to this new approach, but for those in the business of rendering aviation art, accuracy remained a primary objective. And when accuracy is the standard by which an illustration is judged, photography becomes its greatest competitor.

For all these reasons, Clayton Knight and William Heaslip found themselves working in a subject category with dwindling opportunities. They were relatively young—Knight was 54, and Heaslip was 47—and both had put in long hours during the war to meet grueling deadlines for government, military, and corporate clients. Heaslip once admitted to working 67 hours straight to finish a double-page spread for the New York Times, as facts in the story changed hourly.[6] One can only speculate how such stressful routines during wartime took their toll on the health and personal lives of these two artists. Slowing down was certainly an option, but their relative youth and family responsibilities demanded that they remain relevant in their professional lives.

Not surprisingly, the burnout rate was high among such illustrators, especially as they attempted to balance their own artistic integrity against the demands of clients. Aviation artist James Dietz, a 1969 graduate of the prestigious Art Center College of Design, observed that a common remedy from this stress was an increase in the consumption of alcohol and drugs, leading to addiction for an unfortunate few.[7]

Clayton Knight's Post-War Years

During the summer of 1947, Clayton Knight, who was by then recognized as a prominent and well-connected artist/journalist, was invited to participate in the first scheduled passenger flight around the world made by Pan American World Airways. The 13-day journey, which started at New York's LaGuardia field, included Juan Trippe, President of Pan American World Airways, and 19 distinguished guests, some of whom were prominent journalists.[8] It was certainly an honor for Knight to be included with this illustrious group, and the invitation remains a testament to Knight's professional reputation.

But Knight's career path after the war took him back mostly to his pre-war work in juvenile literature. Despite the fact that aviation books had lost some popularity after World War II,[9] Knight took a job in 1945 to illustrate Grosset & Dunlap's Yankee Flyer series. The books, written by Al Avery (a pseudonym for Rutherford George Montgomery) had first been published in 1941 and featured stories of World War II combat missions. Knight illustrated *A Yankee Flyer in Normandy* (1945), *A Yankee Flyer on a Rescue Mission* (1945), and *A Yankee Flyer Under Secret Orders* (1946), all with dramatic art for the covers and simple line drawings for the frontispieces.

Knight had already proven his literary abilities with early ventures into writing and illustrating his own books so it made sense that he would return to this work as a way to improve his future prospects. He expanded his portfolio with Grosset & Dunlap on historical subjects by collaborating on the *We Were There* series, some of which he both wrote and illustrated alongside his wife, Katherine Sturges.

Clayton Knight's drawing from Pan Am's round-the-world flight as it crossed the International Date Line between Wake and Midway, June 28, 1947. (Clayton Christopher Knight)

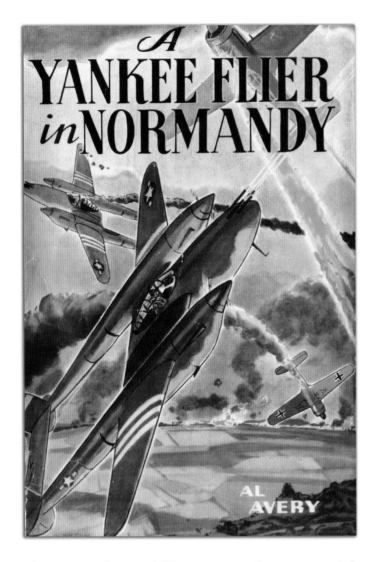

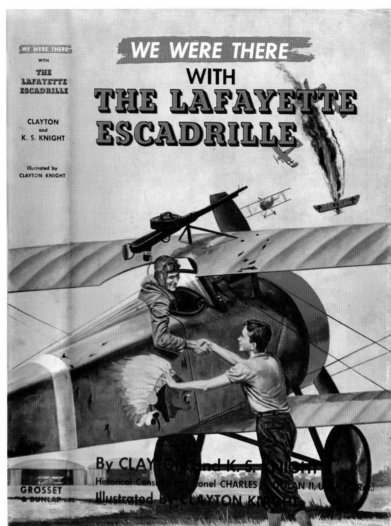

That series advertised "fast-moving adventures with heroes and heroines your own age." In his last contribution to that series, *We Were There with the Lafayette Escadrille*, he superimposed official U.S. Air Force photographs over his drawings of World War I aerial combat, a technique in keeping with then-current illustration trends.

Quest of the Condor (1946) was the first in a series of three adventure books Knight authored for publisher Alfred A. Knopf, Jr. The story was loosely based on a trip to South America taken by the entire Knight family in 1938, including wife Katharine and sons Clayton Jr. (Joey) and Hilary. Years later, Hilary would say that "it was an extraordinary trip for a seven-year-old … one that will live with me forever."[10] While references to aviation were minimal in the book, *Quest of the Condor* won the *New York Herald Tribune* prize for best book of the year in the category for older juvenile literature.

Knight's last book in the Knopf series, *Skyroad to Mystery* (1949), encompassed the theme of aviation in peacetime, laced with intrigue and Cold War espionage. It was also the only one of the three books in the series to depict an airplane in the cover art.

Fred Erisman's survey of boys' aviation series concludes that after World War II these books featured characters who were less focused on the "innovation and individualism of aviation per se," and more on "[striding] into the updated world of corporate- or government-supported electronics, rocketry, nucleonics, and, eventually interplanetary travel."[11] This new emphasis carried through to all manner of publication for America's

Left: *A Yankee Flyer in Normandy* by Al Avery (pseudonym for Rutherford George Montgomery), illustrated by Clayton Knight, 1945. (Grosset & Dunlap, an imprint of Penguin Random House)

Right: *We Were There with the Lafayette Escadrille* by Clayton and K. S. Knight, with historical consultant Colonel Charles H. Dolan II, USAF Retired; illustrated by Clayton Knight, 1961. (Clayton Christopher Knight)

youth during the 1950s, a development that produced a flurry of new book assignments for Knight from established publishers. With a few exceptions, these assignments focused on machines of flight. *The Big Book of Real Helicopters* (Grosset & Dunlap, 1955) and *The Real Book About Our Armed Forces* with Katharine Sturges (Garden City Books, 1959) are typical of this period.

Knight wrote and illustrated *Rockets, Missiles, and Satellites* for Grosset & Dunlap in 1958; and two years later, *The How and Why Wonder Book of Rockets and Missiles* was published, featuring a spectacular cover designed to invoke an emotional excitement for space travel that had previously been reserved for aviation. The research and resourcefulness that went into producing such richly illustrated books "presented in a clear, easy-to-read style—with colorful, accurate pictures,"[12] were intended to inspire future scientists and astronauts.

Skyroad to Mystery, written and illustrated by Clayton Knight, 1949. (Alfred A. Knopf, Inc. an imprint of Penguin Random House)

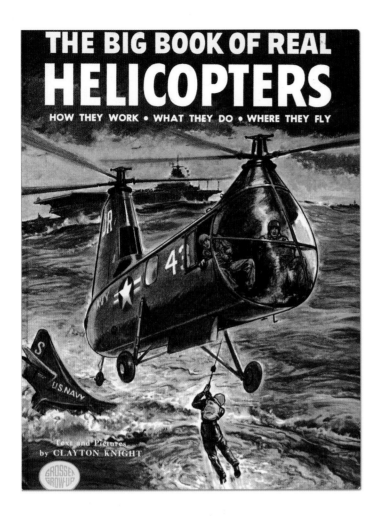

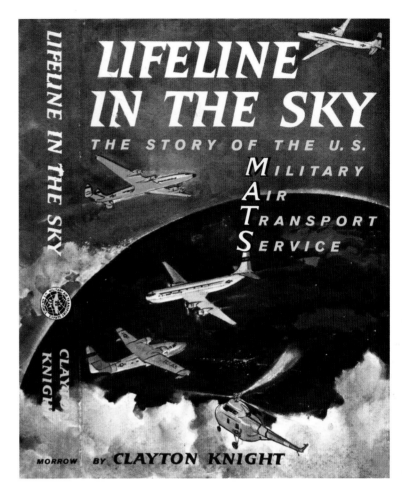

In 1956, Knight embarked on his last assignment for the military when he began a 20-day tour of American military installations abroad in order to write about the U.S. Military Air Transport Service. [13] His book *Lifeline in the Sky* was published in 1957 by William Morrow, with 255 pages of text, 72 on-the-spot drawings, and two full-color paintings.

Left: *The Big Book of Real Helicopters*, written and illustrated by Clayton Knight, Grosset & Dunlap, 1955. (Grosset & Dunlap an imprint of Penguin Random House)

Right: *Lifeline in the Sky: The Story of the U.S. Military Air Transport Service*, written and illustrated by Clayton Knight, William Morrow and Company, 1957.

William Heaslip's Post-War Years

Early in his career, William Heaslip established a reputation for conjuring up fantastical imagery for science fiction stories, particularly in his work for *American Boy* magazine, which ceased publication in 1941. He continued to produce futuristic illustrations for *Boys' Life* throughout the 1950s. His cover for the September 1952 issue of *Boys' Life*, which began a series on interplanetary travel, featured a flying wing. Another cover, this one for the October 1953 issue celebrating the Golden Jubilee of Flight, accompanied a reprint of Orville Wright's own story, which first appeared in the magazine in 1914. In commenting on that cover, the managing editor of *Boys' Life* acknowledged Heaslip's ability to "look ahead as well as backwards."

The last book Heaslip illustrated was *Men of Flight (Conquest of the Air)* by Charles Spain Verrall (Aladdin Books, 1954). For the cover, Heaslip featured a jet fighter test pilot, probably Willliam Barton Bridgeman, even though jet flight is mentioned only in an endpaper chronology.

OCTOBER 1953 · 25¢

Boys' Life

FOR ALL BOYS

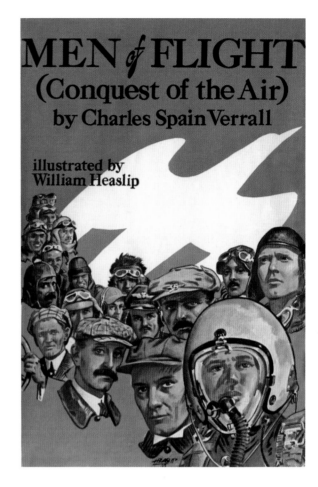

Left: William Heaslip's cover for the September 1952 issue of *Boys' Life*, featuring the article "Tramp Space Ship: a Tale of Interplanetary Travel." (Allan M. Heaslip)

Right: William Heaslip's cover for *Men of Flight* (*Conquest of the Air*) by Charles Spain Verrall.

The Autumn Years

External forces aside, a series of personal losses impacted both Knight and Heaslip and changed their lives in ways inconceivable a decade earlier.

For Knight, the 1950s ended with the deaths of memorable characters of aviation with whom he had worked and socialized. Many of his influential patrons, buddies from World War I days and ranking officers in World War II, had retired shortly after the war, and passed away in the decades that followed. Billy Bishop passed away in 1956, and a few years later Knight lost Elliot White Springs, one of his closest and most supportive friends.[14] But the most devastating personal loss happened in 1963 when Knight and wife Katharine Sturges lost their eldest son Joey (Clayton Knight, Jr.) to cancer.

Joey, who had joined the Army Air Forces during World War II, was the son in whom Clayton Knight invested his dreams of carrying on the family tradition. And Joey did acquire some of his father's interests, becoming both a documentary film writer and a director for the Baltimore plant of the Glenn L. Martin Company, which specialized

Opposite: William Heaslip's cover for the October 1953 issue of *Boys' Life*, celebrating the Golden Jubilee of Flight. (Allan M. Heaslip)

In this post-WWII photograph, Clayton Knight is together with other WWI aviation luminaries. Left to right: Maj. Gen William Ord Ryan, USAS; Meredith J. Roberts, 95th Aero Squadron, USAS; unknown; Clayton Knight, Nos. 44 and 206 Squadrons, RFC/RAF; Lt. Col Harold E. Hartney, No. 20 Squadron, RFC and 27th Aero Squadron, USAS; Kenneth F. Porter, 147th Aero Squadron, USAS; Col. Elliott White Springs, No. 85 Squadron, RAF and 148th Aero Squadron, USAS; Charles S. ("Casey") Jones, Escadrille Spa 96; and Ashley McKinley, 12th Balloon Company, USAS. (Peter Kilduff)

in aerospace manufacturing. But it was younger son Hilary who continued the family tradition as a successful illustrator and writer. His exuberant, highly stylized illustrations for Kay Thompson's classic *Eloise* series of children's books, first published in 1955, have endured to this day.

After the death of Joey, Knight worked on proposals for two books, but they were never published: *Fifty Famous Pilots* carried on the *Hall of Fame of the Air* series; and *Famous Pilots Who Did It First* featured Major James Jabara, the first air ace of the Korean War.[15] He also wrote a 10,000 word article on the Clayton Knight Committee for *American Heritage* magazine, but again, it was never published. He served as an aviation consultant for *American Heritage*[16] and as an advisor to *Grolier International Encyclopedia*, but he couldn't get the latter to commit to a monthly retainer over an honorarium.[17]

Knight marketed himself as best he could,[18] responded to flattering correspondence,[19] and reconnected with old friends,[20] but none of this resulted in sufficient business transactions as demand for aviation illustration continued to wane. His ever-present optimism and good spirits began to flag. And unlike Heaslip, who found peace in teaching and painting bucolic scenes of New Jersey, Knight continued to produce aviation art that focused on war.

Chris Knight (Clayton Knight III) recalls, while staying with his grandparents around this time, his grandfather busy at work on World War I aviation combat paintings.[21] Knight managed to arrange a donation of his World War I paintings to the United States Air Force, including some originals from *Pilots' Luck*. Finding a willing donor for this project was a long and arduous process, one that included intermediaries such as Robert Fawcett,[22] known to his peers as "the illustrators' illustrator;"[23] and Victor Hammer,[24] co-founder (with his brother Armand) of Hammer Galleries in New York. Overtures were made to Floyd Odlum, American industrialist and husband of aviator Jackie Cochran, with a suggestion to get Elliot White Springs involved.[25] In the meantime, Joseph M. Katz, wealthy Pittsburgh manufacturer and head of the Papercraft Corporation, came through as the sponsor. In all, five paintings were purchased for the U.S. Air Force art collection, with the donation staggered over several years.

Knight also assembled a series of illustrations of "every plane that crossed the lines in World War I," including the SE-5, Camel, Fokker D-VII, Bristol Fighter, Spad, Nieuport, and DH-4, all uniform in size.[26] He hoped to sell these, too, with their eventual home being the Air Force Academy, but George C. (Bob) Bales, whose energy had driven the acquisition of historic paintings for the Air Force, had moved to California and retired. There was some interest by the Texas Aeronautical Museum, but a deal was never made.

A coincidental meeting with Clayton Knight, Jr., (Joey) in the office of Navy Supply Command for Antarctica in Washington, DC, during the summer of 1961 offered a young Navy journalist seaman named Peter Kilduff the opportunity to meet the man whom he had followed since the age of 15. Kilduff was on his way to Antarctica, but he was anxious before deployment to connect directly with Clayton Knight.[27] Kilduff would later reintroduce World War I aviation buffs to Knight's history and contributions through a series of articles and books. Their friendship continued through the remainder of Knight's life, and the family credits that relationship with lifting his morale at a time when he felt abandoned by an industry in which he had invested so much.

Clayton Knight continued to attend gatherings of the Dutch Treat Club in New York, but his participation tapered off in the mid-1960s.[28] He also maintained memberships with the Quiet Birdmen and

Clayton Knight at home with Katharine Sturges and her cousin Alice Taggart. Alice served with the Community Service Society of New York from 1933 until her retirement in 1961. (Clayton Christopher Knight)

Peter Kilduff and Clayton Knight in West Redding, Connecticut, April 29, 1966. (Peter Kilduff)

the Society of Illustrators. But his membership in the Wings Club, founded in May of 1942, proved to be most significant. His last major project was to write a history of the first 25 years of the Wings Club, from 1942–67. Ironically, the book includes not a single Clayton Knight illustration—just photographs of the club's many prominent members. Today, only four of the original five paintings in the U.S. Air Force art collection exist, and Knight's remaining World War I paintings are on long-term loan to the Wings Club, where they are prominently displayed. On July 17, 1969, Clayton Knight passed away from complications of diabetes and an enlarged heart.

For William Heaslip, the transition to civilian life after the war was more deliberate due to his purposeful retreat from the stresses of Manhattan: in 1948 Heaslip moved his family from Rahway, New Jersey, to Hackettstown, becoming an integral part of that community. He renovated an old stone barn that had been a prison for British and Hessian soldiers during the Revolutionary War and used it as both his studio and home. He became a founder of the Rahway Art Center and continued there as an instructor even after the move to Hackettstown. He loved to entertain and was well known for his open houses and parties at which attendees would marvel at the cuisine, which was generally potluck dishes.[29]

The Wivel Restaurant was a favorite of the Heaslip's when they would venture into the city as a couple (1951). Located at 254 West 54th Street, the establishment was famous for its smorgasbord dinner and supper dancing revue. (Allan M. Heaslip)

During these years, Heaslip took on the occasional commission and continued work for several of his wartime clients. He shared a studio with other artists in a converted carriage house off Fifth Avenue in New York City. But by 1953, his post-war business had dwindled, and the studio was sold and torn down to make way for a major hotel project. Despite these changes, Heaslip maintained friendships with a close group of illustrators, most notably Dean Cornwell. These artists would arrange *plein air* drawing expeditions in the country, especially in the colorful fall season; and of course, they would also socialize.[30]

The tranquility and stability provided by Clare Wayman, Heaslip's wife of 30 years, came to an end in 1954 with her passing. Heaslip was not religious—perhaps he rebelled against the strict Christian upbringing of his early years—but he was a spiritual person. He refurbished the altar murals at St. James Episcopal Church in Hackettstown, New Jersey, in Clare's memory. The Reverend Clarence Sickles fondly recalls working with Heaslip on this project, and on his own weekly Sunday school lessons, which were illustrated by the artist.[31] This experience led Heaslip to a major commission for a new Seventh Day Adventist publication for young people. The book, *Your Bible and You* by Arthur S. Maxwell, was published in 1959 by Review and Herald Publishing Association, Washington, DC.

Within three years of his wife's death, Heaslip married artist Gilberta Goodwin, head of the art department at Centenary College in Hackettstown. She was primarily a landscape artist with a decidedly modern approach to

style. For a while, they shared a studio in the old stone barn. Goodwin also had a house in Edgartown, Massachusetts, where she introduced her new husband to the Martha's Vineyard art scene. But this marriage was short-lived, and Heaslip soon returned to the security of Hackettstown, where he settled into a life of teaching. His art classes were quite popular as he was a gifted instructor as well as an articulate raconteur, with a lifetime of amazing stories to share. He sold his paintings, mostly landscapes of the neighboring countryside, through local outlets including the Clarendon Hotel, a prominent local establishment. His painting *Out of Alfano Way* is still hanging in the Hackettstown Free Public Library.

In 1969, William Heaslip was diagnosed with terminal leukemia. He sold his formidable collection of Japanese armor and English pewter and embarked on a triumphal world tour accompanied by his daughter Judy, a registered nurse, who functioned as a medical aide and assistant. On that tour, he visited many old friends in Hong Kong, Australia, Alaska, Canada, and England. His lifelong adage—"there are no pockets in shrouds"—was played out until the end. His son Allan, who served as executor of his will, noted that there was $65 left in his father's estate when he died. Allan held no rancor about this state of affairs: his father had gone out in style and on his own terms.[32] Heaslip's funeral service was conducted at St. James Episcopal Church in Hackettstown.[33]

Always striving, forever dedicated, these two artists made

Left: The Revolutionary-War-era stone barn in Hackettstown, New Jersey, that William Heaslip renovated as both a studio and home. (Allan M. Heaslip)

Right: St. James Episcopal Church altar, Hackettstown, New Jersey, refurbished by William Heaslip in memory of his wife Clare. (Paul Bartkus and Rev. Clarence Sickles)

William Heaslip in his studio in the old stone barn, Hackettstown, New Jersey. (Allan M. Heaslip)

William Heaslip's illustration from *Your Bible and You*, by Arthur S. Maxwell. With an eye to applying Holy Scripture to everyday life, the book features imagery reflecting scientific progress through the ages. (©1959 Review and Herald Publishing Association)

visible the sensation of flying in inimitable and tangible ways at a time when few were familiar with the experience. They were uniquely qualified among their peers and shared a lifelong passion for their subject. Their cumulative output was to forever change our perceptions of aviation. Over a 20-year period, they were both on a mission to champion their love of flight, and they did so with enthusiasm, integrity, and generosity. This is their legacy, and with this book, we hope to acknowledge that gift.

Above: Hotel Clarendon, Hackettstown, New Jersey, painted by Wiliam Heaslip. This image was featured on a postcard by the American Aerial Survey Company, Hackettstown, New Jersey.

Left: William Heaslip's painting *Out of Alfano Way* now hangs in the Hackettstown Free Public Library in Hackettstown, New Jersey. (Hackettstown Public Library)

CHRONOLOGY

A Timeline of Important Events in Aviation and Significant Art Works by Clayton Knight and William Heaslip

1891   **Clayton Knight** born in Rochester, NY

1898   **William Heaslip** born in Toronto, Canada

1903   Wright Brothers first flight

1909   U.S. Army's first aerodrome at College Park, MD

1910   **Knight** attends the School of the Art Institute of Chicago until 1913

1914   Aviation Section Signal Corps (ASSC) organized

1914   World War I begins

1917   U.S. enters World War on April 6, 1917

1917   **Knight** enlists in Aviation Section, U.S. Signal Corps; attends ground school in Austin, TX; and ships to England, then France where he joins the 206th Squadron, RAF

1917   **Heaslip** enters Royal Flying Corps, trains as aerial observer and gunner

1918   **Knight** wounded in combat and taken prisoner at Maarke, Belgium

1918   94th Aero Squadron combat operational (first American-trained squadron to enter combat)

1918   World War Armistice ends war on November 11, 1918

1919   **Knight** released from hospital and returns home

1919   U.S. Navy NC-4 Flying Boat crosses Atlantic and lands at Lisbon

1919   Development of reversible and variable pitch props, turbocharger, etc.

1919   **Heaslip** enrolls at National Academy of Design, receives Suydam Silver Medal for Drawing from Life

1920   **Heaslip** attends Art Students League

1921   Douglas Aircraft formed

1921   Billy Mitchell demonstrates that aerial bombing can sink capital ships

Opposite page: William Heaslip's original painting for a Coca-Cola hanger depicts a P-51 Mustang fighter attacking enemy shipping high velocity aerial rockets and .50 caliber machine guns. (USAF Art Collection)

1922   **Heaslip** joins 7th Regiment, New York National Guard

1922   First U.S. carrier USS *Langley* commissioned

1922   Jimmy Doolittle makes cross-country flight record from Jacksonville, FL, to San Diego, CA, in 22 hours

1923   National Air Races held in St. Louis

1924   U.S. Army Round-the-World Flight ends

1925   USN Airship *Shenandoah* destroyed in storm

1925   Doolittle wins Schneider Cup in UK

1925   Billy Mitchell court-marshaled and found guilty of insubordination

1926   Richard Byrd claims first flight over North Pole in Fokker Tri-motor

1927   **Knight** illustrates "The Red Knight of Germany" for serial publication by *Liberty* magazine. *Liberty* remained a major client for Knight, and many of his articles were later published in book form

Charles Lindbergh received his most enthusiastic welcome upon returning to Washington, DC after his historic solo flight to Paris. This Washington newspaper column dated May 27, 1927, looked to the future for this 27-year-old hero.

Welcome, Lindy!

Well, Lindy, you're back home; back under the blue skies of the mightiest and grandest nation on the earth; back with your home folks in Washington, the wonderful capital of that nation whose Chief Executive and people today honor you for deeds that required skill, courage, manhood of the highest type.

You've been greatly honored abroad, feted by royalty, pawed over by low brows and high brows, and yet your head keeps its balance, a good sign that you are truly a real man.

The praises and whooping of the multitudes still ring in your ears, will be ringing today and other days among patriotic Americans who hail with joy your achievements. The noise and din will cease in a short time and you'll be just "Lindy" in the affection of your fellow citizens, and the quantity of that affection will depend upon you and the fine modesty which is yours.

What you've done for your country and for aviation will always be appreciated. Your place in history is as-

sured so long as you continue the manly course you have always followed.

You will realize by tonight how much your fellow Americans think of you, and it will make you happy. You will know that you are indeed welcomed—enshrined in the hearts of your own people.

May all your life be as successful in worthy deeds and ideals as these first years, and may you always wear modestly the honors which come to you.

1927   Pan American begins mail and passenger service from Key West to Havana

1928   LT A. M. Pride makes first landing on new carrier USS *Lexington*

1928   LCDR Marc Mitscher makes first landing on new carrier USS *Saratoga*

1928   **Knight** illustrates *Off the Ground and Go!* published by the Wright Aeronautical Corp, Paterson, NJ

1928   **Knight** illustrates and authors *The Non-Stop Stowaway,* published by the Buzza Company, Minneapolis, MN

1928   **Heaslip** illustrates poster, winning third prize in a competition sponsored by the American Legion

1928   **Heaslip** illustrates his first cover for the *American Legion Monthly*, April 1928

1928   Amelia Earhart, pilot, and mechanic cross Atlantic

1928   Richard Byrd makes the first flight over South Pole

1929   Spaatz, Eaker, and Quesada set endurance record by keeping airplane *Question Mark* in the air over Los Angeles area for 150 hours

1929   First Thompson Race

1929   Doolittle's first public demonstration of "blind flying"

Opposite page: Clayton Knight sent this watercolor to Francis Warrington Gillet, an American who joined the Royal Flying Corps in 1917. He was posted to No. 79 Squadron as a fighter pilot. At war's end, Gillet was acting Captain, Royal Air Force, having amassed a total of 20 victories. He ranked second only to Eddie Rickenbacker among American fighter pilots. (Warrington Gillette, grandson of Francis Warrington Gillet)

To
Cpt. F. W. Gillet D.F.C.

CLAYTON
KNIGHT
1929

1929	Amelia Earhart sets women's record for speed of 184.17 mph
1929	Technical developments: wing flaps and NACA cowling
1929	**Knight** illustrates *Pilot's Luck* with excerpts from stories by Elliott White Springs, Capt. A. Roy Brown, Floyd Gibbons, and Norman S. Hall; published by David McKay Co, Philadelphia
1929	**Knight** illustrates Texaco Company ad "Making Air History," which runs in *Collier's Magazine*, Nov 1929. The ad features Capt. Frank M. Hawks flying solo in Lockheed Monoplane *Texaco No. 5* across U.S. in 37 hours, making non-stop records both ways. (Same ad appears in *Literary Digest*, October 29, 1929.)
1929	**Heaslip** illustrates *Cloud Patrol* by Irving Crump, published by Grosset & Dunlap, NY
1929	**Heaslip** illustrates *The Pilot of the Cloud Patrol* by Irving Crump, published by Grosset & Dunlap, NY
1929	**Heaslip** illustrates cover for *American Boy* magazine, featuring "Haunted Airways, An Air Mystery of 1985" by Thompson Burtis
1929	**Heaslip** designs and illustrates innovative advertisements for Berryloid Aircraft Finishes
1930	Roscoe Turner flies from New York to Los Angeles in a record 18 hours 43 minutes
1930	**Heaslip** illustrates cover for *American Legion Monthly*, April 1930
1930	**Knight** transmits "radio photograph" from an airplane to the ground for the first time in aviation history, during California war maneuvers, April 22, 1930.
1930	Frank Mawler flies from New York to Los Angeles in 12 hours, 25 minutes, setting new record
1930	**Heaslip** illustrates ad for Howard Hughes movie *Hell's Angels*
1930	Technical developments: metal construction replaces wood in airplane construction
1931	Coach Knute Rockne of Notre Dame killed in plane crash; accident hastens all-metal construction of aircraft
1931	**Heaslip** illustrates cover of *Boy's Life*, April 1931
1931	Amelia Earhart awarded Gold Medal by National Geographic for solo flight across Atlantic
1931	Amelia Earhart establishes new distance record for women
1931	Navy flies 242 naval aircraft over San Diego
1931	**Heaslip** becomes consulting art director of *Sportsman Pilot* magazine
1931	Doolittle flies "Gee Bee" to win Thompson Trophy Race; averages 252 mph
1931	Pangborn and Herndon win $25,000 in first nonstop flight from Tokyo to U.S.
1931	Lindbergh inaugurates Pan Am service from Miami to Cienfuegos, Cuba
1931	Technical developments: Sikorsky builds all-metal amphibian, Stinson builds 10 passenger tri-motor, Sikorsky builds 4-engine flying boat for Navy, many

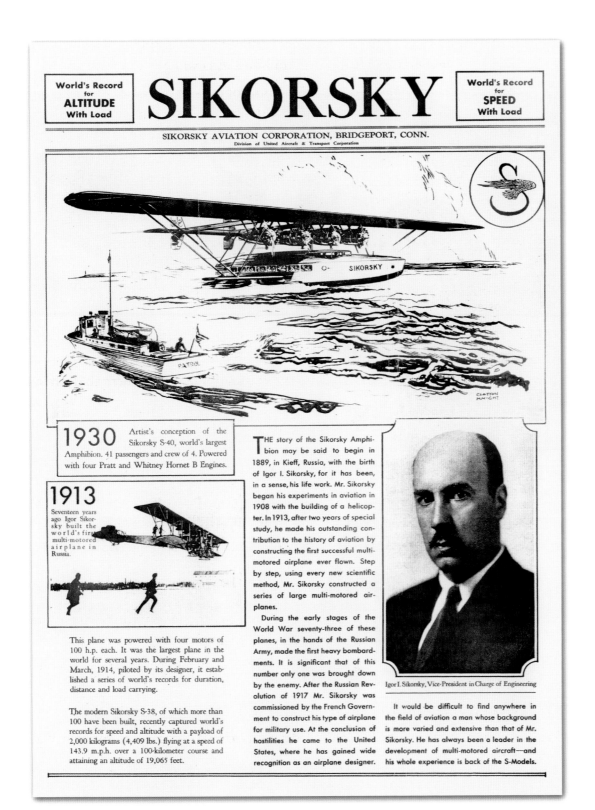

World's Record for ALTITUDE With Load

SIKORSKY

World's Record for SPEED With Load

SIKORSKY AVIATION CORPORATION, BRIDGEPORT, CONN.
Division of United Aircraft & Transport Corporation

1930 Artist's conception of the Sikorsky S-40, world's largest Amphibion. 41 passengers and crew of 4. Powered with four Pratt and Whitney Hornet B Engines.

1913 Seventeen years ago Igor Sikorsky built the world's first multi-motored airplane in Russia.

This plane was powered with four motors of 100 h.p. each. It was the largest plane in the world for several years. During February and March, 1914, piloted by its designer, it established a series of world's records for duration, distance and load carrying.

The modern Sikorsky S-38, of which more than 100 have been built, recently captured world's records for speed and altitude with a payload of 2,000 kilograms (4,409 lbs.) flying at a speed of 143.9 m.p.h. over a 100-kilometer course and attaining an altitude of 19,065 feet.

THE story of the Sikorsky Amphibion may be said to begin in 1889, in Kieff, Russia, with the birth of Igor I. Sikorsky, for it has been, in a sense, his life work. Mr. Sikorsky began his experiments in aviation in 1908 with the building of a helicopter. In 1913, after two years of special study, he made his outstanding contribution to the history of aviation by constructing the first successful multi-motored airplane ever flown. Step by step, using every new scientific method, Mr. Sikorsky constructed a series of large multi-motored airplanes.

During the early stages of the World War seventy-three of these planes, in the hands of the Russian Army, made the first heavy bombardments. It is significant that of this number only one was brought down by the enemy. After the Russian Revolution of 1917 Mr. Sikorsky was commissioned by the French Government to construct his type of airplane for military use. At the conclusion of hostilities he came to the United States, where he has gained wide recognition as an airplane designer.

Igor I. Sikorsky, Vice-President in Charge of Engineering

It would be difficult to find anywhere in the field of aviation a man whose background is more varied and extensive than that of Mr. Sikorsky. He has always been a leader in the development of multi-motored aircraft—and his whole experience is back of the S-Models.

Clayton Knight highlighted the achievements of Igor Sikorsky who designed the prewar, record-breaking, four-engine Ilya Muromets Russian aircraft and the S-40 Flying Boat in 1930. Sikorsky is best known for having developed the first successful helicopter, with a first flight in 1939. (Clayton Christopher Knight)

companies go bust because of Great Depression, Taylor produces Taylor personal aircraft, progenitor of the legendary Piper Cub.

1932   Wiley Post sets record for around the world flight in Lockheed Vega; 15,596 miles in 17 days, 18 hours, 49.5 minutes

1932   James Wedell breaks world speed record in Wedell Williams Special; averages 305.33 mph

1933   **Knight** illustrates *Rhodes of the 94th* by Frederic Nelson Litten, published by Sears Publishing Company, NY

1933   **Knight** serves as consultant on movie set of *Eagle and the Hawk* (starring Fredric March and Jack Oakie) at the request of screenwriter Bogart Rogers, a friend and fellow aviator from World War I

1934   Franklin D. Roosevelt ends commercial airline airmail contract collusion between major airline companies and assigns duties to U.S. Army; this proved disastrous as inexperienced pilots flying poorly equipped planes suffered 13 fatalities

1934   **Heaslip** paints mural, *The First Flight*, for Franklin Institute, Philadelphia

1934   Roscoe Turner sets new record from California to New York in 10 hours, 2 minutes, winning the Bendix Trophy Race

1934   Roscoe Turner wins Thompson Trophy Race

1934   United Airlines Transport Corp formed (from Boeing Air Transport and 5 other airlines)

1935   Amelia Earhart flies from Hawaii to California—the first person to fly this route

1935   Pan Am *Clipper* surveys the route from California to Honolulu as part of the new Pacific route

1935   **Knight** illustrates May 25th cover of *Collier's* ("War Birds are Flying," by W. B. Courtney)

1935   *Luftwaffe*—Nazi Germany's new air force—is revealed by Adolph Hitler

1935   Will Rogers and Wiley Post are killed in a plane crash on August 15th

1935   Boeing 299, prototype of the legendary B-17, is tested

1935   Captains A. Stevens and Orville Anderson set new balloon altitude record of 72,395 feet

1935   Pan Am Martin 130 *China Clipper* inaugurates Pacific route

1935   **Heaslip** illustrates the November cover of *Boys' Life*

1935   **Knight** illustrates the first in the series of *Airmarks of Aviation Boys' Life*, November 1935

1935   **Heaslip** publishes *Air Register for 1935*, showcasing private aircraft and airfields across the country

1935   Major activities include new aircraft: Pan Am Martin 130 Clipper; Boeing B-17; Douglas DC-3

1936   Howard Hughes flies Burbank to New Jersey in 9 hours, 26 minutes

1936   Carrier USS *Yorktown* is launched; later sunk at Midway

1936   Major Ira Eaker flies blind (on instruments) from New York City to Los Angeles

Opposite: William Heaslip did this jolly New Year's cover illustration for the *Elks Magazine* in January, 1932.

Clayton Knight promoted fellow pilots' activities throughout his lengthy career. This cover was done for the Pilot's Reunion Dinner in 1935. (Clayton Christopher Knight)

ALL PILOTS MUST RENDEZVOUS

AT THE

Aviators Annual Armistice Night DINNER AND SHOW

Hotel RITZ-CARLTON

Monday Evening NOVEMBER 11 1 9 3 5

Show written and acted by **Elliot White Springs, Casey Jones, Cy Caldwell, Roger Wolfe Kahn, George Vaughn, Frank Hawks, Frank Godwin, Sam Moore, Roscoe Turner, Clyde Pangborn** and a host of Others

Tickets purchased before the Dinner will be **$5.00**—at the door **$6.00**—Tables seating ten
MAKE YOUR RESERVATIONS **NOW!**

Tickets can be obtained from A. J. HOFFMAN, 180 Broadway, New York, CASEY JONES Newark Airport or

SEPTEMBER 1938

The American

LEGION

MAGAZINE

1937	**Heaslip** receives J. W. Robinson Trophy for printmaking at Los Angeles Aviation Art Competition
1937	Howard Hughes flies from Los Angeles to New York in 7 hours, 28 minutes; average speed 327 mph
1937	Hindenburg dirigible blows up
1937	Amelia Earhart and Fred Noonan lost on round-the-world flight
1937	P-38 fighter designed by Lockheed
1937	**Knight** illustrates cover for the September 4 issue of *Saturday Evening Post*
1937	**Heaslip** illustrates cover for the December issue of *Boys' Life*
1937	**Heaslip** illustrates cover for the December issue of *American Legion Monthly*
1938	**Heaslip** illustrates cover for the April issue of *Boys' Life*
1938	**Heaslip** illustrates cover for the May 25 issue of *Saturday Evening Post*
1938	Douglas "Wrong Way" Corrigan flies from New York City to Dublin, Ireland
1938	Major Alexander de Seversky flies from New York to Los Angeles in record 10 hours, 3 minutes
1938	Hap Arnold succeeds Oscar Westover (killed in air crash) as chief of U.S. Army Air Corps
1938	DC-4E passenger liner prototype introduced; downsized variant becomes successful DC-4
1938	Ercoupe, a safe and easy-to-fly private plane, is introduced
1938	Piper aircraft produces 737 Cub for private flyers
1939	**Knight** illustrates ad for movie *Tail Spin*
1939	Ben Kelsey flies P-38 from California to New York in 7 hours, 45 minutes
1939	Pan Am Boeing 314 Flying Boat surveys Atlantic route
1939	**Heaslip** creates etching *Airport* (included in *A Treasury of American Prints,* edited by Thomas Craven)
1939	Pan Am starts North Atlantic airmail service from Long Island to Portugal and France
1939	Jacqueline Cochrane sets new speed record of 305 mph in P-35
1939	P-39 fighter is tested by Bell
1939	Consolidated delivers XPBY-5A (world's largest amphibian) to U.S. Navy
1939	World War II starts with Great Britain and France declaring war on Germany
1939	**Knight** founds Clayton Knight Committee to recruit volunteer American ferry pilots for the Canadian war effort. The organization is disbanded after the U.S. enters the war in 1941
1939	**Heaslip** begins illustrating the major battles and events of the war weekly for the *New York Times Sunday Magazine*

Opposite page: American Legion Monthly (September 1938) offered this colorful cover by William Heaslip with a challenge to readers to see if they knew their airplanes. A diagram with the correct identification was found on page 62. (*American Legion Monthly*)

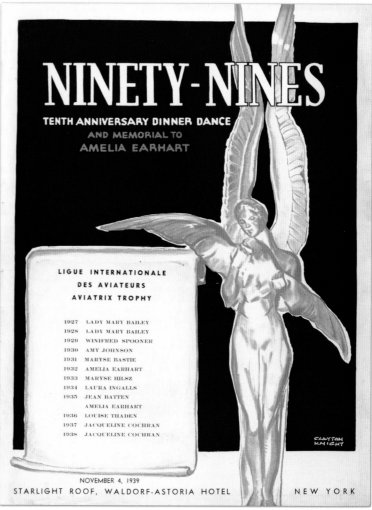

Clayton Knight illustrated these program covers for the Ninety Nines in 1939. The Ninety Nines, founded in 1929, is an organization of outstanding women in aviation. (Clayton Christopher Knight)

1939   Introduction of major passenger, military, and private airplanes during 1930s included: Boeing B-17, Boeing 247; Douglas DC-3, Douglas DC-4; Martin 130, Boeing 314, Lockheed 10 & 14; Sikorsky S-42; B-10; P-38, P-40; PT-13; Lockheed Orion; Beechcraft Staggerwing; Piper Cub; Stinson 105

1940   Nazi forces capture Low Countries; France surrenders in June

1940   Battle of Britain begins

1940   Pan American introduces pressurized Boeing 307 Stratoliner airliners

1940   Jacqueline Cochrane sets record over 200-kilometer course in P-35 at 331 mph

1940   U.S. Army and Navy allow France and England to equip with latest U.S. designs

1940   More new military aircraft designs and enhanced performance of aircraft appear between 1939–47, including the Grumman Wildcat, Vought Corsair, B-24

1941   Igor Sikorsky, design engineer, remains aloft in helicopter 1 hour, 32 minutes

1941   Republic P-47, large and powerful fighter, tested

1941   Soviet Union invaded by Nazi Germany in surprise attack

1941   **Knight** attends Collier Trophy event as director of British ferry command. Collier Trophy presented to the United States Army Air Forces and America's airlines

1941   **Knight** illustrates *Modern Flight* by Cloyd Cleavenger, published by Noble & Noble, New York

1941   **Knight** writes and illustrates comic book *The Romance of Flying*

1941   Innovative Northrup Flying Wing flies

1941   Pearl Harbor attacked by Japan on December 7. U.S. declares war on Japan the next day and on Germany and Italy four days later after both countries declare war on the United States

1941   Flying Tigers (American volunteer group) experience first successful combat mission

1942   Japanese forces sweep through western Pacific, but tide of battle turns with American victory at Battle of Midway in June

1942   **Knight** reports to the American people with illustrations and newspaper columns about his visit to the newly operational USAAF VIII Bomber Command in Europe

1942   Captain Charles Kegelman was decorated by Major General Carl Spaatz with the Distinguished Service Cross for heroism during the first mission of the VIII Bomber Command on July 4, 1942. See page 233 for Clayton Knight's illustration of this event.

1942   Guadalcanal invaded, first American offensive in Pacific

1942   **Heaslip** begins illustrating series of promotional point-of-sale material for Coca-Cola featuring USAAF and U.S. Naval aircraft. New material is developed as new aircraft designs become operational

1942   U.S. and British forces assault Fascist occupied North Africa from the west

1942   **Heaslip** and **Knight** illustrate posters in support of manpower recruitment and military production

1942   **Heaslip** illustrates covers of war industry magazines

1942   **Heaslip** illustrates cover of sheet music *Our Country*, composed by Jacques Wolfe, lyrics by Merrick Fifield McCarthy, published by G. Schirmer Inc, New York

1943   Russians inflict massive defeat on German Sixth Army at Stalingrad, tide of battle turns in the European war

1943   Gen. MacArthur and Adm. Nimitz begin island-hopping assaults along two routes to Japan

1943   **Heaslip** illustrates *Know Your War Planes*, showing 26 American fighting planes in action and 96 authentic silhouettes of warplanes of the world; published by Coca-Cola

1943   **Knight** illustrates *Malta-Spitfire: the Story of a Fighter Pilot*, by George F. Beurling, published by Farrar & Rinehart, New York

1943   Sicily and Italy assaulted by Allied forces; Italy capitulates

1944   **Heaslip** illustrates *The Enemy Knows Your Planes* for War Department, Bureau of Public Relations, Industrial Services Division

1944   D-Day: Allies invade France at Normandy; Paris liberated in August

Captain Charles Clark Kegelman proudly wears his Distinguished Service Cross as Major General Carl Spaatz looks on.

CERTIFIED TO BE A WORK
BY WILLIAM J. HEASLIP.

Estate Executor

from the Painting by WILLIAM HEASLIP ®
AMERICAN ARTISTS GROUP, N. Y.
No. 15413   PRINTED IN U.S.A.

1944 Christmas card by William Heaslip features U.S. Army Air Forces C-47 and C-54 cargo and transport aircraft. (Allan M. Heaslip)

1944	**Knight** begins work as a U.S. Army Air Forces correspondent and artist assigned to Alaska, the Aleutians, and Central Pacific war zones
1944	Nazis begin battle of the Bulge, a last-ditch major assault against British and American forces
1945	Iwo Jima invaded by U.S. Marines
1945	B-29 raids begin to destroy Japanese cities by creating raging fire storms
1945	Okinawa invaded by U.S. Marine and Army forces
1945	Nazi Germany surrenders on May 8
1945	Atomic bombs dropped on Hiroshima and Nagasaki; Japan capitulates
1945	**Knight** invited aboard USS *Missouri* for Japanese surrender ceremony, September 2. Knight creates lithograph of massive overflight of U.S. Army and Navy fighters and bombers as the surrender document is being signed.
1945	World War II ends

Notes

Introduction

1   Robert Wohl, *The Spectacle of Flight: Aviation and The Western Imagination, 1920–1950* (New Haven, CT: Yale University Press, 2005), p. 4.
2   "Publishing," *The New Encyclopaedia Britannica*, vol. 26, Macropaedia, Knowledge in Depth (Chicago: Encyclopaedia Britannica, 1995), pp. 436–444.
3   Dominick A. Pisano *et al.*, *Legend, Memory and the Great War in the Air* (Seattle: University of Washington Press, 1992), p. 35. See also Robert Cunningham, *Aces High* (St. Louis: General Dynamics, 1978), p. 15.
4   "Douglas World Cruiser," https://en.wikipedia.org/wiki/Douglas_World_Cruiser/.
5   "Aviation Becomes Big Business," America By Air, Smithsonian National Air and Space Museum, https://airandspace.si.edu/exhibitions/america-by-air/online/innovation/innovation04.cfm (accessed December 1, 2018).
6   "A History of US Airline Regulation, Part 1: 1911–26: Early Growth Prior to Regulation," https://thetravelinsider.info/airlinemismanagement/airlineregulation1.htm/. See also Nick Komons, *Bonfires to Beacons: Federal Civil Aviation Policy Under the Air Commerce Act, 1926–38* (Washington, DC: Smithsonian Institution Press, 1989).
7   Thomas G. Foxworth, *The Speed Seekers* (New York: Doubleday and Company, Inc., 1976), p.29.
8   Ibid., pp. 49–55.
9   David Ingalls, "Navy Flier and Businessman, 86, Dies April 29, 1985," United Press International.
10 Nick Komans, *Bonfires to Beacons: Federal Civil Aviation Policy under the Air Commerce Act, 1926–38* (Washington, DC: Smithsonian Institution Press, 1989).
11 Receiving less attention was the 1927 Dole Air Race across the Pacific, sponsored by James Dole of the Dole Pineapple interests and inspired by Lindbergh's flight over the Atlantic. The $25,000 prize was won by Art Goebel and William V. Davis, Jr., who flew from Oakland, California, to Honolulu, Hawaii, in 26 hours, 17 minutes.
12 Kenneth S. Davis, *The Hero: Charles A. Lindbergh and the American Dream* (Garden City, NY: Doubleday, 1959), p. 253.
13 Interview with Bob Cavanagh at author Hamady's home, July 15, 1996.
14 Kenneth S. Davis, *The Hero: Charles A. Lindbergh and the American Dream* (Neuilly sur Seine: Ulan Press, 2012).
15 "United Airlines," https://en.wikipedia.org/wiki/United_Airlines/. Note Boeing's earlier connection with United Airlines and Transport Company and its use of Boeing Trimotor airplanes.
16 Lawrence H. Suid, *Guts & Glory: Great American War Movies* (Reading: Addison-Wesley Publishing Co., 1978), p. 33.
17 Donald L. Barlett, and James B. Steele, *Howard Hughes: His Life and Madness*, a reissue of the 1979 title *Empire: The Life, Legend, and Madness of Howard Hughes* (New York: W.W. Norton & Co., 2004), p. 68.
18 "Ford Trimotor," https://en.wikipedia.org/wiki/Ford_Trimotor/.
19 "Tailspin Tommy," https://en.wikipedia.org/wiki/Tailspin_Tommy/.
20 Chris Rojek, *Celebrity* (London: Reaktion Books, 2001), p. 10, 54.
21 Dominick A. Pisano, "The Heroic Age of Aeronautics" in *Flight: A Celebration of 100 Years in Art and Literature*, edited by Anne Collins Goodyear, Roger Launius, Anthony Springer, and Bertram Ulrich (New York: Welcome Books, 2003).
22 Michael Kammen, *American Culture, American Tastes: Social Change and the Twentieth Century* (New York: Basic Books, 1999) p. 171. See also Neal Gabler, *Winchell: Gossip, Power and the Culture of Celebrity* (New York: Knopf Publishing Group, 1995).

Chapter 1

1   *Rochester City Directory* (1908–09) (1909–10) (1911–12) (1913–14), Rundel Public Library, Rochester, NY.
2   Interview with Suzanne Meyn Daniels, February 01, 2006.
3   *Post Express,* Rochester, NY, September 30, 1885.
4   Art Institute of Chicago, Registration Card, October 16, 1911–June 20, 1913.
5   Bulletin of Mechanics Institute, Department Circular, Applied & Fine Arts, Bevier Memorial, April 15, 1910.
6   Rochester Institute of Technology Archive and Special Collections, Wallace Library, Rochester, NY.
7   James Watrous, *A Century of American Printmaking 1880–1980* (Madison: University of Wisconsin Press, 1984), p. 50.
8   Louis S. Casey, *Curtiss: The Hammondsport Era 1907–1915* (Crown Publishers, 1981), p. 64–67.
9   The Art Institute of Chicago, *Circular of Instruction of the School of Drawing, Painting, Modelling, Decorative Designing, Normal Instruction, Illustration and Architecture* (Chicago: The Art Institute of Chicago, 1911–12), pp. 15–17.
10 Art Institute of Chicago, Registration card, October 16, 1911–June 20, 1913.
11 "Drawing the Akron," in *Palladium-Item* (Richmond, Indiana: October 31, 1942), p. 6.
12 Interview with Hilary Knight, February 12, 2006.
13 Everett Shinn declined the invitation to join the AAPS.
14 Bruce Altshuler, *The Avant-Garde in Exhibition: New Art in the 20th Century* (Berkley, CA: University of California Press, 1998), p. 60.

15 Milton W. Brown, *The Story of the Armory Show* (New York: The Joseph H. Hirschhorn Foundation, 1963), p. 89.

16 Altshuler, *The Avant-Garde in Exhibition: New Art in the 20th Century*, pp. 67–69.

17 Ibid., pp. 198–201.

18 Walt Reed and Roger Reed, *The Illustrator in America 1880–1980* (New York: The Society of Illustrators, 1984), p. 84.

19 Interview with Clayton Knight, Aero Society Podcast, Royal Aeronautical Society, London.

20 "Vox Poppers Foiled by the Art of Clayton Knight," mock publication edited by G. Alan Chidsey, Great Neck, NY, July 1938.

21 Harry Kelley, *The Ferrer Modern School* (Stelton, NJ: The Modern School Association of North America, 1920).

22 It should be noted that, unlike other members of the Goldman coterie, George Bellows favored America's entry into the battle raging in Europe, which had been set in motion by the inauspicious assassination of Archduke Franz Ferdinand, heir to the throne of the Austro-Hungarian Empire, in June 1914.

23 Fernanda Perrone, *An Anarchist Experiment: The Modern School of Stelton, New Jersey*, exhibition catalogue, (New Brunswick, NJ: Rutgers University Libraries, 1996).

24 Peter Kilduff, "An Interview with Clayton Knight, No. 206 Squadron RAF" in *Cross & Cockade* (v. 10, no. 4, Winter 1969), pp. 29–30.

25 Ibid., pp. 32–35.

26 Ibid., pp. 36–37.

27 Ibid, pp. 41–42.

28 Burke Davis, *War Bird: The Life and Times of Elliott White Springs* (Chapel Hill and London: The University of North Carolina Press, 1987), p. 86.

29 "Vox Poppers Foiled by the Art of Clayton Knight," mock publication edited by G. Alan Chidsey, Great Neck, NY, July 1938.

30 Ibid.

31 "Conducted by Our Readers," in *U.S. Air Services* (September 1920), p. 33.

32 Another acclaimed artist known for his work with Stehli was the photographer Edward Steichen, who had been an aerial reconnaissance photographer during World War I.

33 Interview with Hilary Knight, April 24, 2006.

34 *Vox Poppers Foiled by the Art of Clayton Knight,* mock publication edited by G. Alan Chidsey, Great Neck, NY, July 1938.

35 Elliott White Springs, "Back in Seventeen," in *U.S. Air Services* (June 1926). Knight may have made a distinction between this work and his earlier magazine covers because those covers were derived from preexisting art work.

36 Clayton Knight, *Log Book: Payments from Jobs 1927–43*, at the Thomas J. Dodd Research Center, University of Connecticut, Storrs, CT.

Chapter 2

1 *The Toronto Daily Star*, February 3, 1902, p. 1.

2 Register of Deaths, County of York, 1900. Archives of Ontario, Toronto, Canada; MS935; Reel: 95.

3 Archives, Merrymount Children's Centre, London, Ontario.

4 Letter from Ethel Heaslip Doherty, London, Ontario, to Owen Billman, Mayfield, New York, December 14, 1970.

5 Excerpt from Protestant Orphan's Home Minute Book, 1906–1917, Archives of the Merrymount Children's Centre, London, Ontario.

6 Archives, Merrymount Children's Centre, London, Ontario.

7 Archives, Children's Aid Society, New York.

8 Interview with Claus Breede, Director/Curator, Royal Canadian Regiment Museum, London, Ontario, September 06, 2006.

9 Interview with Judy Heaslip Biggs, July 21, 2006.

10 Interview with Allen Heaslip, July 17, 2006.

11 Death Records, County of Middlesex, Division of London City, October 25, 1918, p. 294.

12 Interview with Allan Heaslip, July 17, 2006.

13 Interview with Leith River, Archivist, Merrymount Children's Centre, London, Ontario, September 26, 2006; Letter from Ethel Heaslip Doherty, London, Ontario, to Owen Billman, Mayfield, NY, December 14, 1970.

14 Interview with Caroline Wiley, January 13, 2007.

15 News clippings, *London Free Press*, July 1929.

16 Nancy Geddes Poole, *The Art of London 1830–1980* (London, Ontario: Blackpool Press, 1984), p. 79.

17 Ibid., p. 81.

18 Bill Corfield, *The Lawsons of London* (Surrey, British Columbia: Timberholme Books, 2001), pp. 15–31.

19 Interview with Allan Heaslip, July 17, 2006.

20 Walt and Roger Reed, *The Illustrator in America 1880–1980: A Century of Illustration* (New York: The Society of Illustrators, Madison Square Press, 1984), p. 128.

21 *A New London, 1914: Selections from the Orr Photographic Collection*, catalogue, Lorraine Ivey Shuttleworth Community Gallery, 2006.

22 Orlo Miller, *London 200: An Illustrated History* (London, Ontario: Phelps Publishing Company, 1992), p. 159.

23 Bill Corfield & Hume Cronyn, *London's Flying Pioneers* (Canada: Lochaven Publishers, 1997), p. 8.

24 Bishop was credited with 75 confirmed victories by war's end to include 72 aircraft and 3 balloons along with five unconfirmed victories, all aircraft.

25 Bishop visited Heaslip's studio on a promotional visit to New York during WWII. Henry Burden, Bishop's brother-in-law and Canadian war ace, was also an acquaintance.

26 *Aviation in Canada 1917–1918*, compiled by Alan Sullivan, Lt. RAF (Toronto: Rous & Mann Limited, 1919), pp. 234–237.

27 Heaslip received a portion of his training from Vernon Castle, renowned in show business as half of the dance team of Vernon and Irene Castle. Heaslip was on the line waiting for an instructor when Castle and a student died in the fiery crash of a Jenny training plane.

28 Aviation in Canada 1917–1918, compiled by Alan Sullivan, Lt. RAF (Toronto: Rous & Mann Limited, 1919), p. 183.

29 Ibid., p. 184.

30 Ibid., p. 188.

31 Interview with Allan Heaslip, October 14, 2006.

32 Ibid.

33 Ibid.

34 Eliot Clark, *History of the National Academy of Design, 1825–1953* (New York: Columbia University Press, 1954), p. 16.

35 Ibid., p. 158.

36 New York Historical Society archives, NYC: History of the 7th Regiment, NYNG: Volume BV: Report Book, Morning Report.

37 New York Historical Society archives, NYC: History of the 7th Regiment, NYNG: Seventh Regiment Gazette: Folders 1–6.

38 *Faces of Change: The Art of Ivan G. Olinsky 1878–1962*, catalogue and essay by Hildegard Cummings, William Benton Museum of Art, University of Connecticut, Storrs, 1995, p. 9.

39 Interview with Marshall Price, Assistant Curator, National Academy Museum, New York, October 20, 2006.

40 James F. Suydam, elected to the Academy in 1861, bequeathed the sum of $50,000 in his will to establish a permanent fund "the income of which shall be appropriated by the council in such manner as they in their discretion shall deem most desirable to the purposes of instruction in the Arts of Design."

41 National Academy of Design, Registration Card (William J. Heaslip), September 22, 1919.

42 "Londoner Wins Coveted Honor," *The Free Press,* London, Ontario, April 29, 1920, p. 2.

43 The National Academy of Design, one of the oldest and most prestigious organizations of its kind in the country, was definitely "old guard"—and not particularly sympathetic to the new realism embodied in the work of Sloan and others of the Ash Can School.

44 The Art Students League of New York archives, New York.

45 Interview with Allan Heaslip, November 12, 2006. Edith gifted Clare with a set of "Gaudy Dutch" dinnerware to celebrate the birth of Clare's daughter Jacqueline Neva. Letter from Allan Heaslip, June 15, 2018.

46 Interview with Walt Reed, Illustration House, New York, November 27, 2006.

47 Retta Blaney, "The Knights of the Round Table Do Lunch," *American Journalism Review,* vol. 15 (issue 7), September 1993, p. 15.

48 E. Jay Doherty, "Plane Painter," *Flying* magazine, January 1943, vol. XXXII, no. 1, p. 115.

49 Interview with Walt Reed, Illustration House, New York, November 27, 2006.

50 The American Legion archives, National Headquarters, Indianapolis, Indiana.

51 The photos in this book are the sole opinions of the artist and authors. Absolutely no content, except for the use of the words "The American Legion" and/or the use of The American Legion's emblem/logo is endorsed, reviewed, approved or work product of the National American Legion staff.

Chapter 3

1 George Damman, *90 Years of Ford* (Minneapolis, MN: Motor Books International, 1993), p. 15.

2 Howard Mingoes, editor, *The Aircraft Yearbook for 1936* (New York: Aeronautical Chamber of Commerce, 1936), pp. 11–15. A wealth of detailed statistical information on military and commercial aviation sales and development is found in the annual issues of *Aircraft Yearbooks,* published by the Aeronautical Chamber of Commerce between 1919 and 1972.

3 *Liberty* (general interest magazine): https://en.wikipedia.org/wiki/Liberty_(general_interest_magazine)

4 Great War and Modern Memory Gallery, Smithsonian Institution, National Air and Space Museum, Washington, DC. Gallery opened in November 1991 and closed for renovation in 2019.

5 Clayton Knight, *Pilot's Luck* (Philadelphia: David McKay Company, 1929), 13.

6 Galbi Think! New Ideas, Data, and Analysis in Communications Policy, U.S. Annual Advertising Spending Since 1919, www.GalbiThink.org.

7 Walter and Roger Reed, *The Illustrator in America: 1860–2000* (New York: The Society of Illustrators, 1967), 111.

8 Clayton Knight, *Log Book (1927–1943),* (Storrs: Thomas J. Dodd Research Center, University of Connecticut).

9 *Vineyard Gazette,* Martha's Vineyard, NY. July 25, 1958.

10 E. J. Doherty, "Plane Painter," *Flying,* (Chicago: Ziff Davis Publishing), vol. XXXII, January 1943, 58.

11 Galbi Think! New Ideas, Data, and Analysis in Communications Policy, U.S. Annual Advertising Spending Since 1919, www.GalbiThink.org.

12 Clayton Knight, *Log Book (1927–1943),* (Storrs: Thomas J. Dodd Research Center, University of Connecticut).

13 Ibid.

14 Pan American Airways System, (New York, June 1933), p. 20.

15 *Cosmopolitan,* (New York: International Magazine Company, Inc.) month and page not available, 1933.

16 Clayton Knight, *Log Book (1927–1943),* (Storrs: Thomas J. Dodd Research Center, University of Connecticut).

17 Ibid.

18 Frank Tichenor, the publisher of the prestigious *Aero Digest* magazine, became the publisher of the failing *Sportsman Pilot* magazine in 1930. Cyril "Cy" Caldwell, *Aero Digest's* influential associate editor, prevailed upon his boss to appoint William Heaslip as the consulting art director, later art director for the magazine. This is borne out by correspondence (various dates from August 1931) between Heaslip and Caldwell shared with the author by Allan M. Heaslip. Caldwell informed Heaslip of his activities to promote Heaslip's career, and Heaslip responded with a very gracious letter of appreciation. Cyril Caldwell remained a patron and good friend to Heaslip for many years.

Chapter 4

1 Thomas B. Parker, *Frank Von der Lancken: Artist and Educator* (New York: Hirschl & Adler Galleries, 2001), p. 23.

2 Ibid, pp. 1213._

3 Elliott White Springs, *War Birds: Diary of an Unknown Aviator* (New York: The Empyrean Press, 1951), foreword.

4 Curtiss Sprague, *How to Make Linoleum Blocks* (Pelham, NY: Bridgman Publishers), p. 64.

5 Clayton Knight, *Log Book: Payments from Jobs 1927–1943* (Storrs, CT: Thomas J. Dodd Research Center, University of Connecticut).

6 "British Flying Ace Is Guest of Macy's," in *New York World–Telegram,* April 27, (probably) 1928. Clayton Knight family archives.

7 "Macy's Opens Air Show: Week's Display Includes Device for Testing Prospective Fliers" in *New York Times* (March 30, 1928).

8 *Christmas Catalogue 1929* (New York: R.H. Macy), p. 31.

9 "The Greatest Aerial Warfare Photos Go Down in Flames" in *Smithsonian Magazine* (January 1985), pp. 103–113.

10 "First International Exhibit of Famous Aviation Prints and Photographs at G.P. Putnam's Sons" in *This Week in New York* (February 8–14, 1931).

11 "Aviators Dance in Aid of Fund" in *New York Times* (February 12, 1932).

12 "A Sports Exhibition: Art in Review" in *New York Times* (December 13, 1932).

13 Edward Alden Jewell, "Noted American Illustrators Display their Craft in Grand Central Galleries Show" in *New York Times* (November 4, 1933).

14 Alling M. Clements, "Collection of Paintings by American Illustrators Has Strong Appeal to Public" in *Democrat and Chronicle,* Rochester, NY (March 15, 1931), p. 5D.

15 *WPA Artwork in Non-Federal Repositories, Edition II* (U.S. General Services Administration, Public Buildings Service, Historic Buildings

and the Arts Center of Expertise, Fine Arts Program, December 1999), p. iii.

16 Roger Crum, "Constructing the Image of Flight: The Wright Brothers, Photography and their Visual Heritage" in *History of Photography* (vol. 28, no. 1, Spring 2004), pp. 15–17.

17 *Preserving the Wright Brothers Legacy: Proceedings of the Symposium October 22, 1999 with a Guide to Resources on the Wright Brothers* (Dayton, OH: Dayton and Montgomery Public Library), 2001.

18 Clayton Knight, *Log Book: Payments from Jobs 1927–43* (Storrs, CT: Thomas J. Dodd Research Center, University of Connecticut).

19 Unsourced article by Kent Curtis circa 1934. Clayton Knight family archives.

20 Cheryl R. Ganz, *The 1933 Chicago World's Fair: A Century of Progress* (Champaign: University of Illinois Press, 2008), pp. 138–39.

21 Peter Hastings Falk, ed., *Who Was Who in American Art* (Madison, CT: Sound View Press, 1999), p. 2124.

22 Elisabeth Luther Cary, "Present Versus Past: Brooklyn Society of Etchers and Work Shown by the Institute of Graphic Art," in *New York Times* (December 9, 1928).

23 Alexander Gottlieb, "An Ancient Art Linked to a Romantic New Science" in *Brooklyn Daily Eagle* (February 24, 1929), pp. 8–9.

24 Milton W. Brown, *The Story of the Armory Show* (New York: The Joseph H. Hirshhorn Foundation, New York Graphic Society, 1963), p. 273.

25 James Watrous, *A Century of American Printmaking 1880–1980* (Madison: University of Wisconsin Press, 1984), p. 67.

26 "Howard U Artist Exhibits at Smithsonian Institute," in *California Eagle* (April 8, 1948), p. 2.

27 B. F. Morrow, "Highlights of Copper: William Heaslip" in *Prints,* (New York: Prints Publishing Company, vol. v, no. 2, January 1935).

28 Interview with Allan M. Heaslip, November 29, 2006.

29 "First International Exhibit of Famous Aviation Prints and Photographs at G.P. Putnam's Sons" in *This Week in New York* (February 8–14, 1931).

30 Advertisement in *Sportsman Pilot* (August 1932), p. 43.

31 Watrous, *A Century of American Printmaking 1880–1980*, pp. 108–9.

32 Ibid., p. 109.

33 Interview with Allan M. Heaslip, July 8, 2000.

34 *International Aeronautical Art Exhibition* catalog, Los Angeles Museum (February 5–19, 1937).

35 Charles H. Gale , *"Regarding Safety,"* illustrated by William Heaslip, *Sportsman Pilot* (April 15, 1937), p. 6.

36 Thomas Craven*, ed., A Treasury of American Prints: A Selection of One Hundred Etchings and Lithographs by the Foremost Living American Artists,* (New York: Simon & Schuster, 1939), plate no. 53.

37 *The Society of American Etchers Twenty-Fourth Annual Exhibition* catalog, National Arts Club, (Dec 7–28, 1939), p. 8.

38 Letter from John Taylor Arms, President of the Society of American Etchers, to William Heaslip, December 23, 1939. In William Heaslip family archives.

39 Interview with Allan M. Heaslip, November 29, 2006.

40 "Joseph Margulies: New Print Catalogue Raisonné & Retrospective Exhibition," in *Journal of the Print World* (Fall 2006, vol. 29, no. 4), p. 26.

41 Interview with Allan M. Heaslip, July 21, 2006.

42 Advertisement in *Sportsman Pilot* (February 1933), p. 42.

Chapter 5

1 Edgar Wallace, *Tam o' the Scoots* (Boston: Small, Maynard & Company, 1919).

2 A. Scott Berg, *Lindbergh* (New York: G. P. Putnam's Sons, 1998), p. 52.

3 Peter Hunt, ed., *Children's Literature: An Illustrated History* (New York: Oxford University Press, 1995), pp. 120–121.

4 Fred Erisman, *Boys' Books, Boys' Dreams and the Mystique of Flight* (Fort Worth: Texas Christian University Press, 2006), p. 29.

5 Gordon Stuart, *Boy Scouts of the Air at Greenwood School* (Chicago: Reilly & Britton Company, 1912).

6 Harry K. Hudson, *A Bibliography of Hard-Cover Boys' Books* (Tampa: Data Print, 1977), p. 44.

7 Erisman, *Boys' Books, Boys' Dreams and the Mystique of Flight*, p. 23.

8 Roy Rockwood, *Dave Dashaway: Air Champion* (New York: Cupples & Leon Company, 1915), p. 10.

9 Erisman, *Boys' Books, Boys' Dreams and the Mystique of Flight*, p. 19.

10 John T. Dizer, "The Birth and Boyhood of Boys' Life" in *Scouting* magazine (November–December 1994).

11 E. R. Hagemann, "Raoul F. Whitfield: A Star with the Mask" in *Armchair Detective* (Summer 1980).

12 Collectors' Cards–July 1928, in *Boys' Life* magazine (Texas: Boy Scouts of America, 1996).

13 James J. Sloan Jr., *Wings of Honor* (Pennsylvania: Schiffer Publishing Ltd., 1994), p. 219.

14 "Forty Planes Participate in Air Meet on Municipal Field," in *New York Times* (November 12, 1922).

15 Interview with Allan Heaslip, June 21, 2013.

16 Bruce Lambert, "Harold Miller, 89, Navy Publicist" in *New York Times* (May 18, 1992).

17 "Fascinating—Appealing—Achieving," in *Boys' Life* (October 1935), p. 29.

18 Sloan, *Wings of Honor*, p. 219

19 "Boys' Life Aviation Contest," in *Boys' Life* (December 1935), p. 15.

20 "The Press Boys," in *Time* (August 12, 1929).

21 Dave Kyle, "Rocket Ships Came Later" in *Mimosa* (December 2000), p. 27.

22 Walt and Roger Reed, *The Illustrator in America 1880–1980* (New York: The Society of Illustrators, Madison Square Press), p. 125.

23 Timothy J. O'Callaghan, *The Aviation Legacy of Henry & Edsel Ford* (Ann Arbor: Proctor Publications, 2002), p. 3.

24 Ibid., p. 4.

25 Ibid., pp. 19–20.

26 Ibid., p. 48.

27 "Enlist for Air Marking!" in *American Boy* (December 1928), p. 46.

28 "Get Your Airplane Models Ready" in *American Boy* (June 1929), p. 18.

29 "Model Builders Meet the President" in *American Boy* (June 1929), p. 77.

30 Merrill Hamburg, "Here's a Wakefield Cup Plane" in *American Boy* (March 1930), p. 25.

31 "Model Builders Meet the President" in *American Boy* (June 1929), p. 77.

32 "History Preserved: In the Air" in *Model Aviation* (May 2012).

33 "Joan Diehl McCauley: Pioneer Aviator, Arts Patron, Mother of Sen. John Heinz" in *Pittsburgh Post-Gazette* (September 25, 1999).

34 "Noted Aviator Becomes Heinz' Star Salesman" in *Advertising Age* (May 26, 1934), p. 6.

35 Interview with Edwin Lehew, archivist for Heinz, August 9, 2000.

36 "John N. Wheeler is Dead at 87: Ex-Head of NANA Syndicate" in *New York Times* (October 15, 1972).

37 According to an interview conducted on February 4, 2014, with Helena Wright of the National Museum of American History, Smithsonian Institution, Washington DC, other processes in the production of these cards included letterpress and collotype (photogelatine). The introduction of collotype, which produces rich, flat areas of color, would have limited the production run of cards, a fact that may explain the scarcity of the Series One cards. See also Edward B. Gotthelf, "Printing Differentials" in the *Third Annual Edition of the Advertising & Publishing Production Yearbook* (New York: Colton Press), p. 191.

38 Draft Agreement between Maxon Inc./H. J. Heinz Company and Roscoe Turner, March 1935, (Laramie: American Heritage Center, University of Wyoming).

39 *Water Colors and Black and White Drawings by Clayton Knight* catalogue (Washington, DC: National Gallery of Art, Smithsonian Institution), July 6–August 31, 1934.

40 Correspondence from Franklin Bell to Colonel Roscoe Turner, October 15, 1935 (Laramie: American Heritage Center, University of Wyoming).

41 Allen McHenry research posting, Vintage Non-Sports Card Chat Board, November 30, 2011.

42 *Let's Go Flying: Famous Flights and Air Routes of the World,* (Pittsburgh: H. J. Heinz Company, 1937).

Chapter 6

1 Charles J. Gross, *American Military Aviation: The Indispensable Arm* (College Station: Texas A&M University Press, 2004) p. 51.

2 Ibid., p. 64.

3 Ibid., p. 61.

4 Ibid., p. 57–58.

5 Ibid., p. 67.

6 *Aero Digest*, June 1931, p. 35.

7 *Sportsman Pilot*, June 1931, p. 13.

8 Ibid., p. 13–14.

9 Ibid., p. 14.

10 *Aero Digest*, June 1931, p. 36.

11 Ibid, p. 36.

12 *Sportsman Pilot*, June 1931, p. 54.

13 Maj. Gen. Benjamin Foulois and Col. Carroll V. Glines, *Foulois: One Man Air Force* (Dallas: NEXCEL Media/Flying Group, 2010) p. 275.

14 Floyd Gibbons, "Problem 14" in *Cosmopolitan* magazine (May 1933), p. 60–63.

15 Thesis by Ryan David Wadle, *United States Naval Fleet Problems and the Development of Carrier Aviation, 1929–33* (Texas: A&M, 2005) https://core.ac.uk/download/pdf/4269776.pdf.

16 Howard Mingos, ed., *The Aircraft Year Book for 1936* (New York: Aeronautical Chamber of Commerce, 1936), pp. 11–15.

17 U.S. Department of State, Publication 1983, Peace and War: United States Foreign Policy, 1931–1941. (Washington, DC: U.S. Government Printing Office, 1943), pp. 79–86.

Chapter 7

1 Marc Wortman, *1941: Fighting the Shadow War* (New York: Atlantic Monthly Press, 2016), p. 179.

2 Clarence Simonsen's excellent summary of the activities of the Clayton Knight Committee can be found online at http://www. bombercommandmuseum.ca/s,claytonknight.html.

3 Ibid.

4 Stephen J. Monchak, "Syndicates" in *Editor and Publisher* (November 2, 1940), p. 3.

5 Ibid.

6 E. Jay Doherty, "The Plane Painter" in *Flying* (January 1943), p. 116.

7 The Sunday Supplement series, which was distributed by *Wide World Photos* to 22 newspapers around the country, ceased publication in mid-1942. From December 7, 1941, until the series ended, William Heaslip had a brief opportunity to show the United States at war during a time when it seemed that the enemy was unstoppable on all fronts, especially in the Pacific Theater.

8 Wortman, *1941: Fighting the Shadow War*, p. 335.

9 Theodore M Hamady, "Fighting Machines for the Air Service, AEF" in *Air Power History* (Fall 2004), p. 36.

Chapter 8

1 Theodore M. Hamady, "Fighting Machines for the Air Service, AEF" in *Air Power History* (Fall 2004), p. 35.

2 In-depth information on Colin P. Kelly can be found by searching on his name at www.floridamemory.com

3 An excellent summary of Douglas MacArthur's leadership can be found at https://css.history.com/topics/douglas-macarthur

4 *The Romance of Flying* (Philadelphia: David McKay Co., 1942).

5 Combat chronology for 1942 is available at the VIII Air Force Historical Society, www.8thafhs.org.

6 For more information, search on the Boeing 307 Stratoliner *Clipper Flying Cloud* at www.airandspace.si.edu.

7 https://www.newspapers.com (Clayton Knight, Oct., Nov., Dec. 1942)

8 Frederick Allen, *Secret Formula: How Brilliant Marketing and Relentless Salesmanship Made Coca-Cola the Best-Known Product in the World* (New York: Harper Collins, 1992), p. 242.

9 Ibid., p. 253.

10 Ibid., p. 255.

11 Mark Prendergast, *For God, Country and Coca-Cola: The Unauthorized History of the Great American Soft Drink and the Company That Makes It* (New York: Scribner and Sons, 1993), p. 88.

12 Allan Petretti, *Petretti's Coca-Cola Collectibles Price Guide* (Crestline Publications, 1997).

13 Interview with Allan Heaslip, July 16, 2012. Some sources credit William Heaslip with having illustrated all four sets of Coca-Cola World War II military and naval aircraft hangars. The author (Hamady) and Allan Heaslip, son of William Heaslip and executor of his estate, independently concluded that William Heaslip had not done the illustrations for Set No. 1. The reasons are manifold: Heaslip did not sign any of the Set No. 1 hangers, although his signature appears prominently on each successive hanger set. Moreover, Heaslip, who was noted for his careful attention to detail and consistency in portraying aircraft accurately, maintained an extensive photo and article archive. A comparison of the depiction of the B-17 D Flying Fortress in Set

No. 1 with Heaslip's signed portrayals of the same aircraft reveals some significant omissions and errors on the illustration in Set No. 1— among them, the lack of wing panels and ailerons, pitot tubes, and football antennae on the nose, a stylistic difference in the portrayal of the propeller vortices, and an incorrect slope angle to the cockpit windshield.

The author and Allan Heaslip also examined Wiliam Heaslip's illustrations of the B-17 C bomber (similar to the D model, but without cowl flaps as flown by the U.S. Army Air Corps and the Royal Air Force) published in syndicated newspapers on August 31, 1941, and in *Look* magazine on February 10, 1942. Both believe that another illustrator, unidentified at the time of this writing, was hired by Snyder & Black to develop the illustrations for Set No. 1.

14 Gerald S. Beskin, "Public Relations: Publicity" in *National Bottlers Gazette* (March 1947), p. 169.

15 Petretti, *Petretti's Coca-Cola Collectibles Price Guide*, pp. 202-205. All illustrations in the hanger card series are shown in Petretti's book with the exception of Set No. 4, which appeared in 1945. Many of the aircraft illustrated in the final series were updated versions of the same aircraft shown in earlier series, now depicted in a more dramatic and more accurate fashion. The latter achievement was possible because it was clear by then that the Allies were close to winning a decisive victory, and as a result artist Heaslip was able to access a wealth of newly available photographs and detailed information about how the war was being won in the air. Set No. 4 was again offered in 1946, with a note that the pictures remained popular even after the war—in schools, clubs, veterans' hospitals, stores, and various other buildings.

16 For more information on the 315th Bomb Wing, see www.315bw.org/.

Chapter 9

1 Chris McCann, *Masterpieces: The Art History of Jigsaw Puzzles* (Collectors Press, Portland, OR, 1998), pp. 101, 114.

2 For information on the post-war bubble, see https://generalaviationnews. com/2013/02/04/the-post-war-bubble/.

3 Despite the fact that industry unit sales fell precipitously after 1946, a number of important aviation periodicals and associations continued to make wildly exaggerated projections for the future. It was only after predicable bankruptcies and massive layoffs took place that proponents of general aviation growth finally came to their senses and wild claims faded.

4 Walt and Roger Reed, *The Illustrator in America 1880–1980: A Century of Illustration* (New York: The Society of Illustrators, Madison Square Press), pp. 206–207.

5 Ibid., p. 252.

6 "A Commercial Artist Whose Work Has by No Means Been Confined to the Usual Range" in *Vineyard Gazette* (July 15, 1958).

7 Interview with James Dietz, by author Hamady, July 16, 2012. Dietz worked as an illustrator for many years. Today he is renowned as an award-winning artist focusing on World War I aircraft and classic automobiles.

8 "First Scheduled World Air Trip Here on the Dot" in *Chicago Tribune* (July 1, 1947), p. 3.

9 Fred Erisman, *Boys' Books, Boys' Dreams, and the Mystique of Flight* (Fort Worth: Texas Christian University Press, 2006), p. 266.

10 Interview with Hilary Knight, March 26, 2015.

11 Erisman, *Boys' Books, Boys' Dreams, and the Mystique of Flight*, p. 266.

12 Back cover of *Rockets and Missiles* by Clayton Knight, edited under the supervision of Dr. Paul E. Blackwood, approved by Oakes A. White, and illustrated by Clayton Knight.

13 Letter from John E. Carland, Office of the Assistant Secretary of Defense, Washington, DC, April 23, 1956.

14 Clayton Knight and Elliot White Springs continued their professional relationship into the post-WWII era with Knight's occasional commercial work for Springmaid fabrics. That their close personal relationship endured can best be demonstrated by Knight's tenure as a vice-president for the Lancaster and Chester rail line. This private railway served the Springs cotton mills between Chester and Fort Mill, South Carolina, with 29 miles of track—a vice-president selected for each mile. These VPs included such artistic celebrities as James Montgomery Flagg, Clayton Knight, and even Gypsy Rose Lee. The line's facetious train schedules and menus were not meant to be taken seriously: rather, they represented the larger-than-life personalities involved.

15 See the Archives & Special Collections at the Thomas J. Dodd Research Center, University of Connecticut, Storrs, CT.

16 Letter from William Morris, Editor, *American Heritage Dictionary*, to Clayton Knight, September 13, 1966.

17 Letter from Clayton Knight to William Morris, Editor-in-Chief, *Grolier International Encyclopedia*, March 20, 1963. Source: Knight Family Archives.

18 Letter from Clayton Knight to Edward S. Cady, Executive Editor, David McKay Company, January 25, 1966. Source: Knight Family Archives.

19 Letter from Clayton Knight to Lena Young de Grummond, University of Southern Mississippi, Hattiesburg, MS, January 19, 1966. Source: Knight Family Archives.

20 Letter from Clayton Knight to E. V. Rickenbacker, New York, NY, October 4, 1965. Source: Knight Family Archives.

21 Interview with Chris Knight (Clayton Knight III), June 2, 2015.

22 Letter from Robert Fawcett to Lt. Col George C. Bales, USAF, May 22, 1959. Source: USAF Art Collection, Pentagon.

23 Reed, *The Illustrator in America, 1880–1980*, pp. 220–221.

24 Letter from Victor Hammer to Clayton Knight, July 13, 1959. Source: Knight Family Archives.

25 Letter from Lt. Col George C. Bales, USAF, to Floyd Odlum, Atlas Corporation, 1959. Source: USAF Art Collection, Pentagon.

26 Letter from Clayton Knight to Bogart Rogers, March 23, 1966. Source: Knight Family Archives.

27 Interview, with Peter Kilduff, February 3, 2017.

28 Letter from William Morris, Editor of the *American Heritage Dictionary*, to Clayton Knight, January 20, 1965. Source: Knight Family Archives.

29 Letter from the Reverend Clarence Sickles, Heath Village, Hackettstown, NJ, January 19, 2017.

30 Letter, from Allan Heaslip, January 31, 2017.

31 Letter from the Reverend Clarence Sickles, Heath Village, Hackettstown, NJ, January 19, 2017.

32 Letter, from Allan Heaslip, January 31, 2017.

33 On the very day the Heaslip children buried their father, a letter arrived from Owen Billman, a long-time admirer who wanted to meet the man who had so influenced him as a youth through illustrations in *American Boy* and *Boys' Life*. He wanted to write an article on William Heaslip, but he was unable to complete the work. However, the authors are grateful to Mr. Billman for sharing with the authors of this book his compilation of letters and interviews with people long deceased.

Bibliography

Allen, Frederick. *Secret Formula: How Brilliant Marketing and Relentless Salesmanship Made Coca-Cola the Best-Known Product in the World.* New York: Harper Collins, 1992.

Altshuler, Bruce. *The Avant-Garde in Exhibition: New Art in the 20th Century.* Berkley, CA: University of California Press, 1998.

Anderson, John D., Jr., *Introduction to Flight.* New York: McGraw Hill Education, 2011.

Barlett, Donald L. and James B. Steele. *Howard Hughes: His Life and Madness.* New York: W. W. Norton & Co., 2004.

Bellows, Emma S. *George W. Bellows: His Lithographs.* New York and London: Alfred A. Knopf, Inc., 1927.

Berg, A. Scott. *Lindbergh.* New York: G. P. Putnam's Sons, 1998.

Brown, Milton W. *The Story of the Armory Show.* New York: The Joseph H. Hirschhorn Foundation, 1963.

Casey, Louis S. *The Hammondsport Era 1907–1915.* Crown Publishers, 1981.

Clark, Eliot. *History of the National Academy of Design, 1825–1953.* New York: Columbia University Press, 1954.

Cochrane, Jackie. *Jackie Cochrane: An Autobiography.* London: Bantam Press, 1987.

Cohn, Jan. *Covers of The Saturday Evening Post: Seventy Years of Outstanding Illustration from America's Favorite Magazine.* New York: Viking Studio Books, 1995.

Corfield, Bill. *The Lawsons of London.* Surrey, British Columbia: Timberholme Books, 2001.

Corfield, Bill and Hume Cronyn. *London's Flying Pioneers.* Canada: Lochaven Publishers, 1997.

Corn, Joseph J. *The Winged Gospel: America's Romance with Aviation.* Baltimore: The Johns Hopkins University Press, 2001.

Craven, Wesley Frank, ed. and James Lea Cate, ed. *The Army Air Forces in World War II* (7 volumes). Chicago: University of Chicago Press (under the auspices of the Office of Air Force History), 1948-1958.

Damman, George. *90 Years of Ford.* Minneapolis, MN: Motor Books International, 1993.

Davis, Burke. *War Bird: The Life and Times of Elliott White Springs.* Chapel Hill and London: the University of North Carolina Press, 1987.

Davis, Kenneth S. *The Hero: Charles A. Lindbergh and the American Dream.* Garden City, NY: Doubleday, 1959.

Erisman, Fred. *Boys' Books, Boys' Dreams and the Mystique of Flight.* Fort Worth: Texas Christian University Press, 2006.

Erisman, Fred. *From Birdwomen to Skygirls.* Fort Worth: TCU Press, 2009.

Foxworth, Thomas G. *The Speed Seekers.* New York: Doubleday and Company, Inc., 1976.

Gabler, Neal. *Winchell: Gossip, Power and the Culture of Celebrity.* New York: Knopf Publishing Group, 1995.

Ganz, Cheryl R. *The 1933 Chicago World's Fair: A Century of Progress.* Champaign: University of Illinois Press, 2008.

Gascoigne, Bamber. *How to Identify Prints: A Complete Guide to Manual and Mechanical Processes from Woodcut to Ink Jet.* New York: Thames and Hudson, Inc., 1995.

Glines, Carroll V. *Roscoe Turner: Aviation's Master Showman.* Washington and London: Smithsonian Institution Press, 1995.

Gross, Charles J. *American Military Aviation: The Indispensable Arm.* College Station: Texas A&M University Press, 2004.

Hudson, Harry K. *A Bibliography of Hard-cover Boys' Books.* Tampa: Data Print, 1977.

Hults, Linda C. *An Introductory History: The Print in the Western World.* Madison: The University of Wisconsin Press, 1996.

Hunt, Peter, ed. *Children's Literature: An Illustrated History.* New York: Oxford University Press, 1995.

Jeffers, H. Paul. *Ace of Aces: The Life of Capt. Eddie Rickenbacker.* New York: Ballantine Books, 2003.

Kammen, Michael. *American Culture, American Tastes: Social Change and the Twentieth Century.* New York: Basic Books, 1999.

Komans, Nick. *Bonfires to Beacons: Federal Civil Aviation Policy under the Air Commerce Act, 1926–38.* Washington, DC: Smithsonian Institution Press, 1989.

McCann, Chris. *Masterpieces: The Art History of Jigsaw Puzzles.* Portland, OR: Collectors Press, 1998.

Maurer, Maurer. *Aviation in the U.S. Army 1919-1939: Official History of Early American Military Aviation between the First and Second World War.* Washington, DC: United States Printing Office, 1987.

Maurer, Maurer, ed. *The U.S. Air Service in World War I* (4 volumes). Maxwell Air Force Base, AL: Office of Air Force History, 1979.

Miller, Orlo. *London 200: An Illustrated History.* London, Ontario: Phelps Publishing Company, 1992.

Mingos, Howard, ed. *The Aircraft Year Book for 1936.* New York: Aeronautical Chamber of Commerce, 1936.

Morison, Samuel Eliot. *History of Naval Operations in World War II* (15 volumes). Boston: Little, Brown and Company, 1947-1962.

O'Callaghan, Timothy J. *The Aviation Legacy of Henry & Edsel Ford.* Ann Arbor: Proctor Publications, 2002.

Oriss, Bruce W. *When Hollywood Rules the Skies* (4 volumes). Los Angeles Aero Associates, 1985-2016.

Petretti, Allan. *Petretti's Coca-Cola Collectibles Price Guide.* Crestline Publications, 1997.

Pisano, Dominick A. *Legend, Memory and the Great War in the Air.* Seattle: University of Washington Press, 1992.

Poole, Nancy Geddes. *The Art of London 1830–1980.* London, Ontario: Blackpool Press, 1984.

Prendergast, Mark. *For God, Country and Coca-Cola: The Unauthorized History of the Great American Soft Drink and the Company That Makes It.* New York: Scribner and Sons, 1993.

Reed, Walt and Roger Reed. *The Ilustrator in America 1880–1980.* New York: The Society of Illustrators, 1984.

Rojek, Chris. *Celebrity.* London: Reaktion Books, 2001.

Sloan, James J. Jr. *Wings of Honor.* Pennsylvania: Schiffer Publishing Ltd., 1994.

Suid, Lawrence H. *Guts & Glory: Great American War Movies.* Reading: Addison-Wesley Publishing Co., 1978.

Thaden, Louise McPhetridge. *High Wide and Frightened.* Fayetteville: University of Arkansas Press, 2004.

Watrous, James. *A Century of American Printmaking 1880–1980.* Madison: University of Wisconsin Press, 1984.

Wildenberg, Thomas. *All the Factors of Victory: Admiral Joseph Reeves and the Origins of Carrier Air Power.* Annapolis: Naval Institute Press, 2002.

Wohl, Robert. *The Spectacle of Flight: Aviation and The Western Imagination, 1920–1950.* New Haven, CT: Yale University Press, 2005.

Wortman, Marc. *1941: Fighting the Shadow War.* New York: Atlantic Monthly Press, 2016.

Wynne, H. Hugh. *Motion Picture Stunt Pilots and Hollywood's Classic Aviation Movies.* Missoula, MT: Pictorial Histories Publishing Company Inc., 1987.

Index